5

393

1093

6

15 JAN 1997

Gods of Management

Charles Handy

Gods of Management

The changing work of organisations

SOUVENIR PRESS

ACKNOWLEDGEMENTS

To all those who contributed to my thinking I am deeply grateful. If I have not acknowledged them in the text, it only means that they have entered my thought processes in some subliminal fashion. I live by the constant interchange of thought and ideas, in teaching, argument, private discussion or exchange of letters. I am grateful to all those colleagues, students and friends who have, often unwittingly, contributed to my thinking.

Few, if any, of my ideas can be original. The notion of using Greek gods to symbolise cultures has been around for some time. Nietzsche used it, and so did Ruth Benedict. I was first introduced to it by Roger Harrison one sunny morning in the hills of Maine. I am grateful to him for this and many other ideas.

The idea was first developed by me in a chapter in *Understanding Organisations* (Penguin, 1976), where the theoretical underpinnings of the idea are also presented.

I am particularly grateful to Terry Hamaton, who has enlivened the text with his perceptive illustrations, and to my publishers for their constant stimulus and encouragement.

CONTENTS

INTRODUCTION

The gods in this book are the gods of ancient Greece. What, the reader very understandably asks, have the gods of ancient Greece to do with management? An explanation is needed.

To the Greeks, religion was more a matter of custom than a formal theology. Their gods stood for certain things and, to a degree, you chose your god because you shared the values and interests which they represented. You were a Zeus person or an Apollo person, the god of order and reason, a follower of Athena, the warrior goddess, or of Dionysus, to me the most individualist of the gods.

I have used these four gods to symbolise the different ways of managing that can be discerned in organisations, or, to put it another way, the differing *cultures* that exist in organisations. I have done this not just to add whimsy to another book on management but to underline a very important point, that the management of organisations is not a precise science but more of a creative and political process, owing much to the prevailing culture and tradition in that place at that time. Organisations, like tribes and families, have their own ways of doing things, things that work for them and things that don't work. You have to read them right to be effective.

To be sure, there are technical aids to management, principally ways of organising and ordering numbers and materials; there are also some truths about the behaviour of people and groups that seem to hold good in most situations. Wise managers make use of these aids and truths but in themselves they are not enough, otherwise every student from a management course would be an expert manager. Management is more fun, more creative, more personal, more political and more intuitive than any textbook. Nevertheless, whilst every organisation is different, there are patterns which can

9

be discerned, models to be imitated and some guidelines which can be followed.

The patterns and models are those symbolised by the gods, representing different organisational cultures. They add up to what could be called a Theory of Cultural Propriety, which holds that what matters is getting the right culture in the right place for the right purpose. It is called a 'low-definition' theory, one which suggests rather than prescribes, and which is loose enough to allow room for the intuitive and the creative interpretation. No manager wants to be an automaton, nor should any organisation be just a giant processing plant. It is the special privilege of being human that we can go beyond the theories and make our own rules. Organisations will never, therefore, be subject to precise laws and rigid theories. We should, as humans, be thankful for that, even if we might, as managers, occasionally wish it to be otherwise.

Part One of this book (Chapters 1–4) explains the theory of the cultures and how it applies to organisations. The evidence to support the theory has mostly to come from personal experience, because unless concepts gell with one's own experience, creating that Aha Effect ('Aha! So that's why it happens like that!'), the theory will not be of practical use. I have laced the text with bits of my own and other people's experiences by way of anecdote, but the evidence which counts will come from the reader himself or, increasingly these days, herself. If each reader can identify Zeus figures, Apollonian structures and Dionysian attitudes in their own surroundings, then the theory begins to have a reality and a validity.

At one level, the theory helps to explain the comfort or discomfort of an individual in an organisation. A follower of Zeus will not be happy, or effective, in an Apollonian organisation. An Apollonian manager will find Dionysians irritating beyond belief. At a second level, however, the theory becomes a diagnostic tool for a manager or consultant. Inappropriate cultures lead to unhappiness and inefficiency. Communication breakdowns are often the result of one culture clashing with another. Organisations nearly always need a mix of cultures to carry out their different tasks, but each culture has to understand and respect the ways of the others. Too many organisations allow one culture to dominate and thus to impede the others.

Each culture, it will become clear, or each god, works on quite different assumptions about the basis of power and influence, about what motivates people, how they think and learn, how things can be changed. These assumptions result in quite different styles of management, structures, procedures and reward systems. Each will work well in certain situations, but get the wrong god in the wrong place and there will be trouble. The best way to run an efficient chocolate factory will not be the right way to run an architects' partnership, a primary school or a construction site. Different cultures, and gods, are needed for different tasks. Cultures, too, will need to change over time, as the tasks change, as the organisation grows, or as people change. Much of the trouble in organisations comes from the attempt to go on doing things as they used to be done, from a reluctance to change the culture when it needs to be changed. The gods of management, after all, do arouse strong allegiances in their followers. Those who think like Zeus find it hard to accept that Apollo can ever be right.

Cultural confusion, therefore, is one of the principal ills that plague organisations. It shows up in inefficiency or, more obviously, in *slack*, the extra resources, the longer delivery times, the increased overtime, the overstaffed head office; slack is the organisational balm used to ease the pain of inefficiency. It is management's easy option and a way of cushioning a wrong culture. It is, however, expensive and can, in the end, kill the organisation. Managers, therefore, need to be more aware of their own cultural predilections, of which god they personally follow, and more aware of the cultural choices that are open to them and to their organisation. It was always a myth that there is one best way to manage, but it has been a pervasive myth and a damaging one, to both individuals and organisations. The Greeks at least recognised a variety of gods, even if each had his or her favourite. We need a law of requisite variety in management as well as a theory of cultural propriety.

Chapter 4 demonstrates that the choice of gods is influenced by their setting, both by the society around them and its national culture, and by the occupational setting of the organisation. The Japanese are more fond of Apollo than are the Anglo-Saxons. Mexicans have a different way of working from the Swedes. Organisations have to take account of these national differences. But a school has different traditions from a factory, so does a hospital, while a voluntary organisation, or a church, is different again. The choice of organisational culture has to take account of these differences. There is, I am glad to say, no one best way to manage.

Part Two (Chapters 5-8) looks at the major cultural crisis affecting our organisations today. Briefly, it is this, that the chosen route to efficiency via concentration and specialisation which resulted in the multi-layered and multi-structured organisation and in an Apollonian or bureaucratic culture has reached a dead end. Scale creates costs as well as economies; it increases scope but can restrict flexibility; more importantly, it runs counter to the cultural preferences of most of the people it needs to make it work. An Apollonian structure staffed by Athenians and Dionysians will be an expensive disaster.

Chapters 5 and 6 explain why this is so, and why the chosen responses of most organisations are not going to work because they all seek to find ways of perpetuating the Apollonian dominance.

The answer lies in changing the balance of the gods. It adds up to a gradual *organisation revolution*, which may come to be as important as the one which accompanied the industrial revolution. That revolution took people out of the villages into the towns, separated the workplace from the home and transformed communities, family life and the role of women. Whereas people used to work in gangs they now worked in lines of anonymous 'hands'. The 'works' or the 'office' became the day-time, or sometimes night-time, house for most adults, a place where sometimes 20,000 or more worked on one site, often for the whole of their lives. The industrial revolution made the employment organisation the lynchpin of society, the means whereby most people obtained not only their livelihood but also achieved their status and their main purpose in life.

We have come to take the employment society for granted, although Marx and many others saw it as exploitative, alienating and eventually doomed. So pervasive has it been that the right to work has come to mean the right to be employed and was confirmed as that in the Universal Declaration of Human Rights after the Second World War. The job may not have lived up to everyone's expectations but a job was every man's right, and every woman's too if she wanted one.

If the employment organisation, centred around the works or the office, gives way, as Chapters 7 and 8 suggest it will, to a more contractual, dispersed and federal organisation, the effects on society will be profound. It will lead, on the one hand, to more small businesses, particularly in services, and more self-employment. There will be more part-time work in all institutions and therefore more opportunity for more people to combine jobs with other interests in life. More work will be located near where people live rather than where the organisation chooses to site itself. Communities could perhaps become more complete as more people live and work there rather than just sleep there. Flexilives and portfolios of work might become the norm rather than the exception.

On the other hand, the organisation revolution could produce two classes of citizen once again; not, this time, the owners and the labourers, or the managers and workers, but now those with careers and those with just jobs – the professionals and the hired help, who could easily be unhired. There would then be two labour markets, the primary market catering for the professionals and key staff, with job security and fringe benefits, and the secondary fringe of temporary labour, part-time help and self-employment – free, maybe, but often poor.

If more self-employment and tiny businesses are one likely outcome of the organisational revolution then, in terms of the gods, we shall see a resurgence of Zeus and Dionysus, of individualism and personal power. For some countries, Britain in particular, that might be more in tune with the national cultures than the bureaucratic traditions of Apollo, but if these new forms of work are going to be more than an impoverished fringe, there will have to be more thought given to how they can best co-operate and collaborate for their own success. Associations, agents, co-operatives and partnerships belong to these cultures. Will they be the new emerging organisational forms? Can the new businesses learn from the voluntary world and charitable organisations, where the cultures of Zeus and Dionysus thrive, or from professional partnerships, from schools, colleges and the arts? Will the older of society's institutions turn out to be the models for the new ones?

Last but not least, our societies will need to adapt to the needs of the new breeds of organisation. What kind of company law will be appropriate? Will stakeholders' rights still predominate or will there have to be more recognition of the other stakeholders? What education is appropriate for a society of mini-entrepreneurs and semi-professionals? How should taxation, pension and social welfare policies be revamped for a world where full-time employment for life will no longer be the norm? There are more questions than answers in this section, but they are included to demonstrate how an organisation revolution inevitably reaches its tentacles down into every part of society. The gods of management have to be taken seriously when they stage a palace revolution.

This book therefore is an inquiry into the state of our organisations and into their likely future. It is not intended to be a textbook or a manual for managers although managers in all sorts of organisations should find it useful. It is written to encourage more people to think about how organisations actually work and what changes are on the way, because, although 90 per cent of those of us who work still do so in or for an organisation, we still take their ways for granted as if they were part of nature's laws, to be marvelled at or grumbled about but not by mere man to be altered. If this book helps to demystify organisations, to make their ways and their assumptions more understandable to ordinary mortals, and causes more people to think about the way they work and the ways in which they might have to work, it will have served its purpose.

The manager in this book is almost always referred to as 'he'. This is not a deliberate attempt to ignore or demote the female half of the human race, but is done to make the book easier to read. The male gods still predominate in organisations, so please take 'he' to mean 'he or she'; but as the final chapter indicates, times are changing fast and we may soon be using 'she' as the predominant pronoun in management. That will indeed be a sign of an organisational revolution.

PART ONE

The Theory of Cultural Propriety

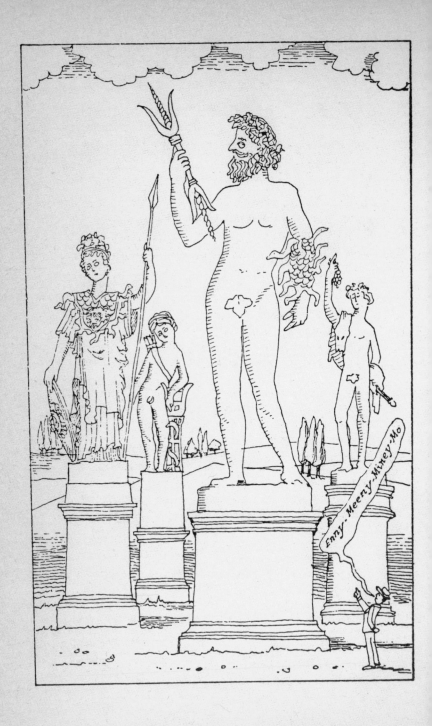

Chapter 1

THE FOUR GODS OF MANAGEMENT

Each of the four gods gives its name to a *cult* or philosophy of management and to an organisational culture. Each of these cultures has also got a formal, more technical, name, as well as a diagrammatic picture. The name, picture and the Greek god each carries its own overtones, and these overtones combine to build up the concept I am trying to convey. They also help to keep the ideas in one's memory.

The Picture

The Culture		*The God*
Club		Zeus
Role		Apollo
Task		Athena
Existential		Dionysus

These names, signs and gods do not amount to definitions, for the cultures cannot be precisely defined, only recognised when you see them. If you know organisations at all, the descriptions should be recognisable as you read on.

17

It is important to realise that each of the cultures, or ways of running things, is *good* – for something. No culture, or mix of cultures, is bad or wrong in itself, only inappropriate to its circumstances. The fact that you do not like or approve of one of them makes it unsuitable for you – not wrong or bad or inefficient in itself. This principle is the heart of the Theory of Cultural Propriety, and I shall revert to it again and again.

The Club Culture (Zeus)

The picture is that of a spider's web. The organisation which uses this culture will, like all other organisations, probably have divisions of work based on functions, or product. These are the lines radiating out from the centre, like the lines of a traditional organisation chart. But in this culture those are not the lines that matter. The crucial lines here are the encircling ones, the ones that surround the spider in the middle; for these are the lines of power and influence, reducing in importance as they get more distant from the centre. The relationship with the spider matters more in this culture than any formal title or position description.

Zeus is the patron God. The Greeks chose, or created, their gods to represent certain features of the world as they saw it. Zeus was the king of their gods, who reigned on Mount Olympus by thunderbolt (when crossed) or shower of gold (when seducing). He was feared, respected and occasionally loved. He represented the patriarchal tradition, irrational but often benevolent power, impulsiveness and charisma.

Historically, this culture is found most frequently in the small entrepreneurial organisation. The boat fanatic who finds he can sell the boats he builds, gets his son to help with manufacturing, his nephew to sell them, his cousin to keep the accounts, is Zeus, and that is the way Zeus slowly builds his web. But the culture also prevails in broking firms, in investment banks, in many political groupings, in start-up situations of all sorts and on the bridge of many a ship.

The club culture is an excellent one for *speed of decision*. Any situation where speed is vital will benefit from this style of management. Of course, speed does not guarantee quality. *That* depends on the calibre of Zeus and of his inner circle – an incompetent, ageing or disinterested Zeus will quickly contaminate and slowly destroy his own web. *Selection* and *succession* are therefore rightly regarded as critical variables in these organisations, and much time and effort are given to them.

The culture achieves speed through an unusual form of communication – empathy. I watched the young executive of a small broking firm at work in the metal exchange one afternoon. He was making a series of rapid purchase and sale decisions of what seemed to me to be alarming magnitudes, with no calculators, formulae or resources to higher authority or expertise. 'How do you make these decisions', I asked, 'and what formal approval and authority do you need from your firm?' 'Oh', he said, 'I make my own decisions, but I try always to double-guess what the old man would do.' 'And if you fail?' I asked. 'Curtains', he said, 'for me.'

The club culture can be a cruel culture if your empathetic guess is wrong. But empathy needs no memos, committees or formal authorities. Club cultures, indeed, are very short on documentation. Zeus does not write, he speaks, eyeball to eyeball, if possible; if not, then by telephone. Many a successful Zeus has been illiterate, if not always innumerate. Instead, empathy depends on *affinity* and *trust*.

You cannot guess what the other man is thinking unless you think like him. There is little empathy between opposites. Your brother's son, your cricketing chum, your drinking companion, are more likely to read your mind intuitively, and quickly, than the stranger off the street. Do not despise nepotism, it can be a good base for empathy. Yet empathy without trust is dangerous, for it can be used against you. Again, it is more difficult to trust a stranger than someone whom you, or your friends, have known long. Selection to club cultures is usually preceded by an introduction, and often confirmed by a meal. You know your friends at table.

These cultures, then, are clubs of like-minded people introduced by like-minded people, working on empathetic initiative with personal contact rather than formal liaison. They are tough clubs, because if empathy or trust is seen to be misplaced the man must go. Weak clubs will not survive because they will either have to inject other methods of communication (and so lose speed), or risk too many mistakes.

Club cultures are cheap cultures to run. Trust is cheaper than control procedures, and empathy costs no pence. Money is channelled to where it matters, to people and the promotion of personal contact: the telephone and travel bills of these cultures are very high, for Zeus will not write when he can talk. They are effective cultures in situations where speed is more important than correct detail, or the cost of a delay higher than the cost of a mistake (which can often be rectified by a subsequent deal). They are good cultures to work in – provided you belong to the club – because they value the individual, give him free rein and reward his efforts.

Club cultures make history, and Zeus figures are the managers most beloved of journalists. (Most organisations started as club cultures, and many have not changed when they should have, for speed of decision and the personal imprint of the leader usually become less important as the organisation reaches its first plateau of routine.) These cultures depend on networks of friendship, old boys and comrades, and can appear, therefore, to be nepotistic closed shops, unpopular in these days of meritocracy and equal opportunity. They smack of paternalism and the cult of the individual, of personal ownership and personal power, the kinds of things that gave the industrial revolution a bad name. They are unfashionable cultures, and derided as examples of amateur management and relics of privilege. They should not be. Of course these methods of managing can be abused and often have been – an evil Zeus will do evil things – but these organisational squirearchies are very effective in the right situation, for trust based on personal contact is not a bad base for getting things done.

The Role Culture (Apollo)

When we think of an 'organisation' it is usually the *role* culture that we envisage. It is a culture which bases its approach around the definition of the role or the job to be done, not around personalities.

Apollo is its patron god, for Apollo was the god of order and rules. This culture assumes that man is rational and that everything can and should be analysed in a logical fashion. The task of an organisation can then be subdivided box by box until you have an organisational flow chart of work, with a system of prescribed roles (specified in things called 'job descriptions') and held together by a whole set of rules and procedures (call them manuals, budgets, information systems or what you will).

Its picture is a Greek temple, for Greek temples draw their strength and their beauty from the pillars. The pillars represent functions and divisions in a role organisation. The pillars are joined managerially only at the top, the pediment, where the heads of the functions and divisions join together to form the board, management committee or president's office. The pillars are also linked by tension wires of rules and procedures. A typical career would involve joining one of the pillars and working up to the top, with perhaps occasional sightseeing visits to the other pillars ('to broaden one's base'). It is a picture of a bureaucracy, if you like, but 'bureaucracy' has come to be a contaminated word and this culture has its merits.

The Apollo style is excellent when it can be assumed that tomorrow will be like yesterday. Yesterday can then be examined, pulled to pieces, and put together again in the form of improved rules and procedures for tomorrow. *Stability* and *predictability* are assumed and encouraged. And thank God for them. That the sun will rise tomorrow can be a most reassuring recollection in some of the bleak moments of the late night. Wherever, therefore, the assumptions of stability are valid, it makes sense to codify the operation so that it follows a set and predictable pattern. Individuals are, usually, indispensable to the operation of the pattern, although, as technology advances, more and more stability can be automated. Individuals in the role culture are, therefore, part of the machine, the interchangeable human parts of Henry Ford's dream. The *role*, the set of duties, is fixed. The individual is he, or she, who is slotted into it. That the individual has a name is irrelevant, a number would do as well. That he has a personality is downright inconvenient, because he might then be tempted to express his personality in his role and so alter the role. And that would throw the whole precise logic of the operation out of gear. In a role culture you do your job – neither more, nor less. Efficiency is getting the train in on time, not early, not late. Efficiency is meeting standard targets. Beat them and it must be assumed that the targets needed revising.

'An interchangeable human part'. It sounds deadening. 'The occupant of a role' sounds like a sort of organisational squatter. To many, the pure role culture is a denial of humanity because of its insistence on conformity. But to others it is blessed release.

How pleasant it can be to know *exactly* what is required of one. How relaxing it sometimes is to be anonymous; how pleasurable not to have to exercise one's initiative, leaving all that creative energy for the home or the community or the sports field.

The Apollo culture is secure psychologically and, usually, contractually. Apollo was a kind god in ancient Greece, the protector of children and sheep as well as of order. Once you join your Greek temple you can nearly always rely on staying there for life. After all, the temple assumes it will be there, may even have a twenty-year forecast of what it, and even you, will be doing. The temple will take over your work life for you, tell you what to do, where to go, what you can earn. It may even arrange your insurance for you, provide a house or a car, make cheap shopping available, or legal advice. It can and will do some or all of these things because of its assumptions about the predictability of the future.

It is no accident, therefore, that life insurance companies are an almost pure example of role cultures. The notion of predictability is built into the whole ethos of their work. Monopolies, including the civil service, state industries and local government, can reasonably assume predictability, too, since there is no competition around to disturb their vision of the future. Organisations with a long history of continued success with one product or service or tradition can also be forgiven for thinking that things will continue as before. And if that is so, then the more you rationalise, codify, standardise, the more effective you will be. If you have the same set of menus for breakfast, lunch and supper every day, the catering operation in your home will be greatly simplified, the costs of labour and materials will be reduced and the managerial energy required will be minimal. It may be boring, of course, but where food is not enjoyment but only the necessary fuel of life, you will find Apollonian catering.

Apollo cultures are efficient when life is predictable. They hate the obverse – change. They will usually respond to a changing environment first by ignoring it, then by doing *more* of what they are already doing. Responses tend to be stylised in these cultures. When costs go up, raise the prices, or the fares. If sales are flagging, sell harder. If the backlog of administration is getting too big, work more overtime. Greek temples are built on firm ground. If the ground starts to shake, the pillars quiver and have to be bonded together. If they aren't, the pediment will fall. Translating the analogy, role cultures respond to drastic changes in the environment (changing consumer preferences, new technologies, new funding sources) by setting up a lot of cross-functional liaison groups in an attempt to hold the structure together. If these measures don't work, the management falls, or the whole temple collapses in merger, bankruptcy or a consultants' reorganisation.

ZEUS OR APOLLO?

I once worked in a Greek Temple organisation. It was safe, predictable and promised a secure career. But at 28 it was boring. An acquaintance with whom I lamented my condition said, 'Why not come and join us? We are looking for an economist to do our project analysis.'

'Who is "us"?' I asked. 'An investment bank,' he replied, 'specialising in the developing countries.' 'But I'm not an economist,' I said. 'I read philosophy at university.'

'Ah! But it was the right university, wasn't it?' he said, as if that made it all all right. 'Come and have lunch with the board on Tuesday.'

I had lunch. We talked long about many things – politics, sport, the world. No one mentioned the job, or economics, or my previous experience. Next week they offered me the job of economist, a new post. Two months later I joined them.

They gave me a fine office, a nice secretary and the Financial Times *– and then left me alone. Nobody phoned, no memos, letters, nothing. After a week I went to see my friend.*

'It's very nice to be here –' I began.

'Good to have you,' he replied.

'But . . .' I said.

'Well?'

'I wonder if I could see my job description, get an idea of my role and responsibilities, reporting relationships, and the general organisation structure.'

'What on earth are you jabbering about, old boy?' he said, looking startled and worried. 'We don't use those sort of words here – what's worrying you?'

'What am I meant to do?' I blurted out.

'Why, what the rest of us do,' he said. 'Search out opportunities to use our resources, get on planes, go and meet people, find some hot news; you know the kind of thing we're interested in, get some more of it.'

I returned to my office, alarmed for myself and for them. But then I thought I saw it. They had wanted an economist because they were secretly very worried about this slap-dash way of doing things. Clearly, some serious professional project appraisal was urgently needed. Luckily, I just happened to have brought along with me from my previous organisation a set of procedures and tables for project appraisal. These could be readily adapted and then I could propose introducing a little more system and procedure into the current craziness.

In a week I was ready. The chairman agreed that I should present my ideas to a meeting of the board. They all listened very attentively and politely.

At the end, the chairman thanked me for all the work I had put into it and then said, 'I suppose a project would have to be very marginal indeed to justify all this analysis and procedure?'

'Well,' I said, 'it's obviously vital for marginal propositions, but you can't even know if it's marginal till you've done this kind of formal analysis.'

'Hmm. You see, we're probably wrong' (in the tone of voice Englishmen use when they know they're not) 'but in this Group we've always thought that we got success not by making better *decisions* than our competitors on marginal *propositions*, but quicker decisions on obvious *propositions*.'

I defended myself, but I knew that he was right. They were brokers, trading in companies. Speed was vital, the accuracy of a decision only relative. They were Zeus. I was Apollo.

I never did get into their club. In the end, I realised that I had a different cast of mind and left before they threw me out.

The Task Culture (Athena)

This culture takes a very different approach to management. Management is seen as being basically concerned with the continuous and successful solution of problems. First define the problem, then allocate to its solution the appropriate resources, give the resulting group of men, machines and money the go-ahead, and wait for the solution. Judge performance in terms of results, solved problems.

Its picture is a net, because it draws resources from various parts of the organisational system in order to focus them on a particular knot or problem. Power lies at the interstices of the net, not at the top, as in the Apollo culture, or at the centre, as in Zeus organisations. The organisation is a network of loosely-linked *commando units*, each unit being largely self-contained but with a specific responsibility within an overall strategy.

Its god is a young woman, Athena, the warrior goddess, patroness of Odysseus, that arch problem-solver, of craftsmen and of pioneering captains. The culture recognises only expertise as the base of power or influence. Age does not impress, nor length of service, nor closeness of kin to the owner. To contribute to your group, talent is what is needed, and creativity, a fresh approach and new intuitions. It is a culture where youth flourishes and where creativity is at a premium. The youth, energy and creativity associated with Athena fit the task culture quite well.

It is a good culture to work in if you know your job. Since the group has a common purpose (the solution of a problem), there is a sense of enthusiasm and joint commitment, with little of the private agenda conflicts that befoul the first two cultures. Leadership in a common-purpose group is seldom a hot issue: instead there are usually mutual respect, a minimum of procedural niceties and a desire to help rather than exploit when others get into difficulties. It is a *purposeful commando*. It talks of *teams* where a role culture has *committees*.

TASK CULTURES IN BLOOM

A friend, employed as an executive with a venerable and traditional British heavy engineering company, went on a working visit to one of the aerospace companies of southern California, towards the end of the sixties, when the space race was at its height and the US Defense Department was the world's largest customer, commissioning a long succession of solutions to high-technology problems, often on a cost-plus basis.

Although he was not to know it, the aerospace companies at that time were the epitome of the successful task culture. Often as much as 30 per cent of their managers had a Ph.D qualification. Their formal structures of organisation were of the matrix type. They worked in project groups which were continually being dismantled and re-assembled. They were at that time financially ebullient.

He returned to Britain with his eyes gleaming. 'It was extra-ordinary,' he said. 'In those companies, not only did the sun shine all day outside, but the managers were young, intelligent, earning high salaries and *having fun,* and *the organisation made money. In my company,' he said ruefully, 'we believed that these things were incompatible.'*

That is the ideal. It works well, indeed excellently, when the product of the organisation is the *solution to a problem.* Consultancy companies, research and development departments, advertising agencies – after all, an advertisement is a response to a client's expressed need – are all one-off problem-solving factories. But put a task culture into a repetitive situation and there will be trouble. Variety, not predictability, is the yeast of this kind of management. Ask Athenians to manufacture pencils and they will devise you the best (and most expensive?) pencil known, or disrupt the process, or depart.

Task cultures come expensive. They are staffed by experts who can demand their market price. They talk together a lot, and talking costs money. Problems are not always solved just right the first time, so there is the necessity for experimentation and the inevitability of errors. Errors cost money, even if they are speedily corrected. Expensive task cultures, therefore, tend to flourish in times of expansion, when the products, technologies or services are new, or when there is some sort of cartel arrangement which provides a price floor. In times of expansion you can get away with high prices – there is more than enough cake to go round. Similarly, new technologies or new products create, for a time, a sort of monopoly situation which lasts until the technology settles down or competitors arrive. During this monopoly situation, the costs or the task structure can be covered by higher charges and prices. In short, task cultures work well when one is venturing into new situations. Luckily, it is in those situations that success is rewarded with the money to pay for it.

Come hard times, however, or an end to venturing, or the need to make the solutions permanent or routine, and the task culture will be seen to be unduly expensive. These cultures are not for plateaux. Athena did not care for domesticity and the routine chores of housekeeping. So task cultures often have a short life. If they are too successful they get big and to pay their way take on a lot of routine or maintenance work – which require Apollonian cultures. Failure, however, is one problem they find it hard to solve (it is hard for a cooperative group to dismiss half of its members), and in hard times a Zeus will usually emerge to deal with the crisis. Or the members may just get older and want more routine, or more personal power.

ATHENA IN A STORM

Ten years ago, the advertising business in Europe was thriving. Advertising agencies competed strenuously, but on quality and service, not on price, which was still fixed at a standard percentage of the cost (effectively a cost-plus system). The agencies were full of well-paid creative talent, usually young.

I was asked to look at the management process of one agency. It was a model task culture. The whole place was a network of temporary project groups (called 'accounts'), pulling in the individual resources from the specialist functions. Most people worked on three or more accounts. Strict standards were applied to the end products (the advertisements), but control and systemisation of the means were minimal. How and when the groups worked was left to them. The allocation of personnel to groups was virtually the only managerial task retained in the centre. Salaries were high, but based on expertise, as recognised by the market-place (there was a lot of mobility between agencies). There was very little formal hierarchy, but an informal class system based on renown, not closely associated with age. Money was not a crucial factor, it was always there. Success was measured by public approval, which meant new clients clamouring at the door. The place resembled a luxurious art school, where everyone seemed to be earning vast sums for indulging in his or her hobby. 'Management' was, in fact, not a word that was used or a concept that was wanted.

Two years later and world recession, inflation and tightened company budgets knocked the bottom right out of the advertising market, whilst hitting the agencies' most vulnerable cost factor _ the salaries of their people, their human assets. Agencies began to compete on price. Companies demanded better and quicker service for reduced expenditure. Costs had to be controlled, since the business could no longer operate on a cost-plus basis in an expanding market.

Budgets, computer print-outs of individual expenses, management committees, redundancy, reductions in office space, a freeze on salaries, lowered mobility, the beginnings of staff unionisation – the symptoms were numerous. Revisiting the agency, the task culture was gone. 'Accounts' were administered. *Procedures abounded. People talked about 'the management', and indeed the top personnel had changed, to bring in a more managerially-minded group, who talked of profit margins and cost-effectiveness and systems. Errors could not be afforded, were controlled for and eliminated – but so were the experiments that accompanied them. Conformity and predictability had begun to flavour the advertisements. They no longer made bad ads, but some thought they no longer made great ones, either.*

Suddenly it was just like another business. The art school had become an ad-factory. The task culture was now a role culture with a few Zeus figures at the top.

Necessary? Perhaps. Sad? Certainly. Task cultures don't easily weather storms.

The Existential Culture (Dionysus)

Dionysus, god of Wine and Song, presides over this culture because he if anyone represents the existential ideology among the gods. Existentialism starts from the assumption that the world is *not* some part of a higher purpose; we are not simply instruments of some god. Instead, although the fact that we exist at all is an accident, if anyone is responsible for us and our world, it is ourselves. We are in charge of our own destinies. This is not a recipe for self-indulgent selfishness, for Kant's categorical imperative applies, that whatever we ordain or wish for ourselves must be equally applicable to the rest of mankind. Wine and orgies won't work unless someone makes the wine, and that someone must potentially include us.

The organisational implications of existential thinking are great. In all the other three cultures, the individual is subordinate to the organisation: the style of the relationship may vary, but the individual is there to help the organisation achieve its purpose, and is paid in one way or another by the organisation for doing that. In this fourth existential culture, the organisation exists to help the individual achieve his purpose.

How might this be? Well, think of doctors: four of them, each an individual with his own speciality, but who agree to share an office, a telephone, a secretary to form a partnership association. Or think of architects, or barristers in their chambers, or a co-operative of artists. Theirs is a commune culture, existing for its participants. Its picture is a cluster of individual stars, loosely gathered in a circle. But the picture will remain essentially unchanged if a star or two departs. The stars are not mutually interdependent.

The existential culture is excellent, therefore, where it is the talent or skill of the individual which is the crucial asset of the organisation.

This is the culture preferred by professionals. They can preserve their own identity and their own freedom, feeling owned by no man. And yet they can be part of an organisation, with the colleagues, the support and the added flexibility, and even bargaining power, that association brings.

Dionysians recognise no 'boss', although they may accept co-ordination for their own long-term convenience. Management in their organisations is a chore, something that has to happen like housekeeping. And like a housekeeper, a manager has small renown: an administrator amongst the prima donnas is bottom of the status lists.

Dionysian cultures are splendid places to work in. I have worked in one myself – a university. Professionals usually have job security, agreed fee scales, allocated territories or spheres of influence, guarantees of independence. This is marvellous for them. But not for those who have to lead or organise or manage such people.

For there are no sanctions that can be used on them. Dismissal, money, perks or punishment are all outside the jurisdiction of the leader. Even promotion or selection decisions are made, as a rule, by groups of equals. Professionals do not willingly receive orders, fill in forms or compromise on their own plans. Every teacher likes to be the uninterrupted king in his own classroom, just as every doctor is god of his consulting room. You enter by invitation only, criticise on request, command by consent. For these are the organisations of consent, where the manager governs with the consent of the governed, and not with the delegated authority of the owners. It may be democracy, but it is very difficult, and exhausting, to deal with.

One would not expect to find many such organisations around, certainly not in the business or industrial scene, where organisations, by their charters, have objectives that outlive and outgrow their employees. Indeed, the Dionysian culture is something which causes shudders in any more usual organisation or manager – precisely because of the lack of mandated control. Where you can manage only by consent, every individual has the right of veto, so that any co-ordinated effort becomes a matter of endless negotiation. Only where every individual can do his own thing, and could in fact operate without the organisation at all, is there less problem. Antique hypermarkets, where individual dealers ply their trades independently although under one roof, a marketing co-operative for independent growers or craftsmen, can usually be managed (they would not use the word) without too much difficulty. There would be few conflicting objectives, few needs to compromise individual desires for a common good.

Organisations, however, put the common good before the individual need and so they tend to try to translate Dionysians into Athenians, the existential into the task culture. They are, of course, right, as judged by their own interests, to try to do so. Individuals, however, like the notions of individuality and personal professionalism which reside in the Dionysian idea. There is a growing band of 'new professionals' – individuals who define themselves according to their trade, not just doctors and lawyers, but now also the 'systems analyst', 'research scientist', 'public relations adviser', 'consultant'. These individuals see themselves as independent professionals who have temporarily loaned their talents to an organisation. They are often young, usually talented and can command an open market salary and reputation. They behave as Dionysians, and as long as they are talented they can get away with it, for the organisation needs them enough to manage them on the terms of their consent. Increasingly, therefore, the specialist groups and any research or development activities are acquiring an existential flavour.

Wherever individual talent is at a premium, the Dionysian flavour is probably necessary, and organisations do well to recognise it and accommodate it. But the cult of Dionysus is growing and is no longer related to individual talent. We would all like the benefits of existentialism without its responsibilities and risks. Existentialism on the shop-floor is a new phenomenon. We shall return to it in the second part of this book.

FAMILY CULTURES

Have families changed their cultures?

Once upon a time, the paterfamilias ruled as Zeus over his table. He was master and all knew it. They did as he commanded when he commanded.

Then Apollo became the fashion. To each his duties and his status. The men made the money, women the food, children the beds.

Democracy brought Athena into the family. Not duties but tasks, projects and small group activities became the feature. 'Why don't you both . . .?' or, 'Shall we . . .?'

And now Dionysus? A temporary liaison of individuals. If individual interests start to diverge the liaison cannot be enforced. Joint activities (e.g. holidays) cannot be assumed or imposed, only negotiated.

Do organisations follow a similar sort of cultural inevitability? If so, where are we on the route?

Gods of Management

Which are you?

You will probably not identify yourself completely with any of the
four gods. Most people, the Greeks included, are too complex to do
that, and pay homage to more than one philosophy. Similarly, your
organisation will probably include aspects of all four cultures.

Do my classifications apply to your experience? Only you can
judge that for yourself, but in some recent research on US corporations, Michael Maccoby* produced his own four classes of organisational characters:

The Jungle Fighter
His goal is power. He experiences life and work as a jungle,
where winners destroy the losers. There are two sub-types, the
lion and the fox, different in the way they walk their jungles.

The Company Man
His sense of identity is based on being part of the powerful
protective company. He is concerned with the human side of the
company, his interest is in the feelings of the people around him
but he also has a commitment to maintain the organisation's
integrity.

The Gamesman
The gamesman is the new man. His main interest is in a challeng-
ing competitive activity. He enjoys new ideas, new techniques,
fresh approaches. He is a team player, playing for the corporation.

The Craftsman
His interest is in the *process* of making something, in doing a
craftsmanlike job. Many scientists in organisations fall into this
category. They want to do their own thing rather than to master
or manage the system.

The resemblance to the four Greek gods is unmistakable.
There is, too, some historical significance in the order in which I

* M. Maccoby, *The Gamesman: The New Corporate Leaders*, Secker and Warburg,
1978.

have placed the gods. Most organisations originated as club cultures, almost squirearchies built around the personality of the founder, the owner or the patriarch. These are the traditional tribes – the first form of organisation, I suppose, informal, intuitive and personal. This form of Zeus management lasted for a long, long time. Take even the railways of England, built in the nineteenth century, incredible examples not only of engineering but of co-ordinated manual effort, in which over 200,000 men were at one time working with pick and shovel – even their organisation was based on sub-contracting to gangs of navvies working for a Zeus figure. It was the introduction of the factory that changed things, with the idea that work could be broken down into its component parts rather than multiplied out, so that, instead of having 100 gangs working on 100 different engines, you divided up the bits of the engine. This change in the technology of work required rules and procedures – the role culture. The role culture produced enormous cost reductions when linked to the new self-powered technology of steam, and then electricity. It turned out, however, to be a very expensive culture for one-off jobs and to be slow at reacting to the unexpected.

The committee of experts, on the other hand, had always been around. But it was not until the pace of change hotted up that it began to be a widely-used basis for management, called the project team or task force. As so often, it was probably the innovative pressures of war that fostered the task culture as a method of organisation.

And now, today, the increased specialisation of technology is beginning to make Dionysians of us all. The idea that armies, for instance, will soon be just groups of scientists is not such a remote possibility.

If you examine the history of most organisations, you will find that they have progressed through the club (Zeus) culture to the role (Apollo) culture, to which they have subsequently added the task (Athenian) and existential (Dionysian) cultures as they have needed to change and develop. By now, most organisations of any size are some mix of all four.

Organisations, however, need to do more than merely equip themselves with a mix of cultures and their attendant gods. The cultures must first be internally consistent for Apollonian assumptions of order and rationality will not produce results in the task culture (Athenian) part of the organisation, or vice versa. Second, of course, you need the right culture for the right job: a club (Zeus) culture for the accounts department would nearly always be inefficient. These are the two most common causes of mixed-up management, and we shall go on to examine them. Meantime, the Dinner Party Game may enliven the occasional boring evening.

THE DINNER PARTY GAME

Try this rudimentary form of cultural diagnosis when at your next party. Ask your neighbour what he does for a living.

If he replies, 'I work for X', naming an individual whom you are supposed to have heard of, he will turn out to be in a Zeus culture.

If he says, 'I work with Y company or organisation', going on perhaps, to define his job title, he will be in an Apollonian role culture.

If he puts his title first and then his organisation, as for example, 'I am in marketing, with W. company;' then he probably sees his part of the organisation, and himself, as a task culture.

If he just says, 'I am a barrister' or, 'I paint', he is a Dionysian.

The mix of differences

Why would these very different gods be required in the same organisation? Well, looked at one way, life is just a set of jobs to be done. Organisations are just larger sets of jobs to be done. These jobs seem to fall into three types:

> **Steady-state**
> **Development**
> **Asterisk**

Let me explain.

STEADY-STATE describes those jobs which are programmable, because they are predictable. They can be handled by systems and routines, by rules and procedures. In a typical organisation, they might actually account for 80 per cent of the quantity of work to be done.

DEVELOPMENT jobs are those which attempt to deal with new

situations or problems. In many cases, the result may be a new system or routine, which ensures that the next time the event occurs it will not be a problem, merely an incident in the steady-state. These are the jobs which ensure, if they are well done, that the organisation adapts. In many organisations, the groups responsible for them will include the word 'development' in their title (as in 'Product Development' or 'Systems Development').

Not all problems are development jobs, however. Some are what I can best describe as ASTERISK situations. Asterisk situations are the exceptions, the occasions where the rule-book has failed, the emergencies where instinct, and speed, are likely to be better than logical analysis or creative problem-solving. These situations have to be resolved by personal intervention.

Each of these job-types has its matching symbol and its god. The wrong god matched to the wrong job causes mixed-up management and its consequence, inefficiency.

The steady-state is a square ⬜ , and Apollo, of the role culture, is its god.

Development activities require a creative cell and Athena is their goddess, with her problem-solving capacity.

Asterisk situations are represented, naturally, by an asterisk *, and here Zeus and Dionysus share the honours (a liaison which has caused some confusion).

'Management' happens when these activities are linked together in an appropriate fashion and given some common purpose or direction. Symbolically –

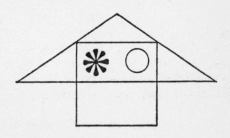

The 'manager' therefore has to embrace within himself all four cultures. He has to be able to emulate each god in the appropriate circumstances. If you want an explanation for the lure of management, this is it – the simultaneous call of four gods. And if managers look weary, well they might after this quadruple culture shock – cultural schizophrenia.

Most people can't do it, of course. Most people revert, particularly when tired or stressed, to their favourite culture. So organisations, which are made up of managers and managees, after all, tend to get culture-bound. When individuals or organisations get culture-bound they start to define jobs to fit their cultural inclinations. Zeus characters will see development problems as asterisk situations calling for their personal intervention. Apollonians will make everything fit into the rule-book, even if that is obviously the most complicated way of doing it. Athenians love creation. They are prone to inventing fine solutions to unnecessary problems (the 'Concorde' phenomenon), or to devising answers which, though immaculate, are hugely expensive to implement. To be adequate is not a challenge to Athenians, only to Apollonians. Mixed-up management.

ZEUS IN THE CARPET WAREHOUSE

My wife has in her time worked as an interior designer and decorator. She used, then, to complain that the problems of management did not require the complex and elaborate theories of management academics for their solution. 'Commonsense', she said, 'and the ability to read and write.' 'Consider', she would say, 'the carpet problems that I have. Last week I ordered a red carpet to be sent on Tuesday to Kingston. Instead, they sent a blue carpet on Thursday to Richmond. No great problem for me,' she added. 'I got on to Fred up in the warehouse, cursed him and chatted him up. "That's all right, luv," he assured me. "Bill will get the van out, pick up the blue carpet, bring it back here and get your red carpet to your customer by this afternoon." And so they did. They always get it right the second time. But the cost to them must be tremendous. Efficiency just means getting it right the first time.'

She was right, of course. But getting it right the first time would mean a system of checks and controls, matching orders to delivery chits to lorry schedules to calendar dates. All very straightforward but involving bits of paper and files and checks. Boring stuff, at least for Fred, who has been running the warehouse for thirty years and likes to keep everything in his own head. That way, he can spend his day giving orders, dealing with questions, settling disputes, placating angry customers and allocating drivers, all by personal intervention. His idea of bliss is to have three telephones ringing, one face at the window, another at the door, all needing him, at once. Then he feels indispensable, powerful, valuable.

He is a Zeus sabotaging the steady-state. An asterisk in a square. A mismatch of cultures equals expense, in this case Bill running unnecessary errands in his van.

So it is that organisations often, even usually, end up with the wrong cultures in the wrong places, with jobs defined by favourite gods rather than gods assigned to jobs. Even as individuals, in our daily lives, we are guilty of this theistic favouritism. As a confirmed Dionysian with streaks of Athena, I cannot find it in my heart to do the routine tasks of household maintenance, which I designate as 'suburban trivialities'. Inevitably, our house is prone to endless emergencies calling for creative solutions and personal inspiration. The steady-state is minimal, asterisks and cells abound.

More instances of mixed-up management:

● Developmental cells may be required to solve the co-ordination problems of the steady-state, with all its systems. If they don't, then asterisk situations arise and Zeus-style action is needed. Too much of this, however, and the steady-state becomes pitted with cells and asterisks, depriving it of much of its strength. Reverting to earlier symbols, the pillars of the temple get affected by a sort of cultural dry rot. A plethora of projects is a danger sign in a Greek temple organisation.

● In an attempt to minimise costs, Apollo organisations may attempt to standardise and systematise *everything*, even developmental jobs. An Apollonian will tend to use the past to forecast the future. Apollonian planning, for instance, will be a euphemism for 'projections'. Initiative will then be stifled by 'proper channels', and the energies of the Athenian or Zeus characters diverted into beating the system.

● In the 1960s, there was a vogue in large organisations for corporate planning departments. In many cases, these rightly became creative cells with an Athenian task culture. Staffed by young, talented and enthusiastic individuals, scenarios, alternative futures and forecasts poured out of them. Unfortunately these had often little impact on the mainstream organisation (the steady-state of manufacturing and marketing, or of administration and services). The cells were rather like hornet's nests hanging from the gutters of the Greek temple. Often the departments were housed, territorially, at the edge of the headquarters' building and attached, structurally, to the management through the most junior of the directors. Often they found it easier to communicate with other creative cells, even those in competing organisations (at conferences or courses or conventions), than with their own steady-state colleagues. But this 'organisational irrelevance' made it easier to amputate the cells when economic stringency was needed in later years.

● In a competitive talent hunt, large organisations tend to try to restock their manpower bank with an annual intake of young graduates, or MBA's, or professionals. Rightly or wrongly these people have often been educated in a problem-solving mode, the Athenian task culture. If the interest and commitment of these individuals is to be retained, they need to work on developmental tasks in problem-solving cells. But, for many organisations, the key managerial posts lie in the steady-state. The transference is not easy. Athenian notions of project teams, participative management and every man an expert can actually get in the way of routines and administration. The alternative – putting the young Athenians in as apprentices at the bottom of the steady-state pillars ('get their hands dirty', 'learn the ropes the hard way', 'a few months on the road never did anyone any harm') can be a huge culture shock to the new recruit, breeding a disillusionment with life in organisations which he may never lose.

Asterisk situations are interesting ones. They properly occur where you might least expect them. Not at the *top* of organisations but in the *middle*. At the top, the decisions have long-term implications – they are developmental problems which are more appropriately and productively solved by Athenian cells. Asterisk situations usually get thrown up by dilemmas in human relationships – which are of all situations the least amenable to prediction or programming. Personal conflicts, imminent disputes, inter-group rivalries, private crises, crucial selection or promotion decisions – these are the sparks which start an asterisk job. Of course, they can occur in the boardroom or the council chamber as well as in the factory or office, but numerically and proportionately they will be of less significance. It is at supervisor and middle management level that Zeus should reign, or out on the road, where the salesman, or driver, has to act on his own and use his initiative when the rule-book runs out. Unhappily, it is at the middle and edges of organisations that Zeus figures are least tolerated. They are most numerous at the top, although times are changing in some organisations, where the idea of president's office, a triumvirate or quadrumvirate of top talent acting as a team (or cell), is becoming more frequent, as an adaptive recognition that the prime task of the directorate is one of development, not of personal intervention. (There remain, of course, the ritual and ambassadorial duties of a tribal head. A Zeus figure is appropriate here, to represent the organisation on formal or external occasions, a sort of constitutional monarch.)

Differences, then, are necessary and good for organisational health. Monotheism, the pursuit of a single god, must be wrong for most organisations. But the choice and blend of gods cannot be haphazard. The wrong god in the wrong place means pain and inefficiency.

Apollonians At Work

Chapter 2

THE GODS AT WORK

You have now been introduced to the current gods of our organisations. An introduction is, however, only an invitation to get better
acquainted. One would be foolish, on the basis of so short an
acquaintance, to start restructuring one's organisation. The ways of
each culture need further exploration and explanation should
anyone want to act on them. Our next tasks will be to unravel the
differences between the cultures and then to suggest how the
cultures can be knitted together again to make up the balanced and
efficient organisation which would solve the first level of problem in
our organised society.

Balance and efficiency eliminate 'slack'. Slack in organisation
means the waste of resources, be those resources money, men or
materials. Slack is today the slow cancer of our organised society. It
is explained in more detail later.

I have argued that each organisation needs a mix of cultures, a
different culture or god for each major activity, process or job. But
within each activity or section of the organisation, cultural purity
should prevail. The cultures must be *internally* consistent, for whilst
organisations need more than one god, *individuals* are monotheists,
they want one god at a time, cultural purity.

Apollonian assumptions, for instance, applied to Athenian individuals produce resentment, cynicism and reluctant conformity,
like the signs of guilt in an individual who knows that he denies
himself. A healthy organisation is therefore one that is culturally
true in its parts. Where Apollo is needed and where Apollonians
work, Apollonian ways are healthy. But if the *work* demands
Apollo and your *people* are Dionysians, what then? Do you change
your clothes to suit your job or change your job to suit your clothes?
Which is an organisation's true culture? The one that the logic of the

41

work demands, or the one that exists in the existing complex of the individuals and their cultures?

Each culture makes its own assumptions as to how individuals *think and learn,* can be *influenced*, may be *changed* or might be *motivated*. These assumptions result in theories and practices of individual development, in philosophies of change, systems of control and mechanisms of reward. But what works in one culture will not work, or not work so well, in another. Cultural harmony is health as well as happiness. Fashion, that insidious agent of change, may bring Management by Objectives, or Appraisal, or Team-Building into vogue. These, however, are all mechanisms best suited to their own culture. Transplanted to another they are ineffective – worse, they generate artificial behaviour, the rituals and rites of organisations that so often are the outward signs of corporate malaise. Without cultural awareness, organisations too easily find themselves genuflecting to false gods. The only universal sin, it is held, is to be untrue to oneself. Organisational 'sin' is committed when a culture is untrue to itself. We shall look, then, at each culture in turn, at its assumptions and practices in the three critical areas of

thinking and learning
influencing and changing
motivating and rewarding

The Club Culture (Zeus)

WAYS OF THINKING AND LEARNING

Zeus individuals tend to think intuitively and in wholes. They move fast to a possible solution and test that, moving to another if the first solution looks unsuitable. A logical step-by-step analysis is not their way, for they like responding to stimulus and get bored easily. Thus they like a jumble of events (nine-minute shots, as one research study shows), and days which are full of maximum variety. They rely a lot on impressionistic, 'soft' data and set little store by the conventional hard data of reports and analyses. They think holistically or in totals, seeing the full picture and assessing that, instead of building it up bit by bit from its parts.

CHIEF EXECUTIVES IN ACTION

Henry Mintzberg watched five chief executives at work.* He concluded:

1. *The chief executives strongly favoured verbal communication, rather than written communication.*
2. *Analytical inputs – reports, documents, budgets – seemed of relatively little importance to these chief executives. They attached more weight to the soft and speculative data – impressions and feelings, hearsay, gossip. Given this data they* synthesized *rather than* analysed.
3. *The chief executive is usually the best-informed member of the organisation, but has difficulty in disseminating that information to the rest of the organisation, perhaps because his information is 'soft', intuitive and not formalised.*
4. *The chief executives had a simultaneous, experimental, hectic, unplanned work pattern. Half of their activities were completed in less than nine minutes, there were no evident patterns in their days, they preferred interruption (leaving meetings, keeping doors open), and disliked routine (only 7 per cent of verbal contacts were regularly scheduled).*
5. *'Leader', 'Disturbance Handler' and 'Liaison Man' were the words that best described their main roles.*
6. *In only 14 of 25 decision processes observed was there an explicit diagnosis stage. Chief Executives preferred to jump straight to the solution.*
7. *'Timing' was of great importance in the chief executive's assessment of actions.*
8. *In only 18 out of 83 choices made by the chief executives did they mention using explicit analysis. 'Intuition' and 'Judgment' better describe what they did.*

This Zeus-like behaviour is typical of many chief executives. The question we must ask is whether it is *appropriate* at the top of that organisation.

Zeus individuals do not learn logically or analytically or sequentially. They learn by *trial and error* or by *modelling*. And that is how

---

* Described in his book *The Nature of Managerial Work*, New York, Harper and Row, 1973.

they expect others to learn. The methods of training and development which Zeus cultures apply to their youth can be categorised as *apprenticeship* methods: 'Work with me for a while, see how I do it, and when I think it's right I will let you have a go.' In Zeus cultures, one will find systems of personal assistants, or a chief executive's cadre of young hopefuls. People will speak of protégés and crown princes, of heirs to the succession, who will be tested out in some organisational proving-grounds, by giving them their own small commands where they will be free to demonstrate their ability without causing too much damage to the parent concern. It is possible to succeed whilst still young in these cultures, given a strong patron and success in early trials. Choosing your models is perhaps the key to successful learning, for a man will then model the kinds of behaviour and values which lead to success in that business or trade or profession.

The senior figures in a Zeus culture will find *their* models in other organisations. A Zeus man will not inquire, 'What is current theory?', but rather, 'What is so-and-so doing?' He will use the luncheon tables of conferences and the receptions of society to unearth new models for his own development. Above all, to Zeus men learning must be secret. To a Zeus man, an admission of a need to learn is an admission of a deficiency. I was once asked to advise the Zeus-type board of an organisation: 'But come after the office closes,' they said, 'and use the rear entrance, if you wouldn't mind.' A professor on the premises might be an omen of disaster! After all, these are club cultures, clubs where like learns from like and outsiders have little to contribute.

WAYS OF INFLUENCING AND CHANGING

In the club cultures, it is the control of resources and personal charisma that count. If you own the club, you can tell people what to do. If you have a track record of success, then you have that certain smell which gets called charisma. A rather charming piece of leadership theory talks of 'idiosyncrasy credits', earning the right to do what you want the way you want. But the credits have to be earned, since there can be no overdraft of idiosyncrasy credits, while any man's bank balance of credits can get used up by too many idiosyncrasies and need renewal by another run of success. Wise men in Zeus cultures do not overspend their credits.

From those power bases of resources and charisma, the Zeus culture creates change by changing *people*. Individuals are the link pieces in these cultures. If a link is failing – replace it. A Zeus thinker will instinctively respond to an organisational problem by saying, 'Whose job is that? Change him.' Change *can* mean reform or education, but often, in these organisations, it means literally, replacement. Clubs can be tough, and Zeus cultures do not always respond to the logic of the argument so much as to the signature at its end. 'Who said that?' is a more pertinent question than, 'What was said?' Results speak louder than reasons and actions than arguments, for you do not change the course of these organisations by reasoning, but by reasons in the mouths of *credible persons*.

Hence the reputation of Zeus cultures for organisation politics. If the source of the argument counts more than its logic, then your choice of individuals and of clubs within clubs will be crucial. You will succeed or not, and be judged, by *whom*, not *what*, you know, although whom you know will depend on what you *do*. Inevitably, these cultures are therefore political. But that word 'political' is only a sneer when used by men of other cultures. Zeus people accept and enjoy a world of personalities and of power based on credits and ownership.

CREDIBILITY WINS

I had been asked to investigate the economics of a possible investment in North-west Africa and to advise the chairman on what action the board should take.

After a week of careful research, two late nights and much analysis, I had produced a report, full of charts, estimates and calculations. At the front was the mandatory half sheet of paper with a summary of my conclusions, summed up (conclusively, as I thought) in the properly discounted annual rate of return of 15.7 per cent after tax. It must be a good thing.

The chairman looked at it.

'Thank you,' he said, 'you've put a lot of work into this. You think we should go ahead?'

'Of course,' I said, *'no doubt about it.'*

'I see, I think I'll just have a word with Aubrey,' said the chairman (mentioning the name of a well known merchant banker). He contacted him on the phone, briefly stated the situation and there followed a five-minute conversation of which all that I heard was

'Yes . . . I see . . . Really? . . . Hm . . . Naturally . . . Quite so . . . Thank you very much, Aubrey'.

He put the phone down.

'No,' he said. *'It's not on. Aubrey says "wrong place, wrong time, wrong company". Thanks all the same, old boy.'*

I was grossly offended by this victory of old-boy network over rational analysis. In time, however, I came to recognise that the credibility of Aubrey, with much successful experience in overseas investment, was rightly going to be more important in that Zeus organisation than my untested technical reasoning.

MOTIVATING AND REWARDING

Zeus characters look for power over people and events. They like to see things happen as a result of their personal action or intervention. It is their desire that, personally, they should make a difference.

The implications are fairly clear. They enjoy situations where they have a great deal of discretion, where they have power over resources, and where personal intuitive decisions are important. To be confined in their responsibilities, or to preside over an area where technical expertise alone provides the answer to the crucial questions, are to them constraints upon their potential, and therefore de-motivating.

In Zeus cultures, money is highly valued; but it is, usually, money as an enabling factor or money as a symbol of results achieved. Many a Zeus will not think to spend heavily on personal goods, regarding this as the wasteful use of a means of power. People, or information, as well as money can be the object of their collector's instinct, knowing intuitively that these commodities are often at least as powerful as money. To this end, they will invest considerable time in creating and maintaining *networks*, potential sources of useful people, useful information, or even cash. Such men seldom rest from their labours, because they do not work for rest but for zest: in resting, they might miss an opportunity to make a difference. They like uncertainty (including gambles), because uncertainty implies freedom to manoeuvre.

It all fits well into the club culture: trust and empathy backing up intuitive decisions; personal charisma based on a track record of success; money as a thermometer of success; politics, people and networks as a way of life. Reward these people with responsibility: give them resources, a challenge and your trust. Control them by results, or the look in their eyes, not by pension schemes or titles or even office cars.

PERCY AND THE POTATOES

After one long hot European summer, potatoes got expensive in the shops. One Saturday I went shopping with a friend – a successful ship broker, one of those men who was clearly very wealthy but always needed to borrow money, for his own was all committed. We were staggered by the price of potatoes and walked out refusing to buy any.

Two weeks later, I saw him again:

'Remember those potatoes?' he said. 'What did you do about them?'

'I went home and decided to buy rice instead,' I replied. 'Why, didn't you?'

'Oh, no, I rang up a contact in Calcutta, ordered 2,000 tons of Indian potatoes at £100 per ton, arranged freight and insurance for £30 per ton and sold them in advance to a London merchant I knew *for £230 per ton.'*

'But, Percy,' I said, 'that's £100 per ton profit and on 2,000 tons . . .'

'Don't worry,' he said, smiling, 'it didn't come off. The Indian Government stopped the shipment on the docks, but for three phone calls it was worth the chance.'

I switched to rice. He nearly made £200,000. But he maintains an extensive network. I would not have known who to ring even if I had thought of it. Besides, what would I do with £200,000 – invest it? He would have staked it all on another deal.

The Role Culture (Apollo)

The role culture is quite different. Apollonians think differently and therefore make different assumptions about influence, control and the motivation of others. It may have something to do with which side of the brain got developed first (see below), the environment of one's youth or even the first organisation encountered in life. Apollo followers will find Zeus people crude, irrational, unpredictable, frightening at times, certainly different. The two cultures do not mix. A Zeus will chafe under an Apollonian regime and forget to trust his intuition or his network. An Apollo can be useful to a Zeus superior, but his more logical ways must be understood and tolerated by the Zeus figure if his true capacity is to develop.

ARE YOU RIGHT OR LEFT BRAINED?

There is an emerging consensus that our talents may have something to do with which side of our brain got developed first. Scientists have known for some time that the brain has two distinct hemispheres. In the left hemisphere of most people's brains are located the logical thinking processes. This left side of the brain works sequentially, in a linear manner. Language is one common example. The right hemisphere looks at patterns, complete images or relationships.

Speech seems to belong to the left side, but movement and emotions to the right, logic to the left, inspiration and creativity to the right. Much of education is linear or sequential or verbal – stimulating the left side but perhaps neglecting the right. Those who are bad at logic may be good at art. Lawyers, scientists, accountants may have a developed left brain; artists, politicians – and some managers? – a developed right brain.

Henry Mintzberg has suggested* that successful chief executives rely more on 'feel' and intuition than systematic reasoning (right more than left), that they 'synthesise' rather than 'analyse', that they know, intuitively, more than they can communicate, revel in

---

* H. Mintzberg, 'Planning on the left side, managing on the right', *Harvard Business Review*, July-August 1976.

ambiguity and dislike regularity. He goes on to propose that planning is a left-brained activity, which can be made systematic, but that creative strategy needs right-brain thinking, which usually comes from one man.

Are Apollo and Athena left-brained, Zeus and Dionysus right-brained?

WAYS OF THINKING AND LEARNING

Apollo definitely prefers the left-hand side of the brain. Apollonian thinking is logical, sequential, analytical. Apollonians would like to believe in a formally scientific world, where events move according to predetermined formulae. They like to proceed from problem definition to the identification of the appropriate solution mechanism ('This is a logistical distribution problem, therefore apply the appropriate operations research technique'). On the whole, the more of these mechanisms you know, and can use, the more problems you are likely to be able to deal with. Efficiency tends to mean simplification, getting things down to the bare but essential features.

Intelligence is a useful indicator of ability, but it will be intelligence of the convergent rather than divergent kind – straight rather than lateral thinking.

Learning, therefore, in Apollonian cultures, is to do with the acquisition of more knowledge and skills; it is additive, and it is acquired by a *transfer* process (called 'training'), in which those who possess the desired knowledge or skills pass them on to those who don't. It follows that individuals can, to a large extent at least, be classified according to their possession of knowledge, experience (another sort of knowledge) and skills, and allocated to roles which require particular sets of these. If the requisite skill is lacking it can, by training, sometimes be provided.

This way of looking at thinking and learning fits routine predictable activities very well. These activities *can* be broken down into sets of required knowledge, skills and experience. It is therefore in Apollonian cultures that you will find individuals spoken of as 'human resources' – resources which can be planned, scheduled, deployed and reshuffled like any other physical asset. To this culture, then, belong the formal techniques of manpower planning:

assessment centres, appraisal schemes, training needs diagnosis, training courses, job rotation – in fact, all the paraphernalia of traditional management development.

The contamination arises when these attitudes and approaches are used in other cultures. In fact, in most organisations these techniques peter out as the higher echelons are reached; for most organisations will have a Zeus-cum-Athena culture at the apex, with individuals who have the power to ignore amongst themselves the rules they set for others. The mechanisms of Apollo are thus often confined to the lower and middle regions. Though many might mutter about one law for the rich and another for the poor, there may be intuitive wisdom in this apparent flouting of democracy.

WAYS OF INFLUENCING AND CHANGING

It is in Apollonian organisations that 'authority' becomes a recognisable concept. 'With what authority do you do that?' is a meaningful question in the steady-state, whereas in a Zeus culture it would be seen as ritualistic mumbo-jumbo. Power in the role cultures stems from one's role or position or title. Written into that role is a list of rights as well as responsibilities. The organisation chart (an indispensable piece of equipment in role cultures, although often unheard-of in club cultures) is a diagrammatic way of showing who can give orders to whom or via whom. If you don't have the title you can only *ask,* not *tell.* The authority of your position not only entitles you to tell someone to do something, it also allows you to create a complex of rules, procedures and systems for your own domain. These rules, procedures and systems are the railways of the steady-state. They direct and steer the flow of information and activities which turn inputs into outputs. And, as with railways, the driver (manager) is there to influence the speed, not to control direction. In an Apollo culture, the manager is the person *in* authority, whereas the Zeus manager *has* authority (his own, not that of the organisation).

It is a misconception to believe that managing means decision-making in the role culture. Decisions are in fact few in number and are very much of the processing category ('Do we let that go, start this one, direct that one?'). It is the design of the organisation's railway system which is crucial: its operation only requires an adherence to timetables. Administration is a word that fits Apollo cultures but is anathema to Zeus.

It follows that, to change Apollonian systems, one must change either the sets of roles and responsibilities (the *structure*), or the network of rules and procedures (the *systems*). Changing any individual (the engine driver) has a minor impact compared with changes in the structure or systems (the lines of track or the time-table). Astute Zeus men trapped in an Apollo culture will adapt their own cultural instincts, and use the rules and procedures and role descriptions of Apollo to lock in their competitors and to free themselves. In so doing they distort the logic of the organisation, and so contaminate that culture and their own. This is an example of the unconstructive politics of organisations – the manipulation of the Apollonian systems for personal advantage.

BUDGETS IN APOLLO

Budgets in Apollo cultures are one way of defining one's organisational territory and personal discretion. It is tempting to any man of self-conceit to enlarge his domain by bidding for an increased budget. But one man's increase must be another man's decrease, unless an enlarged budget for the total organisation is accepted.

An enlarged total budget has, of course, to be accompanied by a matching increase in output – if not, then organisational inflation occurs, an increase in the 'money supply' of the organisation without an accompanying increase in productivity. In organisational terms, the 'money supply' is activity. Under budget inflation, activity or 'busyness' rises, but output remains constant. In physics, it is known as Brownian motion.

Apollonians prefer compromise to conflict. The mechanics of compromise breed budget inflation. It takes a tough and ruthless new arrival, or the imminence of catastrophe, to slash budgets. Apollo cultures, when thriving, tend therefore to be prone to a creeping inflation, with 'activity' increasing faster than output.

Are budgets, one must ask, an underlying cause of the progressive paralysis of large organisations?

WAYS OF MOTIVATING AND REWARDING

Apollo men are tidy men. They value order and predictability in
their lives as in their affairs. Things need to fit into place, with
contracts precise and honoured, roles prescribed and kept to.
'Duty' is an important concept to them, as is the notion of obligation, or responsibility to keep one's own part going. They are
seldom curious, believing that the world around them is on the
whole organised by people who should know what they are doing
(even if the evidence is sometimes lacking!).

It is not easy to describe the motivation of Apollonians without
making them seem dull. That is because they pursue certainty as
avidly as a Zeus man shuns it, and because the role, or the job to be
done, is at least as important as the deeper purpose behind it all. If it
sometimes seems remarkable that life goes on with its seed-time and
harvest, buying and selling, fetching and carrying, despite the erup-
tions of economic crises or armed rebellions, it is Apollonians that
we must thank for it. Head down in their role, they prefer to assume
the certainty they cannot always see. This gives them a particular
slant on life. An Apollonian believes in life insurance and pension
funds, confident that life has sufficient predictability for it to be
sensible to make long-term provisions for the future. A Zeus sees a
pension only as a source of realisable assets. An Apollonian finds
sense and security in the budgets and job descriptions of a formal
organisation, even if he may debate the details, whilst a Zeus will
view them only as constraints on his opportunism.

Again, these characteristics fit the requirements of the role
culture, which relies on predictability to be effective. The complex
of long-term careers, pension schemes, career planning, role descriptions, rules, procedures and operating plans which a role culture
needs to do its work, all fit the 'psychological' contract required by
Apollonians. They are very contractual people, in fact, and are
more inclined than most to formalise that psychological contract,
turning it into a full legal contract in many cases – a tendency which
can frustrate the Zeus personalities who often sit at the top of their
organisations.

Because Apollonians value the power that is conveyed by the
formal authority of their role, they are appropriately rewarded by
an increase in formal authority and its outward visible sign, status. It
is in role organisations that people most avidly compare and

compete for the status symbols of the organised society: the company car, the expense account, the executive suite. It is appropriate that they should, though to another culture this would seem a meaningless and petty game.

The Task Culture (Athena)

This is the culture of the group, the group of experts focusing on a common task or problem. It is the organisational culture which most suits those who have been rationally educated in a democratic society, people who would like to think that they are living in a meritocracy and who would not be offended to be called meritocrats themselves. Success, to organisational Athenians, is desirable if it has been earned. Such men will see Zeus people as over-privileged, or lucky, or unduly thoughtless. They may admire the forcefulness of a Zeus on occasion, but would wish it had been preceded by more counsel and deliberation. Apollonians will be seen by Athenians as useful but boring people, desiring to perpetuate the present rather than explore the potential of the future and of change. Most of the new professionals in organisations, those who think of themselves as 'marketing men' or 'corporate planners' or 'product managers' will see themselves as task culture people, Athenians. It is, in fact, the form of management that most people accept and aspire to. Unfortunately, as the last chapter indicated, it is an expensive and luxurious way of running organisations, so it is frequently contaminated: a problem solved by Athenians has to be administered in Apollonian ways. But the people are often the same, and there lies the *rub*.

WAYS OF THINKING AND LEARNING

Athenians are problem-solvers. Problems are solved best, they think, by a mix of creativity with some applied logic. Fundamental, too, to the process of problem-solving is the ability to work with others. Many brains make better solutions, as long as they work with, not against or for, each other. Learning, therefore, is acquiring the ability to solve problems better. Some technical aids may help and a little Apollonian instruction can sometimes be

useful, but the crucial learning is by continual exploration or discovery, successive problem-solving of the hypothesise-test-
rehypothesise variety. Mix with this the requirement to learn to
work with others, and you get the kind of group problem-solving,
discovery learning, project-based approach of so many schools,
courses, and training centres. The case study of law schools and
management courses is the most frequent vehicle for this type of
learning, supplemented by 'group-effectiveness' training embrac-
ing such devices as 'T-Groups', 'Power and Influence Workshops'
and 'Team-Building Laboratories' – all admirable in their own
cultures.

Athenian cultures tend to think of individuals as resourceful
humans rather than human resources, regarding them as people
who are responsible for their own ultimate destinies but who at the
moment are available for assignment to particular problem areas.
In these cultures, therefore, there is more likely to be a bidding
system for jobs and positions than in the Apollonian steady-state.
Leaders recruit teams, or individuals apply to join groups. Assignment is usually subject to the agreement of both individual and
leader. A commando unit where the commander has had no say in
the choice of his men will not be very effective. If there are appraisal
and development schemes in these cultures, they will be likely to be
so devised that the *individual* initiates any discussion or action.
Self-development will be encouraged and mobility between organisations will not be frowned upon.

WAYS OF INFLUENCING AND CHANGING

Organisational Athenians bow down to wisdom and expertise. To
command in a task culture, you must have earned the respect of
those you command. This command can then be exercised through
the socially acceptable form of *persuasion*. Obedience is replaced
by agreement. There is a lot of talk, argument and discussion in task
cultures, where discussion documents abound and it is expected
that what is written is read. In this culture, unlike those of Zeus and
Apollo, you begin to rely on the rational strength of your case to win
your way. To do so, however, it is first necessary to define the
problem and win agreement to that definition and to its priority for

the group. 'Problem-solving', say Athenians, 'starts with problem-finding.'

Task cultures work best when a heterogenous group of talents finds its homogeneity through identification with a common cause, task or problem. The first step to influence in these cultures, then, is to change the definition of the focal *problem or task*. Change the problem and you change the direction of activity. Only in cases of imminent disaster can the new problem be *imposed*. More usually it grows out of a changed consensus in the group. Any newcomer wishing to change things must first remember that he cannot even raise the problem of the critical problem until he has the respect of the group. But this respectability can be imported. It can be earned in one place and transported to another. Athenians are cosmopolitans to a degree – that is, they believe that expertise travels, and that one is a citizen of the world, not of one organisation.

The task culture is beloved of the 'new' professional (the marketing, production, planning and development experts of modern corporations) because of this transferability of expertise. In a task culture you can gain the credibility of an expert without the kind of personal charisma necessary in a Zeus culture. These qualifications act as an introduction in the Athena culture, whereas you need a patron or a track record in the world of Zeus. Of course, if your subsequent actions give the lie to your qualifications, these quickly get eroded, while in time a track record amounts to a qualification and can then be transported to another organisation.

Athenian task cultures tend, therefore, to deal with change by 'boxing the problem'. This is an organisational technique which consists of identifying the problem, allocating staff time to dealing with it, and recognising this new distribution of resources and priorities by putting a new *box* on the organisation chart: a box whose title is, in effect, the problem. If, for instance, the problem is one of Co-ordinating Subsidiary Plans, a group (permanent or temporary) can be set up to deal with this dilemma, and legitimised by the allocation of a box on the chart and the appropriate title of Division, Department, Unit, Group, Committee or Task Force (depending on its size and permanence). In a task culture, it is usually possible to identify its major concerns by examining the titles of its current committees or study groups.

A predominantly Apollonian or role culture will, sensibly, surround itself with many task culture groups to attend to its needs for change. A Greek temple organisation, finding itself in a changing market or technology, will rapidly become cross-strutted with a whole variety of co-ordinating teams, planning groups and investigating committees. This is fine. The confusion arises when such groups believe that the effectiveness of their reasoning will influence the Apollonian part of the organisation, or when the steady-state Apollonians ignore the task groups because they are inadequately enmeshed in the formal authority structure. Problem-solving, you see, is fine as a method of influence *inside* the task culture, but to influence another culture you have to play its games.

ATHENA INTO ZEUS WON'T GO

The top echelon of the consultancy company was being reorganised. Times were leaner and a new, tougher and more directive style of management was, probably rightly, thought to be required at the top. The four chief barons conferred privately, off-site, meeting in their own homes. The large, consultative top management group was to be disbanded. Its leisurely, reflective, debating style would be too cumbersome for the new urgency they wanted to implant. Instead, these four would comprise the Chairman's Group, which would be the top power group in the consultancy.

Then there would be an administration committee to look after what we would call the steady-state activities. Although very necessary, this was, in this organisation, very much the housekeeping role and consequently of low status.

But the consultancy had other longer-term problems: its future, for instance, and the question of standards and product quality, of talent, development and recruitment. In a typically Athenian fashion, part-time committees were set up to 'deal with' these matters, and the chairmanship given to the most appropriate people in the firm.

One of them refused the task – to the amazement of the chairman (after all, the appointment was by way of being a compliment). 'You do not understand the nature of power in this organisation,' said the refusing manager. 'Unless the chairmen of your committees are also members of the Chairman's Group, their work will be ineffectual and I do not want to be busy being ineffectual.'

The chairman was puzzled, angry and hurt. A proper Athenian by nature, he saw the other's response as a greedy and irresponsible bid for personal status. The manager, probably rightly, saw a Zeus culture forming at the top of a rather fuzzy and extravagant task culture, a Zeus culture in which membership of the club would be an essential prerequisite to the exercise of influence at the top. Talking from different, but undeclared, cultural assumptions, the argument degenerated into a personal quarrel.

The committees exist. They do not matter very much _ Athenian appendages to the new Zeus club. The chairman is contemplating joining them, 'to beef them up a bit'. The manager, like Achilles, sulks in his tent. A cultural misunderstanding clutters up the organisation.

WAYS OF MOTIVATING AND REWARDING

Athenians like variety and get bored by certainty. But they are problem-solvers rather than difference-makers, looking for a dilemma rather than a vacuum. In this way they differ from Zeus, although, just as in the myth Athena sprang fully-armed from the head of Zeus, so, in a way, the Athenian culture can provide the brains to Zeus's impulse. Athenians, however, also respect expertise and professionalism and are concerned, therefore, with their own self-advancement, self-advancement in a professional rather than hierarchical sense, although promotion can often be the outward sign of professional success.

When Athenians talk of 'getting the job done', they bring a different flavour to the phrase than when Apollonians say it. Athenians imply a problem solved and dealt with – something finished once for all; whereas Apollonians work in a continuous present and might more commonly say 'getting on with the job'. Thus it is that an Athenian prefers the task to be defined rather than the role, for he wishes to keep discretion over the means to any given end. 'Objectives' he will buy, not 'Role Descriptions'. Teams, the personalities and talents who make them up, interest him greatly, whereas the Apollonian would prefer to know the rules governing their interaction. The Athenian is content to be judged by results, whilst in Apollo cultures the results can seldom be attributed to any individual or set of individuals, so that it must be means, the performance in a role, which has to be judged.

Athenians therefore flourish under conditions of variety, problem-solving and opportunity for self-development. They respond to payment by results, to group assignments and to 'defined uncertainty' – the solution of identified challenges. Appropriately, they work in the development areas of organisations, in predominantly task cultures, such as consultancies, research groups, advertising agencies, or, increasingly, at the very top of very large organisations. They get restless in the steady-state and can be indecisive in crises.

MONEY OR . . .?

Lisl Klein* tells of an experience which illustrates the difficulty of pinning down the precise nature of motivation.

A maintenance mechanic in a chemical process firm was being interviewed. It was an unstructured interview, during which he talked freely for two hours about his job. At first he took a fairly instrumental line: 'All I'm interested in is the money. This firm pays well and that's the only reason I stop here. What a working man wants from his job is the pay packet, and don't let anybody kid you about other fancy notions.'

Half an hour later he was talking about the firm, and discussing various things which he thought were wrong with it. The interviewer said nothing, but the mechanic seemed to think he was being inconsistent, because he stopped himself. Then he said, 'Well, you see, when you get a bit older, and the kids are off your hands, and you've paid for the house, and your wife's got a washing-machine – you don't need money so much any more. You find you start noticing the firm. And by God, it can annoy you!' (Some Athena urges?)

Half an hour after that he said, 'You know – what I really like is when the machine goes wrong and I'm the one who knows how to put it right.' (Zeus in a crisis?)

(Klein comments that any definition of his motivation would depend on where the interview finished).

---

* L. Klein, *New Forms of Work Organisation*, Cambridge University Press, 1976.

The Existential Culture (Dionysus)

Dionysians, of course, are very different again. It is anathema to a Dionysian to be classified except as *not* belonging to another classification! They like to be individuals, exceptions to all generalisations. It is therefore very difficult, and perhaps mistaken, to describe them as a class. Nevertheless, the growth of individualism in organisations is becoming one of the central dilemmas of society, and I have defined it so in this book, so the difficult must be attempted.

WAYS OF THINKING AND LEARNING

Dionysians, for example, defy rigid classification in their thinking habits. These depend a bit on their chosen profession: scientists may well think like Apollonians, artists like Zeus. To be a Dionysian, however, is to think, whether it be true or not, that you have nothing much to learn from any man. Only from life. For those at the top of their profession this may well be true in fact as well as in perception. In others, less eminent or less skilled, it can seem like unfounded arrogance, disrespect, or, at times in youth, downright rudeness.

Dionysians therefore prefer to learn by immersion, by new experiences. It often happens that a Dionysian will give up a job or a post or a project when he is total master of it, just because he is a total master of it and therefore has nothing left to learn. It is a habit infuriating to employers and clients alike.

DIONYSIAN MASOCHISM?

André Previn, the conductor, was being interviewed on the radio. 'Why', asked the interviewer, 'did you leave Hollywood and the composing of musical scores for the films just when you were doing so well and had that world at your feet?' 'Because', said Previn, 'I began to wake up in the morning without any pain in my stomach. I was no longer unsure of my capabilities.'

A publisher said, 'Academic authors are always bored by the books we *want them to write, which build on their established reputation, while publishers are always worried by the books* academics *want to write, which are about fields and topics new to them.'*

'What I hate about careers', said the young arts graduate, 'is that you know what's going to happen to you. It's so boring. It's the unexpected that develops you, swimming out of your depth.'

Dionysians will resent any attempt by others, particularly an organisation, to plan their futures or develop their abilities. They want opportunities, but demand the right to choose between them. They will talk of sabbaticals, of second or third careers, of dropping out or dropping in. In one or two organisations, the notion of 'educational credits' has been developed as a way of meeting the developmental needs of Dionysians. Educational credits are, like paid holidays, made a legal entitlement of the individual. A credit is one week's leave plus expenses for development purposes (usually a 'course'). An individual might qualify for two credits per year, which could be accumulated for up to five years. He can spend his credits any time, subject to the agreement of his superior on the exact dates and on the 'developmental' character of his proposed activity. In this way, opportunity is provided by the organisation but the choice and final decision is the individual's.

WAYS OF INFLUENCING AND CHANGING

It is hard to influence Dionysians. Since they do not acknowledge the power of the organisation, or conceive themselves as working *for* the organisation (as opposed to *in* it), there are no organisational weapons to deploy against them. Dionysians respect only *people* – but there is no predicting what they will respect them for. It can be for their talent, or for their faces. Or it may be talent one month, and personality the next.

It is this very unpredictability that gives them the personal freedom essential to the culture. Even the words 'influence' or 'change' smack of an infringement of liberty to a Dionysian. It follows that any attempt to influence or change a Dionysian is going to be much more a *contracted* procedure than in the other cultures, although in a sense any process of change or influence involves some notion of 'exchange', in which one person or persons do or get something in recognition of something else.

A Dionysian negotiation always starts with the stated or implied opener, 'What will induce you to . . .?' Only from an intimate knowledge of the person involved can one begin to make predictions as to what the particular inducement will be. As in all Dionysian situations, everything is particular, peculiar to the time, place and person, not general. Dionysians are therefore very difficult people to 'manage'. To anyone used to working on broad assumptions of similarity between similar people, it is very confusing to find that what works with A does not produce the same results with B, who is apparently a doctor, or architect, or activist, or professor in exactly the same situation.

Of course, we all have Dionysian streaks in us, but most people confine these to certain portions of their life – their gardens, their social life, their holidays. To carry them into organisations of work can make it very difficult for those in charge, for the endless series of individual negotiations involved make life both unpredictable and exhausting. It is for this reason that Dionysians have to put on the cloak of another culture, or to be irreplaceable, if they are not eventually to be evicted or discarded by their employer.

Dionysian organisations (partnerships, usually) are therefore managed in a one-on-one fashion. The 'leader' interacts with each individually, meetings being called only for the dissemination of information or to ask for ideas on a situation of common interest.

WAYS OF MOTIVATING AND REWARDING

In these areas Dionysians are, of course, the most individualistic of the lot. Once again, they are hard to characterise as a generality precisely because they insist on, almost exaggerate, their individuality. Like Zeus characters, they want personally to make a difference to the world, but it does not have to be through power or people or resources. It does not even have to be noticed. A poem in a corner, a picture unseen, a patient healed unnoticed, can also be reward enough to Dionysians. It is interesting that the true Dionysian professions actually forbid any form of advertising, whilst the more Athenian professions (consultants, estate agents, architects) find more or less discreet ways to promote their fame.

Dionysians value personal freedom above all, freedom to act and speak as they wish, but particularly freedom of their time. Obligation to a community or organisation they recognise as a necessary part of the social contract, but they will, without rancour, try to incur as little of it as possible in return for their own rights. They like to be consulted, with a reserve right of veto, but not to participate; to be asked for their views, but not obliged to give them.

If this seems an essentially selfish view of the psychological contract, one must remember that these people do not really want to work in organisations at all. They are loners who gather in organisations or communities or partnerships purely for convenience, their convenience. As part of a larger and more culture-mixed organisation, these Dionysian values, or psychological contracts, can only be tolerated if the individuals have great personal talent, if they are full professionals. As we shall see, the problems arise when the untalented begin to demand Dionysian contracts.

The first essential, then, of organisational efficiency is cultural purity. To each his own god. Harmony is health. It is when the gods compete within one activity that confusion results, for then the law of cultural propriety is infringed.

If harmony is health, the healthy (happy) organisation is one that uses the appropriate methods and assumptions of influence in a particular culture. Thus persuasion, logical reasoning (Athenian), is effective in a Zeus culture only if it comes from a member of the club; in an Apollo structure, if accompanied by the requisite authority. Techniques and rule-books (Apollonian) get ignored by Zeus figures unless it suits their purpose to use them, or they respect the author (if he can be identified). Changing people around has little impact on an Apollonian organisation, although it can be a major learning experience for the individual. Hence 'job rotation' as a favoured form of individual development in Apollonian organisations – it develops the individual whilst leaving the organisation untouched. Conversely, changing the structure or the procedures (Apollonian) has little effect on Zeus organisations if the key people, the club, remain the same. In these organisations structural change is often only a means to changing key people without too much trauma.

My descriptions of the motivational contract were of course

drawn in stereotype. As I have already pointed out, we are none of us, individuals or organisations, culturally pure. All of us like a little predictability in our lives as well as a little variety. All of us want at some time to make a personal impact. But if we are honest with ourselves (and who has more incentive to be?), we can admit that the proportions of the cultural mix differ in each of us. And there lies the problem of motivation. There is no one answer, no universal panaceas to be found in piecework systems, in job security, in lowered taxation, in job satisfaction.

Harmony, as always, is health. Reward systems designed for Apollonian role cultures, linking role performance to hierarchical promotion, can be ineffective if the psychological contracts operating are those of a Zeus culture. Apollonians understand deferred gratification – they can wait a longer time for their ultimate glory. Zeus and Athena people want quick results and rewards, discounting the future at a high rate, living for today or tomorrow rather than the year, or the decade, after next.

DISCRETIONARY DIFFERENCES?

Elliott Jaques has plausibly suggested that individuals differ in their innate capacity for discretion.* He measures discretion by the maximum time that the individual can operate without a review of the quality of his performance. Simple tasks usually have a short 'time span of discretion', maybe even of hours, whilst senior management roles have discretion spans measured in years.

A large number of studies has pointed to a consistent number of strata of discretion spans in organisational roles, as follows:

Time-Span	Stratum
(?) 20 yrs	7
10 yrs	6
5 yrs	5
2 yrs	4
1 yr	3
less than 1 yr	2
less than 3 months	1

* See further E. Jaques, *A General Theory of Bureaucracy*, Heinemann, 1976.

Giving people work that requires more discretion than their current capacity is very stressful. Jaques goes on to argue that large organisations have most jobs at the fifth, sixth and even seventh strata, but that there are few people around with those capacities.

It is intriguing to speculate whether the cultures, and cultural types, differ in the levels of strata involved. Maybe Zeus cultures operate with short time-horizons and levels of 4 and below? If so, such individuals would find the top of large organisations very stressful places. Athenians, too, may not feel comfortable with time-spans longer than two years. And Dionysians? And some Apollonians?

We don't know, but Jaques' research may be yet another reason to explain why cultures don't mix.

The confusion between Zeus and Dionysus is a very real one. Both act as individuals in situations which, whether real or imagined, demand their personal intervention. The difference lies in the power behind their action. Zeus relies on his control over vital resources and the force of his character, or charisma, backed by his experience and record of success. Dionysians are accepted because of their professional competence, because they are unique crafts-men whose skills cannot easily be replicated. A bad Zeus can make things happen, albeit wrong. A bad Dionysus is ignored. A Zeus can be incompetent in the eyes of others. A Dionysus depends on the respect of others to have any impact. On the other hand, nature is fair. Zeus needs power and wants impact. Dionysus often does not care. 'Take it or leave it' is not a Zeus remark, but it could be a Dionysian one. Dionysians are more self-contained, inner-directed and concerned about their craft. A Zeus without people to interact with will die, and the entrepreneur who claims that he will retire to his orchard when he has made his pile, is usually lying: his need to intervene in the affairs of others is not going to be satisfied with apple trees. The Dionysian, on the other hand, can be happy cultivating a garden visited only by himself. Yet, because both Zeus and Dionysus characters intervene personally, relying on their personal prowess, it is often hard to distinguish them by their behaviour. The dedicated scientist, intent on an idea, can be just as dominant, even ruthless, as the Victorian mill-owner. Many a Zeus will define himself as an organisational craftsman, an enthusiastic professional, and be both surprised and hurt by accusations of dictatorship.

Formal documented schemes of Management by Objectives will turn into time-consuming rituals in Athenian cultures, who will find their own ways of defining the common purposes of their groups. To apply the 'group-effectiveness' training of the Athenian culture to the steady-state is only to foster insecurity and uncertainty or, in Zeus cultures, outright rebellion. The notion of patron and protégé is anathema to Apollonian cultures, who regard crown princes as disruptive to their grading schemes. Yet, in their proper place, these devices work. You cannot run a factory like a trading company, nor a trading company like a consultancy. So the habits of thought and of learning are just as unlikely to be identical. They are, in fact, very different and need to be seen to be so. Cultural propriety must be preserved.

THE MISSING REFUSE BAGS

In one local authority area, it was the practice to collect refuse in plastic bags, which were distributed to householders for this purpose by the drivers of the refuse-collecting lorries.

These plastic bags had a value on the open market, as some of the lorry drivers apparently discovered. At least, it soon became clear that many of the new bags were not reaching the householders for whom they were intended.

It was, therefore, decided to set up a separate unit, with its own vans, to distribute these bags independently of the refuse vehicles.

Now lorry drivers are a special breed. Their cab is their kingdom, the road their territory. Once on the road, they answer to no man. They are the Dionysians of the motorways or the Zeuses of the delivery services. In their own spheres, they wield dictatorial power, as any housewife who offends the delivery driver will know. Refuse collectors are no exception. They are individuals with their own freedoms. Leash them if you can, and dare.

Private marketeering can be one of the side attractions of this mini-buccaneering. This is often more a game than a crime, and losing is getting caught. To stop the game as a penalty for catching some losers is seen as unjust, even, perversely perhaps, as an infringe-

*ment of liberty. Zeus is humiliated, Dionysus snubbed. Their inter-
ventionist energies, their wish and ability to be noticed, will now be
turned inwards on the system instead of outwards. Their power will
be negative.*

*In this case, the local authority sought to reduce the number of
drivers to compensate for manning the vans. The drivers retaliated by
working to rule and threatening a strike. The action of the authority
brought the drivers together as nothing else ever had. From now on,
muttering increased, morale decreased.*

Zeus will not willingly, or cheaply, submit to Apollo.

ENTER ATHENA

*The new chief executive – the radical son of his more traditional
founding father – was keen to put more life and humanity into his
father's viable but unspectacular dye-manufacturing company. This
company employed 150 people and produced a range of dyes from
base-stocks for a number of long-standing customers. Their
methods, both of manufacture and of accounting, were old-
fashioned but reliable, and adequate in a world where things did not
change very much, where growth was slow but steady, and where the
labour turnover was under 5 per cent.*

*'Groups', he announced, 'were the way to work: groups where we
earned respect from our colleagues by an honest sharing of both
problems and perceptions, where the pursuit of a common goal by
equals would produce a new synergy.'*

*Although most of the managers and supervisors did not even
understand the words he was using, he did after all pay them, so they
reluctantly agreed to attend a weekend 'Group Dynamics Workshop'
to find out about these new ways of working. A Group Dynamics
Workshop is a T-Group, a method designed to help the individual
explore the way groups work and how he can work in them by a mix
of discussion, exchange of perceptions, small tasks and a shared
reflection.*

*By the Saturday night, Bill had revealed his true feelings about
Fred, who was unlikely to forget them in a hurry; the chief executive
found that the group could discover at least one common enemy –
himself; Tom, the accountant, had withdrawn behind a wall of
silence; and, overall, a new sense of unease and defensiveness had*

entered the usual bantering conversation of the group.

The young chief executive was puzzled. It had worked so well at college and in that consultancy group he had been attached to for a while. What had gone wrong?

Athenian ways do not, however, fit the more staid and formal roles and ways of an Apollo organisation, which, like it or not, was what he had inherited.

The questionnaire at the end of this chapter provides one way of analysing and codifying the cultural preferences of your organisation and yourself. Questionnaires, of course, are fallible, particularly when one fills them in for oneself about oneself. Add to that the fact that organisations are not hard objective realities, like chairs, which can be objectively measured and described; nor is your character or personality (in spite of the attempts of some psychologists to define them). So it is clear that the scores that you arrive at can only be your view, from where you stand at this point in time, of the organisation and yourself.

The interesting thing would be to give the questionnaire to a variety of people, and then to compare their ideas of the organisation (and of you?) with yours. A lot would depend on where they worked in the organisation, whether they were looking up or down or across it when they filled in the questionnaire, and how satisfied they were in their own lives. To some extent, they probably change their cultural behaviour as they do different parts of their job. And so they should.

Questionnaire on the cultures of organisations*

To complete the questionnaire, proceed as follows:
a) Consider the organisation you work for, the whole of it. What sets of values, what beliefs, what forms of behaviour could be said to be typical of it? Look at the four statements under each of the nine headings in the questionnaire. Under each heading, rank the four statements in order of 'best fit' to the organisation as you see it (i.e. put '1' against the statement that best

* The questionnaire is adapted from one originally developed by Dr Roger Harrison.

represents the organisation, '2' against the next best, and so on). Put the figures in the column under 'Organisation Ranking'.

b) When you have done this for the organisation, then go through the whole process again, this time for yourself, reflecting your own preferences and beliefs. Try not to look at your rankings under 'Organisation' while you do this, so that your second ranking is truly independent.

When you have ranked all the statements under each of the two columns, add up the scores for all the statements that are marked (a) under each heading, then the scores for all the statements listed (b), and so on (e.g. a total score of 9 for all the (b) statements would mean that you had ranked the (b) statement '1' in each of the nine headings).

You should now be able to complete the following table.

	All (a) Statements	All (b) Statements	All (c) Statements	All (d) Statements	Total
The Whole Organisation					90
You					90

As in most questionnaires, you will want to qualify all your answers with the remark, 'It all depends . . .'. You will find it hard in some instances to find any great difference, in your own mind, between some of the statements. Do not let this deter you. The questionnaire results will not be precisely accurate, but they should provide useful indications. You will find that the best way to proceed when trying to rank each set of statements is to trust your first, almost intuitive reactions. Do not linger over them too long.

When you have completed the questionnaire and added up the scores, turn to page 72 for an explanation of the total scores.

Own ranking	Organisation's ranking
1.
(a)	*A good boss*
	is strong, decisive and firm but fair. He is protective, generous and indulgent to loyal sub-ordinates.
———	———
(b)	is impersonal and correct, avoid-

<table>
<tbody>
<tr><td></td><td></td><td>ing the exercise of his authority for his own advantage. He demands from subordinates only that which is required by the formal system.</td></tr>
<tr><td>(c)</td><td></td><td>is egalitarian and influenceable in matters concerning the task. He uses his authority to obtain the resources needed to get on with the job.</td></tr>
<tr><td>(d)</td><td></td><td>is concerned and responsive to the personal needs and values of others. He uses his position to provide satisfying and growth stimulating work opportunities for subordinates.</td></tr>
</tbody>
</table>

Own ranking	Organisation's ranking	
2.		
(a)		*A good subordinate* is hard working, loyal to the interests of his superior, resourceful and trustworthy.
(b)		is responsible and reliable, meeting the duties and responsibilities of his high job and avoiding actions which surprise or embarrass his superior.
(c)		is self-motivated to contribute his best to the task and is open with his ideas and suggestions. He is nevertheless willing to give the lead to others when they show greater expertise or ability.
(d)		is vitally interested in the development of his own potentialities and is open to learning and receiving help. He also respects the needs and values of others

and is willing to give help and contribute to their development.

Own ranking	Organisation's ranking	

3.   *a good member of the organisation gives first priority to*

(a)   the personal demands of the boss.

(b)   the duties, responsibilities and requirements of his own role, and the customary standards of personal behaviour.

(c)   the requirements of the task for skill, ability, energy and material resources.

(d)   the personal needs of the individuals involved.

4.   *People who do well in the organisation*

(a)   are politically aware, like taking risks and operating on their own.

(b)   are conscientious and responsible with a strong sense of loyalty to the organisation.

(c)   are technically competent and effective, with a strong commitment to getting the job done.

(d)   are effective and competent in personal relationships, with a strong commitment to the growth and development of individual talents.

5.   *The organisation treats the individual*

(a)   as a trusted agent whose time and energy is at the disposal of those who run the organisation.

(b)   as though his time and energy

were available through a contact having rights and responsibilities on both sides.

(c) ─── ─── as a co-worker who has committed his skills and abilities to the common cause.

(d) ─── ─── as an interesting and talented person in his own right.

6. *People are controlled and influenced by*

(a) ─── ─── the personal exercise of rewards, punishments or charisma.

(b) impersonal exercise of economic and political power to enforce procedures and standards of performance.

(c) ─── ─── communication and discussion of task requirements leading to appropriate action motivated by personal commitment to goal achievement.

(d) ─── ─── intrinsic interest and enjoyment in the activities to be done; and/or concern and caring for the needs of the other persons involved.

7. *It is legitimate for one person to control another's activities*

(a) ─── ─── if he has more power and influence in the organisation.

(b) if his role prescribes that he is responsible for directing the other.

(c) ─── ─── if he has more knowledge relevant to the task at hand.

(d) ─── ─── if he is accepted by those he is controlling.

Own
ranking

Organisation's
ranking

8.   *The basis of task assignment is*
(a) _____   _____   the personal needs and judgment
                                    of those who run the place.
(b) _____   _____   the formal divisions of functions
                                    and responsibility in the system.
(c) _____   _____   the resource and expertise
                                    requirements of the job to be
                                    done.
(d) _____   _____   the personal wishes and needs for
                                    learning and growth of the indivi-
                                    dual organisation members.
9.   *Competition*
(a) _____   _____   is for personal power and advan-
                                    tages.
(b) _____   _____   is for high-status position in the
                                    formal system.
(c) _____   _____   is for excellence of contribution
                                    to the task.
(d) _____   _____   is for attention to one's own
                                    personal needs.

Interpretation of questionnaire scores

The (a) statements represent a Zeus 'Club' culture,
the (b) statements represent the Apollo 'Role' culture,
the (c) statements represent the Athenian 'Task' culture,
the (d) statements represent the Dionysian 'Existential' culture.
The *lower* the total score for any set of statements the *more
prevalent* that culture is in your organisation or in you. A score of 9
for the (a) statements (the lower possible total) would mean a
totally pure Zeus culture. You are unlikely to have any totals as low
as that.
A table that reads, for example:

	(a)	(b)	(c)	(d)	Total
Whole Organisation	14	12	27	37	90
You	29	24	16	21	90

would mean that your organisation was a mix of Apollo and Zeus, while you prefer to be Athena backed up by Dionysus.

First – Balance Your Gods

Chapter 3

THE GODS IN BALANCE

It is now necessary to look a little more closely at the forces that influence the balance of gods or cultures in any organisation, at the problems of changing the mix of cultures when necessary, and at the way of holding that balance without contaminating the individual cultures. If the mix is wrong, or badly balanced, or is not changed when change is needed, the result is this phenomenon called 'slack' or ineffectiveness, the lurking cancer of organisations.

Effective organisations have usually formed their own balanced mix by experiment and continual adaptation. They have achieved cultural propriety and minimised slack. But success, if it is to continue, must be understood. History, the story of how it happened, is an inadequate explanation for others to use, for history cannot be relied upon to repeat itself. I shall therefore attempt to explain, functionally rather than historically, how it is that effective organisations achieve the proper balance of gods. The organised society needs more cultural propriety in its organisations, and it needs it now: it cannot wait for some Darwinian process of evolution to get there in the end.

We shall look in turn at the *forces* that influence the *choice* of mix, and the ways of *changing* and of *managing* that mix.

HOW DO YOU EXPLAIN YOURSELF?

An American visitor to Europe commented that, every time he asked the reason for something in Europe, he received the historical explanation: 'Because the King met with his nobles in this way.'

or

'Because my grandfather liked to see the mill from his bedroom.'

or

'Because my family did not approve of schools.'

or
'*Because originally they got free travel when this firm was owned by the railway.*'

'*In my country*', said the American, '*I normally get a functional explanation. Perhaps that's why you all are so interesting, while we are more efficient.*'

The influencing forces

Organisations have to live with the pressure of several counter-vailing forces. 'Management' is the act of reconciling these forces in some blend of jobs and cultures. There can be no universal formula, for the pressures will be felt differently by each organisation. The best way to express these forces is to describe their effects as tendencies: 'the greater the force, the more likely . . .'

> *The principal forces are:*
> Size
> Life-cycles
> Work patterns
> People

If we describe their effects briefly we can then come back to a discussion of what one can do about them.

Size: How many people can you relate to as individuals at any one time? Fifty? One hundred? One thousand? It all depends on how well you want to relate to them, of course, but for most people the answer must be nearer fifty than one thousand. All the cultures, except the role culture (Apollo), depend on the people within a work group knowing each other. Knowing each other implies an awareness of personality, talents and skills, as well as just a name.

The bigger you are, the more like Apollo you will be
That is the general tendency. My own inclination is to follow Antony Jay's empirical rule of ten as the breakpoint. Once you have more than ten individuals in a group, ten groups in a division, or ten divisions in a company, you have to rely on formal methods of control and co-ordination. The farmer with his three farmhands has

no need of the Apollonian devices of managerial textbooks. It can all be done intuitively and personally. The small primary school can run perfectly well with a minimum of impersonal co-ordination, hierarchies and forms. Not so the large secondary school. Small is non-Apollonian, which is not the same as saying it is beautiful, but many a small company takes growth as its goal, achieves it and hates the changes it brings. From Zeus or Athena to Apollo is quite a violent transition. Parkinson's Law that the administrative component always grows faster than the rest, ignores the influence of other factors which we have yet to examine; but, if translated and downgraded from a law to a tendency, it does emphasise that increasing size means an increasing proportion of the steady-state, a larger square. □

RESEARCH AND SIZE

As with much descriptive research on organisations, the conclusions of research on the effects of increasing size cause little surprise:*
- *As the size of the organisation increases, so does the need for co-ordination and supervision.*
- *As co-ordination and supervision increases, so does the bureaucracy.*
- *As bureaucracy increases, so do impersonal controls.*
- *Impersonal controls are accompanied by increases in absenteeism and staff turnover.*
- *The larger the size, the smaller the average amount of communication between members.*
- *As size increases, so does specialisation.*
- *As specialisation increases, the complexity of each job reduces.*
- *It is NOT always true (in spite of Parkinson's Law) that the administrative component increases faster than the rest.*
- *Apollo thrives on size.*

Life-cycles: This is another way of referring to the old chestnut of management, 'rate of change'. The tendency can be expressed as *'The higher the rate of change, the larger the influence of Athena'.*

* Based on B. P. Indik, 'Some Effects of Organisation Size on Member Attitudes and Behaviour', *Human Relations*, 1963, 16, No. 4, pp. 369-84.

The difficulty is that it is very hard to assess the rate of change. As overall measures of societal tendencies, it may be appropriate to use indicators such as speed of travel or quantities of data processed. But these are of little value to an individual organisation, to which it is more useful to think in terms of life-cycles – products, technologies, systems. How many years will each last? When the solutions of the fathers were good enough for the sons – a generational life-cycle – the Athena component in organisations was very small. When, at the other extreme, the useful life of any idea is shorter than the time it took to create it (as in some very new technologies), the Athena influence is huge.

The idea of life-cycles, too, should not be confined to industrial or commercial products. Diplomatic rules, educational policies, housing plans, co-ordination systems – all have their life-cycles. When you get to minimum life-cycles – only one of anything is ever made (in consulting firms, some architects' offices, art studios and the like) – there is an almost pure Athenian culture, with the Apollonian methods reserved for the housekeeping duties of the 'services and administration'.

It is impossible to quantify the proportions in general terms. It would be nice to be able to state that, if the life-cycle equals the creative cycle, Apollo will equal Athena; if double, then double Apollo. Life is not that simple, but such a rule of thumb will do for a start, as a quantification of this tendency alone. Remember, however, that there are other factors at work to influence the final mix.

In practical terms, this tendency means that organisations adapt to shortening life-cycles by, for instance:

pulling people out of straight production into production development, or from sales to market development;

setting up task forces or study groups;

calling in consultants;

cutting down the production or administrative component, leaving development groups intact;

creating a top management group, removed from operational responsibility.

In all these cases the *problem-solving capacity* (Athena) is increased, not the *administrative capacity* (Apollo).

Work patterns: There are three different ways to arrange the work to be done in an organisation:
as *flows* (where one section's work is the input for the rest);
as *copies* (where the work of each section is identical);
as *units* (where the work of each section is independent).

An assembly line is the most familiar example of a *flow pattern*. It is a logical way of organising complex, repetitive work, allowing specialisation and economies of scale at each stage. A chemical process plant is an automated flow pattern. A local government office is often a clerical flow pattern, as a particular piece of paper goes through successive official stages in the office. A school, or a hospital, can also be regarded as a flow pattern, with students or patients as the pieces.

Branch banking, multiple stores, gasoline stations are familiar examples of *copy patterns*. Economies of scale and co-ordination depend on each unit being a replica of the others. If airline tickets were not filled in, identically, in every ticket agency, it would be much more difficult to arrange interchanges among airlines, or communal booking facilities. If every outlet of a multiple store did its own purchasing and pursued its own billing procedure, the economics of mass purchasing and of centralised accounting would be impossible.

Unit patterns apply where standardisation is impossible or unnecessary. Trading and dealing activities, craftsman manufacture (pottery, painting or architecture), the self-employed, small organisations, such as farms or independent shops, are all familiar examples of this pattern.

The tendency is for flow and copy patterns to require Apollonian (role culture) methods.

Unit patterns can be Zeus-like (most frequently), or Athenian (if the collaborative work of a group is needed), or Dionysian (as with most professionals). Teachers, for instance, are Dionysian in their own approach and prefer to operate as single units, yet often find themselves part of a flow or copy organisation. Dilemma! And the experiments at Saab and Volvo automotive plants have been attempts to create unit patterns in a traditional flow pattern industry.

It is not, however, only the economics of standardisation that

drive organisations towards flow or copy patterns. The concept of
control is also at work. Control is important if you need to regulate
or inspect quality *before* the event. It is very hard to do this syste-
matically or efficiently in unit patterns, because quality control in
unit patterns is a post-factum feature. If you make a bad deal, or a
bad picture, or sell the wrong item in your store, the mistake will not
be discovered until *after* the event. In many businesses and offices,
this is not critical. Although errors are always undesirable, it is often
impossible and unnecessary to avoid them altogether. We can and
do learn by them. But some errors are too critical to be left for
post-factum discovery. This particularly includes errors which
might cost human lives, and in such cases antecedent checking is
usually required by law (e.g. in aircraft manufacture, the drug
industry, housebuilding and food manufacture). Even when it is not
a legal requirement, an organisation can decide that the financial
cost of an error is punitive and it must be stopped before it happens.
It will then find itself insisting on copy or flow patterns of work, and
an increase in the role culture (Apollo).

   The takeover of a small firm by a larger one can often result in the
unit pattern of the small firm changing to conform to the copy
pattern of the larger one. This causes a culture change, usually from
Zeus to Apollo. Once again, the culture shock to the individuals can
be severe, the more so because it is not understood.

THE KALMAR PLANT

*Volvo's Kalmar car-assembly plant is the most visionary experiment
in job redesign yet.*
   *The shape of the building is designed to provide a lot of sides and
corners. Each corner provides a home for teams of 15-20 workers
with their own workshops. There are more than 20 of these small
shops, each with its own entrance and facilities, such as change room,
sauna bath, coffee and conference room, coffee machines and even a
view. Duplicate facilities are built in to provide for a possible second
shift with its own territory. Employees are allowed free use of phones
for local calls to keep in touch with the outside world.*
   A true little village.
   *Around these villages glide wagons, silently controlled by elec-
tronic impulses from under the floor. A wagon, a low platform*

carrying the chassis or body, can be called in by one of the workshops when the workers are ready for it. The wagon can be tilted to any angle, stops instantly if it bumps into any person or thing, and is constantly checked by computer for work faults, which are fed directly back to the workshop for rectification.

Teams are required to produce a daily quota; breaks and idle time are not monitored or controlled. The quota was fixed by union negotiation, not imposed by management.

'It all sounds too good to be true,' comments John O'Meara, of Witwatersrand University Business School, in South Africa, after visiting Kalmar, 'but is it really working? The answer was that the new plant had so far exceeded expectations.

FROM UNIT TO COPY – ZEUS TO APOLLO

The old man was sawing my length of timber for me with quite unnecessary care and precision in the timber yard.

'You look as if you love that wood,' I said. 'Were you ever a professional carpenter?'

'Yes, indeed,' he replied. 'I used to work for X,' (naming a famous furniture designer)

'Why did you turn to a timber yard, then?'

'Well, X got taken over by YZ company [a conglomerate with a furniture division] and everything had to be made to fit their standard designs. Suddenly, it wasn't fun any more. All the pride went out of the work. And then they said they didn't need so many people, so the older craftsmen went – the more expensive ones, you see. In the old days, Terence [the owner and founder] used to be around – we all knew him and knew how he wanted things – great man. After "they" came, it was all forms and regulations and inspectors. Not the same at all. So now I just work to get money. It's OK here. Just a job.'

People: Much as one may sometimes deplore it in others, people are different! This is not going to be an excursion into personality theory – that is an unnecessarily complex field for our cultural preferences. But there is probably a bit of each god in each of us and we are all to some degree adaptable – that is, when we have to, we will live in alien cultures, though usually unwillingly and at a price.

Our cultural preferences are probably thrust upon us by our early experiences and environments. No doubt some are born as Zeus or Dionysus, but since these cultures describe the ways we relate to our fellow men, it is likely that our attitudes to them are due more to our environments than to our genes. There is good evidence to suggest that certain cultures are more popular in certain societies, indicating that there is some kind of societal conditioning.

Japanese are different from Italians, aren't they? But were they *born* different in their cultural preferences? Our education can bend us towards cultures or away from them, as can the values and customs of our early homes. Father's occupation is still the best predictor of the son's choice of job – and probably of culture as well.

And though people certainly can adapt, they do not necessarily adapt easily. If your organisation is currently manned by Apollonians, wanting a secure life and a fair day's pay for a fair day's work, it will be hard to create a range of developmental cells and Athenian attitudes. You have got to work with what you've got in the way of people. That applies to the organisation, to the catchment area of your work and to society as a whole. Deportation is becoming as rare in organisations as in society (it is almost necessary to prove an illegal offence before dismissing a man), and wholesale re-stocking of an organisation is unthinkable in democratic societies.

The tendencies of the 'people forces' are too varied to be easily summarised. Some of them are obvious:

Youth does not relish Apollo, with that culture's need to play down individuality;

The more you've been educated, formally, the further down the scale of cultures you are likely to be (e.g. doctors and architects, with unusually long training periods, are often Dionysian, the illiterate driver or entrepreneur a Zeus);

Educational philosophies which emphasise the individual and his development (as opposed to the inculcation of received wisdom or values), will produce people with Athenian or Dionysian preferences;

The hungry obey, the contented argue. Apollo cultures rely on an *economic* contract between organisation and employee, a contract that works best where economics matter most;

Personality characteristics affect cultural preferences. A restless intuitive extrovert will find Apollo tiresome. Individualists dislike

Athena, with her group emphasis, as much as they do Apollo. Conformists prefer Apollo.

And so on.

Remember that these are tendencies, not laws. As humans we have the delightful ability to be the exceptions to our own generalisations.

DO THE GODS HAVE PERSONALITIES?

In his popular book, Know Your Own Personality,* *Eysenck has related two of the personality dimensions which he uses to categorise personality (Introversion-Extraversion and Stable-Unstable) with the traditional divisions of the ancients. It is interesting to speculate (there is no factual evidence) whether the quadrants provide clues to the personalities which I have associated with the different gods. Dionysus is the difficult one to fit into the picture. A law unto himself, a Dionysian can perhaps be found in any quadrant, although some of the characteristics of the 'empty' quadrant (Melancholic) must fit many a 'loner'. (see diagram on p. 84).*

The choice of blend

Where do we go from here? The organisation is a mix of four activities (steady-state, development, asterisk and management), each with its cultural god or gods. The proportion of each activity is influenced by the four forces. Thus a *large* organisation with *long life-cycles*, operating in a low-technology *facsimile pattern* with *minimally educated* workers from a depressed area, is very likely – almost certainly, in fact – to have evolved with a large number of steady-state activities and to be dominated by an Apollo role culture. Some canning factories, perhaps; the automobile industry, in some of its parts; 'nuts and bolts' manufacturers of any size; the textile industry of yesterday.

A *small* organisation, making hand-made objects *to order* on a *unit* basis, with highly-trained *craftsmen*, will resemble a Dionysian partnership; whilst the account teams of an advertising agency, *smaller*, with *short life-cycles* and requiring *talented groups* of

* H. J. Eysenck and G. Wilson, *Know Your Own Personality*, Pelican, 1976.

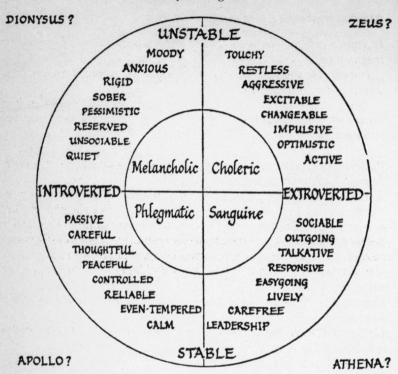

DIONYSUS ?

ZEUS?

UNSTABLE

MOODY
ANXIOUS
RIGID
SOBER
PESSIMISTIC
RESERVED
UNSOCIABLE
QUIET

TOUCHY
RESTLESS
AGGRESSIVE
EXCITABLE
CHANGEABLE
IMPULSIVE
OPTIMISTIC
ACTIVE

Melancholic | Choleric

INTROVERTED

EXTROVERTED

Phlegmatic | Sanguine

PASSIVE
CAREFUL
THOUGHTFUL
PEACEFUL
CONTROLLED
RELIABLE
EVEN-TEMPERED
CALM

SOCIABLE
OUTGOING
TALKATIVE
RESPONSIVE
EASYGOING
LIVELY
CAREFREE
LEADERSHIP

STABLE

APOLLO ?

ATHENA ?

people, will be very Athenian if successful; although some agencies have been built up by the careful selection of a few Zeus characters with their own webs (mini-agencies, in fact under one umbrella).

If you want to know how you arrived where you are, this method of cultural analysis will explain it. If you want to know why there are more creaks and groans in the organisation than you would choose, this may provide the clue (a culture-mix out of line with the principal forces). If you, individually, are unfulfilled or uninspired or underpaid, this analysis may show you why (an Athenian trapped in a temple?). More generally, cultural analysis will indicate the underlying reason for much of the incompetence in our organised society.

WORK-TYPES AND PEOPLE-TYPES

Is your work pattern recurrent (a repeating schedule of events) or fragmented?

Is it trouble-shooting or long-term requiring sustained attention? Is it responding or self-generating?

These questions come from Rosemary Stewart's investigations into the pattern of managerial work.* She finds three basic patterns, and some mixed.

Pattern 1 – Systems Maintenance *(Works Manager, Production Manager, Branch Manager)*
Exception-handling, responding to problems, monitoring performance. A fragmented work pattern, particularly in a variable market or work-flow situation, more crises than predictability. Frequently found in middle and junior management positions, not usually found in senior management except in small companies or with individuals who like to work this way. Will suit individuals who are energetic, resourceful, decisive and perhaps restless. Zeus perhaps?

Pattern 2 – Systems Administration *(Financial Accounting, Staff Manager)*
Concerned with the accurate processing of information and the administration of systems. The more formalised the organisation the more of these administrative, recurrent, time-deadline jobs there will be, particularly in the middle of junior levels. Suits those who like security and dead-lines. Apollo?

Pattern 3 – Project *(Research Manager, Project Leader, Product Sales Manager)*
Long-term tasks, often of a one-off nature. Little recurrent work, more need for sustained attention. There will be a greater need for self-generation and any fragmentation will be self-imposed. Found at all managerial levels. Suits those who can sustain a self-generating interest over a long time. Athena?

Pattern 4 – Mixed *(General Manager, Production Engineer)*
A mixture of the previous three. The occupant of the job has to vary his work pattern. Management?

* See further R. Stewart, *Contrasts in Management*, McGraw-Hill, 1976.

Changes in the balance

Any balance of gods and cultures, once achieved, is bound to be only temporary. Organisations must respond continually to their environment, even if they do not themselves set out to change that environment. Growth is one typical, self-induced problem of cultural change.

A small pottery of craftsmen, inspired by its success to grow and mechanise, will run into conflicts as Dionysians are confronted with Apollonian systems. The people will resent the new need to keep count and to record, to itemise and to cost. They will dislike the necessity of employing non-potters at comparable salaries to sell or keep the accounts. They may hire an 'administrator' and hope that these new features of their life will go away. They won't. Although they themselves have created these new forces, their creatures have lives, or at least cultures, of their own.

This 'stage of growth' problem is a common one. Zeus begets Apollo as the system grows. Then Athena is needed to maintain the development. 'Management' comes to mean the co-ordination of all three, and sometimes four gods in one whole. Previously, 'management' meant 'Zeus'. Now it only sometimes does. Naturally, people find it hard to realise that a way of behaving which worked yesterday does not, cannot, work today. Self-imposed culture change of this sort is very stressful. It seems to carry with it a loss of identity as the culture shock gets personalised – 'I can no longer make things happen, what has gone wrong with *me*?'

The irony of success often lies in the fact that the methods which brought success are not those which are best suited to maintaining it. The commander who won battles was often the wrong person to administer the territories he had conquered. The planners are often the wrong people to implement their plans – culturally wrong, I mean – as the saga of the Bosco Chemical Factory demonstrates.

THE BOSCO CHEMICAL SAGA

Bosco Chemicals UK Ltd had been doing well. Their eight lines of imported pharmaceutical products had produced an annual growth of 25 per cent in turnover and profits. Hitherto, they had been essentially a field sales force based on a warehouse in London, but they decided in 1970 that their turnover now justified doing the blending and formulation in a factory of their own. Based on estimated factory costs and the expectation of a continued growth in sales, the economics of the venture appeared good, for the base stock was available locally and the imported finished products had been expensive.

Being historically only a distributing organisation, they had no manufacturing competence. So they bought some, the best. They hired a group of nine people to oversee the design and construction of the factory and then to be its first management team. The nine were young, highly qualified, well paid, and between them they covered the range of competences required. They were headed by Martin, 34, the factory manager designate. Martin typified his team. He was idealistic, enthusiastic and saw this job as an opportunity to show that factory work could be meaningful and interesting as well as profitable to individual and organisation.

For two years, the nine worked together in one large room, dominated by a model of the new factory in the centre. They were planning everything, from the layout of the machines to the decor of the refreshment room; from pay scales to uniforms. They sat in a circle. This in itself mirrored Martin's approach to management – a collaborative problem-solving activity, spurred by mutual respect between colleagues. Hopefully, the whole factory of 400 people would work like that. The room, when you visited it, was bubbling with excitement, ideas and lively good fellowship.

In the autumn of 1973 the factory opened, only a month behind schedule. There was a backlog of orders, piled up in anticipation of own-manufacture. But there was also a start of worldwide recession in the industry and a consequent tightening of margins. Inflation in the UK was starting to rise. The first months were difficult (teething problems, they called it), with machines breaking down, operators without experience, unanticipated quality problems. 1974 was a disaster. Sales were falling and the sales force were putting great pressure on the factory for immediate delivery, shorter production runs, special orders, etc. But the factory was planned on the assumption of long, computer-calculated, standard production schedules. The planned system could not cope. Instead, endless interim arrangements had to be made. Day was lived by day. Costs escalated. Tempers flared. The planned room for expansion (in staff and faci-

lities) now looked like over-capacity without the expected increase in sales. Redundancies were ordered. Unions moved in.

The 'nine' met in almost constant session. In accordance with their tradition, every problem was classified as a project and assigned a project team. In June 1974, there were 47 projects, and Bert (the production engineer) was involved in 23 of them. Martin was losing his hair and getting divorced. There was a general feeling in the group of puzzlement, dismay and irrational anger at fate. 'How could it be going wrong? We are all talented, young, hard-working, committed people. Why isn't it working?'

The company boss blamed Martin. He should get tough. Kick a few people. Shout more. Less of this endless committee work. Martin wanted time. You can't start up a factory in under two years. Participative problem-solving must be the best way. Mike (production manager) blamed participative problem-solving. 'It's just a pill factory,' he said. 'You don't need brains, only blokes and some system.' Everyone else blamed the 'nine'. 'Why don't they do their job?' they said. 'Always asking us to help with their problems. It's their business to manage, not ours. We knew there was a catch to all these fringe benefits and luxury coffee rooms.'

And then they started leaving. Three of the nine left for other companies, seeing no promotional prospects in Bosco. Martin fired one after an argument (which did a lot for his self-confidence). Redundancy slimmed down the workforce. Experience began to keep the machines working. Martin was unexpectedly offered the job of New Product Manager in the US parent company and accepted. Mike took over. Systems superseded projects. Participative problem-solving was replaced in the jargon by 'role and responsibility'. The 'nine' was now 'three', reporting to Mike. There were regular monthly meetings for information exchange. Mike solved the problems and told the others.

They say it's boring, but the results look good. Athena for creating, Apollo for running a factory. But it's hard for the same men to excel in initiating and in steady-state activities. Organisations do adapt, but with pain and time, unless they understand what's happening to them.

The general pattern is that change of any magnitude involves a subsequent change in the balance of cultures and gods. If that cultural change does not take place, there is a mismatch between the demands of the work and the ways of managing it – success has bred inefficiency through cultural imbalance. But cultural change of the order needed in these situations is hard to bring about deliberately. We are creatures of cultural habits and do not change gods easily, particularly when those gods have served us well in the past. It need cause us no surprise, therefore, to find that we have to be frightened into cultural change – a kind of organisational culture shock is needed. The sequence of major change in organisations is well-established. It goes like this:

THE CHANGE SEQUENCE

An analysis of the major organisational changes of recent years reveals an almost invariable sequence of events:
Fright: *The organisation is faced with unmistakable signs of alarm – imminent bankruptcy, a slump in sales, major strikes, a squeeze in margins, massive operational difficulties, might be some of them.*
New people: *New people are brought in to the top of the organisation, most frequently a new chief executive, to do the necessary and often painful restructuring. Because there is a need for incisive action, quick decisions with inadequate information and a certain ruthlessness, the new person at the top is often a Zeus character.*
New directions: *The new team at the top re-organise priorities. Some lines of activity, or some products, are dropped, others are started. Bits of the organisation may be sold off or closed down, so that everything can be concentrated on the best of what is left. A new strategy emerges.*
New groupings: *The new strategy leads to new structures, which in turn mean individuals changing roles and responsibilities. New methods and systems are simultaneously introduced.*

Only in the case of **additive change** *where an organisation of its own accord takes on another component, does it seem possible to avoid this traumatic sequence. It seems that it needs an organisational earthquake to change the balance of gods when things are going wrong.*

(An excellent analysis of the causes and process of forced organisational change is provided by Stuart Slatter in Corporate Recovery, *Penguin, 1984.)*

Linking the gods

Given the right mix, the organisation still needs to be held together.
The gods need to be linked. Failed linkages in institutions show up
most dramatically in the scrapbook of 'goofs' held in the institutional memory of any organisation – the creations of the research
department developed by someone else, the sales drive that ran out
of goods to sell, the product switch which no one mentioned to the
purchasing department, and so on. More insistently, they show up
in the arguments, bickerings and tribal wars that proliferate in
organisations, particularly the bigger ones.

Cultural harmony within one part of the organisation is often
nurtured and supported by deliberately distinguishing it from the
other parts. Enmity without encourages harmony within. But this
cultural isolation can destroy the total institution. Linkage between
the cultures is essential, and effective linkage has three elements:

● cultural tolerance;
● bridges;
● a common language.

When these fail, a fourth element, slack, will cover up the cracks,
but slack is only the thermometer of inefficiency or incompetence,
the outcome of mixed-up management.

CULTURAL TOLERANCE

Each culture has its own preferred ways of co-ordinating and controlling. The club cultures rely on trust, empathy and personal
inspection. The role culture links defined jobs or roles by rules and
procedures, and an inspection system to make sure that the rules
and procedures are enforced. Task cultures dealing always with new
problems, plan and re-plan, using past data to correct future
estimates and forecasts. Existential cultures relegate and delegate
the co-ordinating function, calling it 'administration' (a denigrating
term for them).

But since, as I have shown, the ways of one culture are anathema
to another, the personal visitation of a Zeus seems to an Apollonian
an intrusion on private territory, reeking of distrust: 'Does he

not believe my reports or understand the figures?' Zeus people, on the other hand, are bored by the formalities of Apollonian co-ordinating mechanisms and find them hard to use. The discussions and committees that lie behind the planning of Athenians seem like inefficiency to Apollonians, just as the disregard of Dionysians seems like irresponsibility.

But to impose your ways on others is bigotry, cultural sin. The first step, then, to effective linkage is to allow each part of the organisation to develop its own appropriate methods of co-ordination and control and to tolerate differences between the cultures. Otherwise, one enters the 'spiral of distrust', when what seems sensible co-ordination to you appears intrusive control to the other.

THE SPIRAL OF DISTRUST

The principle of 'balance' keeps cropping up in life. There seems to be a reciprocal 'balancing' relationship between trust and control, so that where trust is increased control diminishes, and if you increase your control the perceived trust is decreased, as on a balance:

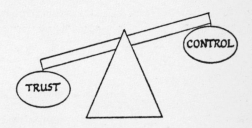

The farmer had been successful, he now operated three small-holdings (each of about 120 acres) in addition to his own home farm. Each smallholding was managed by one of his three sons (indeed, he had bought them for this purpose). Clearly, he thought, good management required that he co-ordinate the work of the four farms so that he got optimum use of the central pool of capital equipment, better purchasing and sales deals, etc. The principle was so obvious that he didn't need to discuss it, he merely asked his sons for a weekly detailed advanced schedule of their work, followed up a week later by

a matching report on work done with, where appropriate, details of quantities.

The sons met in the house of the eldest. 'Father has been conning us along,' one said. 'He told us that he trusted us to run our own farms and would finance the start-up. Now it's clear that he wants to check on everything we do both before and after we do it. We are just employees – not his trusted sons. I propose that we demand that he hand us over the legal ownership of our farms, otherwise he is quite likely to sell them over our heads once we've put them in order.' 'And another thing,' said the third son, 'he's deliberately adding together all the proceeds so that we can't tell whose is what.'

The father was astonished. His attempts to start his sons off as independent farmers had resulted in outright rebellion. It must, he muttered, be the result of this new mood of distrust and independence in the youth of the country.

The possibility that his well-meant attempts at co-ordination looked like control, *which suggested, in that Zeus-like culture, a measure of* distrust, *simply did not occur to him.*

The spiral of distrust starts with good intentions and is often invisible.

But cultural tolerance is only the *prerequisite*, the necessary condition, of a balanced organisation. Much more, of a more positive nature, is needed to link the cultures.

BRIDGES

Some well-known work in organisation theory* has demonstrated that the more 'differentiation' there is between the people, the work, ideologies and time-horizons of different parts of an organisation, the more methods of 'integration' are needed. The idea of balance again. Like many of the precepts of organisation theory, this is blindingly obvious once it has been stated. In our terms, the more diverse the cultures the more bridges you need.

Bridges range from copies of correspondence, through joint committees (with appeals to superior courts or umpires), to co-

---

* P. R. Lawrence and J. W. Lorsc, *Organisation and Environment*, Boston: Harvard University, 1967.

ordinating individuals, liaison groups or project teams. In between them are what might be called pontoons, or the temporary bridges of task forces, study groups or 'confrontation meetings' between the arguing groups.

Without bridges, the cultures go their separate ways (resulting usually in lowered efficiency and the occasional goof), or they have to be held together at the top by imposed directives, decrees and referee-like decisions. Using the top of the organisation as the principal 'bridge' not only distorts the structure and corrupts the cultures, but occupies an undue proportion of the top people's time.

THE PARADOX OF DELEGATION

The chief executive was explaining his way of management.

'*I've taken my job,*' *he said,* '*which is running the organisation, I suppose, and then I've split it down into its constituent parts (such as planning, financial control, sales, etc.) and then put a man in charge of each. That way I've delegated my total work and am free to act as a counsellor, consultant or arbitrator to any of them as and when needed. Look,*' *he added,* '*an empty desk, an empty diary: perfect delegation, wouldn't you say?*'

Three months later I saw him again.

'*How's it working?*' *I asked.*

'*The* system*'s* fine,' *he replied,* '*it's the* people, *they're not up to it. They are very blinkered, can't take an overall perspective. Do you think they can be educated to think like directors of the company?*'

'*How do you mean?*' *I asked.*

'*Well, everything I push down to them seems to come back to me as an argument to be resolved. Our board meetings consist of a set of functional viewpoints, leaving me to take the company view and make the decision. They can't see beyond their own function, yet in their position every functional problem concerns others as well as themselves.*'

'*But that's what you wanted, wasn't it?*' *I asked.* '*You delegated everything except co-ordination, compromise and linkage, so that remains your job.*'

'*I suppose that's true,*' *he said ruefully.* '*But it wasn't what I intended. Now I'm busier than I ever was before I delegated it all so neatly. I'm so busy I don't have time to think, let alone be counsellor, consultant and all those other things I talked about. I've got back more than I gave away, it's like delegating into the wind.'*

'Perhaps you should try delegating some of your linkage responsibility as well as your functional supervision. After all, if you can only cross the river at its top it will not only be a very busy bridge, but other people are going to have to do a lot of walking.'

The 'matrix organisation' (in which the demands for co-operation between functions are met by full-time project groups made up of representatives from the functions, operating under project leaders) is the ultimate 'bridged' organisation. In this design, the cultural priorities of the functions are exported into the project groups. In these groups, much depends on the leadership capacity of the project leader to make an effective bridge, bonding the capabilities of the functions to a common good. He is helped in this task if he has the power of *selection* and/or promotion; if the projects control the allocation of *new investment*; and if the project group has full use of each individual's *time*. On the other hand, putting too much emphasis on the 'bridge' may be to weaken the individual cultures or functions. The balance can be restored by giving some of the powers (of appointment, or production) back to the functions, or retaining them for the centre or top of the organisation. This will weaken the power of the projects but strengthen the functions. It has been argued that projects pursue the practical, functions the ideal, in a matrix organisation. Balance would suggest the need for a constantly shifting distribution between these two.

Few organisations will find that the complexity justifies the cost of a full matrix organisation. Few will be content with a bridge only at the top. Most will locate a bridge at the points of major interaction between the cultures – where research meets production, for instance, or where purchasing, production and sales combine in a production schedule. Some will include bridges between policy management and executive supervision. The first question clearly is – how many bridges and where? The temptation for management is always to overdo it. It feels lonely at the top when you don't know what is going on or know who does know. The danger of too much co-ordination is not only its cost, but the ever-lurking spiral of distrust. The danger of too little is, of course, the goofs and sub-optimisation referred to earlier. On balance, experience would suggest that we should make do with as little as we can, even at the risk of a goof. There is an established connection between the *quantity* of co-ordination and the degree of apathy in organisations. The more co-ordination, the greater the apathy. The invisible apathy may well cost more than the occasional but visible goof. If, of course, goofs are either illegal (e.g. in hospitals or government) or extremely costly, the apathy may have to be endured.

The second decision to be taken on bridging is the method. There are essentially *three* ways of achieving formal co-ordination in organisations, by *grouping, central information*, or *liaison*.

Grouping. Essentially this means putting all the functions concerned with a problem into one group with one objective. In a factory, instead of having a production unit serviced by engineers, quality control, maintenance and production development, there is one of each of these in the unit, so that all the bits to be co-ordinated are represented there. The matrix organisation applies this method in the extreme. It is effective but clearly very expensive, since to work it properly you need to have an engineer, quality controller, maintenance officer and development officer for each group or problem.

Central Information. By this method, all the information necessary for co-ordination is routed, by manual documentation or computer, to a central point, usually at that position in the hierarchy which could be called the lowest cross-over point in the organisation chart of the points to be linked. In a predictable world, it is quite possible to work out what information is needed when and where, in order to allow particular decisions to be made. One can even state in advance the criteria for these decisions, so that they can be made automatically by the computer when the decision is at hand. The impact of the computer on organisational decision-making (as opposed to record-keeping) is here – in this form of bridging. The airline booking operations, the computerised stock-control systems, even the automatic entry gates to car parks, rely on this vertical information system of linkage. Central information works well in predictable situations, if the humans involved can live up to the accuracy required. Most systems, however, are over-designed and very vulnerable to human error. One fool can gum up the whole works.

Liaison. This is the most tenuous form of bridge. It relies on one man telling another what he is doing, wants to do, or cannot do. Liaison can be helped along by the disciplines of committees, by formally circulated information, or by permanent liaison officers (a sort of human bridge), but ultimately it does depend on the willingness of individuals to talk, discuss and compromise on both means and ends.

There are cultural affinities to these bridges. The Athenian culture prefers liaison, with its flexibility and emphasis on trust and informal ways. Apollo cultures like central information and the kind of certainty and predictability that this involves. And Zeus cultures, quite properly, like the group, with all that they need under their own command.

But organisations remain a cultural mix and require a mix of bridging mechanisms. The temptation is to overdo one's preferred mechanism and to attempt to apply it to the other cultures. The tidiness of the data and the forms of central information cannot apply throughout the organisation without reducing its flexibility. Apollonians must show some cultural tolerance in their bridges with the task cultures. Zeus cultures must allow more systematisation than they are comfortable with. One must, in short, resist the instinctual pull of one's own culture if the bridge is with another culture.

The cultural split implied by bridging two different cultures occurs in its most obvious form in the role of the liaison man who must stand with a foot in each. The 'integrator', as he has been called, has become a prized person in the complex organisations of today – and a special person. The successful liaison man, we know from research, is knowledgeable about each of the areas he has to bridge and is respected by both, is of high status in the organisation, so that he can get things done, is skilled in interpersonal relationships and has a high tolerance for stress. Not a job for a weakling! Nor a very young man, or for someone who has failed in the mainstream. The stress arises, in my view, from the great difficulty of having to live in two cultures simultaneously. It is hard to sustain this dual nationality. Most liaison men become identified in time with one side or the other, thus reducing their efficiency as a bridge and turning liaison into negotiation. A better understanding of the cultures and their preferences might make it easier for these human bridges to carry out their very difficult but necessary role.

Nowadays the supervisor and the junior manager are often liaison men parading under more formal titles. Their job is to link a number of lateral forces, often without the formal authority to do so. It is at their level that the asterisk situations we have referred to earlier arise – situations where the possible is to be preferred to the ideal, where trust and intuition and empathy are quicker than formal communication, and where interpersonal relationships are critical: Zeus situations, in fact. Good liaison men are Zeus characters, but they often act as bridges between Athenian task forces. They need cultural self-discipline.

Any inhabitant of organisations will have perceived the law of the pendulum at work as the organisation centralises, then a few years later decentralises, only to centralise again in due course. Here the organisation is intuitively searching for a new balance: it swings from central information to a mixture of groups and liaison and back again. The search for balance is never-ending. The swinging is inevitable but, if done with cultural understanding, the pain is less.

A COMMON LANGUAGE

The third aspect of linkage is a common language. 'An organisation that talks together walks together', one might say. But the vocabulary of organisations differs from our everyday conversation. What is it that goes across the various bridges in the linking systems? What does the organisation choose to talk about? Is it sales? Or costs? Or productivity? What concealed but central values are revealed by its private codes or the fashionable jargon of the day?

What are the critical figures or columns in the formal reporting system? Do the internal memoranda refer to people, or reports, or departments? What does the private humour reveal as the 'in' buzz-words? What are the failures you mustn't make?

A supervisor was studying the 40 pages of internal information circulated monthly to all departments of the great integrated multi-department corporation. 'Do you use all this?' he was asked. 'Oh, no,' he replied. 'I only look at this figure on page 22. If it's up I'm OK, down and I'm in trouble.'

The choice of what you count, what you compare with what, what you show to whom, has a clear effect on behaviour. Do you compare performance with past performance or with planned performance? Do you count functional results or overall results? There is little point talking profits if the reporting system only counts sales and costs except at the very top.

The code will indicate where the power lies and what method of linkage is most important.

ORGANISATIONAL CODES

An internal memo in a Zeus culture will often read like a private family letter. For example, 'In view of Jeremy's information, JGH suggested that we suggest to Bob H that he try to win over Peter McK in the hope that his support will be conclusive. RTC agreed to follow this up after talking to TStJR and GJS.'

Apollonian communiques bristle with terms like MKR/Z, PROD/ EVR/S, JDRs and FSPs, which refer to departments or regular documentary returns.

Task cultures are full of commando language – 'Bill's Gang', 'the Television Group', 'the Forward Planning People'.

Dionysians use professional rather than organisational codes, demonstrating their true allegiance.

All these codes are baffling to the outsider, but serve a function in linking the organisation together, as long as both sides understand them. Language, however, can be a barrier as much as a bridge.

The slang, the buzz-words and the current jargon will point to current priorities – 'objectives', 'participation', 'quality' or 'health and cleanliness'.

It is easy to be quietly humorous about the languages of organisations, but words do affect behaviour. Language is normally but a mirror of its society, but it can be used more deliberately to shape and direct the preoccupations and priorities of that society, or to reinforce new bridging mechanisms. If, for instance, a 'group' system is introduced, the reporting mechanism must reflect the new system by producing 'group' data. If quality is more important than quantity, the informal vocabulary should reflect that. And the languages should coincide. It is no use preaching productivity to the unions if the statistical vocabulary does not contain appropriate productivity statistics. You can detect an organisation's heart by looking at its language.

The temptation is to follow one's personal cultural instincts. The quandary is how far to 'sin', to go against the instincts in the interests of cultural propriety, to use new vocabularies deliberately to send new messages, in order to achieve a new internal balance in the organisation. The instinct of a Zeus to rely on informal conversations to inject new values and goals may not carry over to the Apollonian part of the organisation, which will expect these changes to be reflected in the statistics of the reporting system. Athenians won't believe them unless they are incorporated in revised group assignments.

Slack – the price of imbalance

If linkage is not achieved, the gaps get filled in by slack and organisational slack indicates some fat somewhere in the system. A small degree of slack is no bad thing: a fully lean organisation will find it hard to cope with any irregularities in its planned activities. Slack can be used to iron out bumps, to live through difficult periods, take advantage of unexpected opportunities. But slack that conceals poor linkage, or a mismatch of gods, is a cancer in the body of the organised society. Like cancer, it can grow unnoticed, until it gets so bad that the whole body begins to decay. By then, it is too often too late to intervene.

Slack takes various forms:

Investment. Equipment and facilities are provided to cope with the peaks of quality or quantity, leaving 'slack' in the troughs. Seasonal industries (e.g. soft drinks, photo-finishing, tourism) invest for summer peaks. Quality-conscious industries tool up for the highest quality even if such small tolerances are required only for a small portion of their work.

Staffing. Many organisations staff up to meet all contingencies, including sickness and holidays as well as peak-loading. Industries which peak daily (catering, commuter transport) have a daily slack problem. Slack in staff can create self-fulfilling prophecies: over-recruitment to cover wastage can actually encourage it, as people see a visible excess and leave before they are pushed.

Systems. Systems can be designed to cope with an expanded operation, but may not flex with the varying size of the operation, so that a small workload incurs the full weight of co-ordination,

systems and controls, or trivial decisions get the full boardroom
policy routine.

Time. The more time you have at your disposal, the less you need of
other forms of slack. In the quality furniture trade, it is customary to
manufacture only against a firm customer order. This practice
allows one to carry minimum stocks (no investment slack), but
makes production planning very difficult, so that one probably has
to carry excess personnel (staffing slack).

Margins. High margins permit one to carry other types of slack,
including error slack. Technologies where speed is more important
than accuracy (e.g. trading) often carry high margins to allow for
error slack. It is an established fact that stock-market ratings of
earnings per share rise in relation to the likelihood of risk, or error.
It is then the customer who pays.

Errors. Error slack usually accompanies high margins, on the assumption that the errors will be corrected. The existence of room
for errors in the tradition of the industry allows one to skimp on
systems, but of course results in poor quality and shoddy work if the
errors do not get corrected in time.

We can choose our slack, although usually we fall into line with
the traditions of our industry, occupation or society. It can be
argued that it is Britain's tradition of using staffing slack rather than
investment slack that has been a major contributor to her successive
economic crises. Labour has historically been cheap in Britain, and
investment more lucratively routed overseas to the old Empire. As
a result British firms tended to be over-manned and under-
equipped, compared with, for example, the USA, where capital
was readily available and labour scarce. Now, of course, the labour
slack in Britain is no longer cheap. In cutting down that slack, a pool
of unemployment is created, but, and possibly more serious, the
slack has not been replaced by investment slack. Margin slack is
seldom possible in the conditions of international competition
(although continual devaluations can help), leaving any needs for
slack to be met by time (overdue delivery dates) or error (poor
quality), or high domestic prices. The organised society pays for its
slack through its consumers.

On an organisational scale, there are cultural preferences for
slack. Club cultures prefer margin slack. This gives room for experiment, allows people to learn by their mistakes without ruining the

institution, and permits flexibility. When appropriate they would like to back this up with investment slack as a form of equipment back-up to their key resource – individuals.

Role cultures believe in system and staffing slack. In their way of thinking, the capital assets of the operation can be used efficiently or inefficiently depending on the way the work is planned and carried out. They like to play on the slack of human resources (believing these to be the most flexible of resources) and on chains of systems. The ability to draw at will on a pool of retained labour has, for instance, long been at the heart of the automobile industry's way of working.

Task cultures like investment slack, again as equipment for their talents to work upon, and time. Where time is unavailable they will tend to staff up – more brainpower will produce good results quicker.

Luckily, existential cultures have small linkage requirements. Luckily, because these cultures seldom have the resources to create investment slack, they abhor systems slack and are unlikely to add deliberately to their number to create staffing slack. When, therefore, the Dionysians of an existential culture have to be co-ordinated, there are usually delays (time slack) or mistakes (error slack).

It is when the comparative costs of the different forms of slack change, as in Britain in the 1980s, that management has to reconsider, and often to act against, its cultural instincts. Club cultures, for instance, are often accustomed to working in a mini-monopoly situation where, for reasons of geography (they are in a regionally distant market), size (they are too small to bother with) or custom (the norms of the cartel or industry or occupation), they have price discretion and could use the slack of high margins. When they expand, they encounter competition and have to cut slack in order to compete. If they do not at the same time improve their linkage they will have to find another form of slack. If they are not careful, that slack will be of the time or error variety. Thus it is that growth in Zeus cultures can often result in inefficiency.

Role cultures, used to a pool of cheap labour, and with decision routines which examine investment projects with a microscope, whilst overlooking major staffing decisions, may have to change their ways if the pool gets expensive and can no longer be fished at will. Investment may then be the appropriate form of slack if linkage fails.

LABOUR AS 'A' FIXED COST

A friend was attending an international management course in Belgium. The British executives were complaining loudly and long that management in Britain had become impossible, due to the burden of legislation and the impossibility of moving your labour force around, or reducing it, as you wanted.

'Aw, shucks!' said an American. 'We've lived with that situation in Scandinavia for years. It's easy. You just treat your labour as a fixed cost.'

There was a perplexed silence.

'And so . . .?' asked a timid voice.

'Why, then your investment is your variable. You build lots of small plants and close down or open whole plants. Play around with the operation, not the people.'

It's only a change in slack.

The role of the missionary manager

Cultural propriety might appear a rather obvious virtue. Surely every organisation intuitively reacts to the influencing forces in its environment and seeks to minimise inappropriate forms of slack? Indeed, if it does not, will it not be starved of profit and therefore of its prospects for survival? Why, then, should not a purely mercenary approach be in fact the best way of securing that cultural propriety, which will in turn remove any unwanted slack or unnecessary incompetence?

This is the essential premise of capitalism. I shall argue at more length later that this premise will not hold much longer. Here we can at least recognise that the principle is fallible even now. It is true that *gross* incompetence or excessive slack usually results in a loss of clients and thence in organisational death, given a free market. But how many markets are free? For a start, all professions have a protected market, as do all Government agencies. These are organisations just like any others, and often affect one's lives more deeply than those of commerce and industry. Incompetence or slack in these areas is protected by regulation – a slow-moving and ineffective device, particularly where, as in the case of the professions, the police and the civil service, it is self-policed. Then the industrial and commercial organisations owned by the state normally have protected markets, at least in their own countries. There are exceptions, notably the automobile industries in France, Britain and Germany, but the exceptions are rare enough to be noticeable. Finally, in the private sector of commerce and industry, how effective a policeman is competition among rivals? Where monopoly is outlawed, most businessmen would prefer an oligopoly where a number of firms run *parallel* businesses, competing in defined ways in defined areas but usually mirroring each other's cultural patterns. True competition comes from outside, from another country or another technology carrying with it different assumptions about cultures and slack. And when that true competition arrives, there is no shortage of squeals of anguish, pleas for tarriff barriers and for technological protection (once it was for textile workers, now for shoe-makers).

Profit – the major mercenary objective – is more easily guaranteed by seeking to win an area of price discretion than by eliminating slack. In these days, where profit margins are increasingly regulated, decreased costs can actually result in decreased profits. Indeed, profit can be the result of inefficiency, rather than efficiency, in a situation where *margins* are controlled but not the final price.

PROFIT AS THE MEASURE OF INEFFICIENCY

In my early days in the oil industry, a marketing cartel still operated in various parts of the world, a cartel in which the major companies agreed to preserve their existing market shares in each territory (the 'As Is' agreement).

Under this arrangement, the oil companies became essentially monopoly distribution systems for a vital commodity: justifiable, perhaps, in an age when oil supplies were limited and capital could have been wasted in unnecessary fields at the consumer end. However, profit was still used as the measure of efficiency.

One of my first tasks was to compile the price lists for lubricating oils. It was a simple task, actually. There was a printed list of cost items for each brand. I got the relevant figures from Accounts and added on the 15 per cent profit margin (not excessive, the companies saw themselves as non-exploitative), and put the final total down as the new price.

After a couple of weeks, I commented to the sales manager that this system was a recipe for inefficiency, since the higher our costs the higher would be the 15 per cent margin. He was horrified at the thought. Conditioned to believe that higher profit was always good, he could not bring himself to consider that it might only indicate inefficiency in a monopolistic service industry.

This particular cartel ended soon afterwards when oil supplies increased and the companies went on the search for new markets. The counterparts to this story continue, however, in many industries and trades in many pockets of society.

In most western countries, over 50 per cent of gross domestic product is already in the public sector with protected markets. If an honest evaluation were made of the remainder, a large part would consist either of professional fees, practical oligopolies of parallel businesses, or territorial monopolies equivalent to the small regional equipment rental operation, or the village store whose monopoly is too small for others to wish to intervene. All these areas have price discretion to some degree. The discipline of competition and the whip of profit will punish only *gross* incompetence or *excessive* slack. No, cultural propriety, like social propriety, cannot be enforced, only desired. Mercenary organisations and mercenary managers are not in themselves enough. They must be missionaries, too, if incompetence, mixed-up management, that first dilemma of the organised society, is to be resolved.

Dionysus Turned Zeus?

Japanese were behind them in serrated ridges that seemed to stretch

Chapter 4

THE GODS IN THEIR SETTINGS

People are different, as we have noted. Different personalities favour different gods. But it goes further and deeper than that. An organisation is not only a culture in itself, it sits surrounded by a culture, be it of Japan or Italy, of schoolteaching or medicine. The *setting* in which an organisation operates will have a major impact on the blend of gods, even if the demands of size, life cycles and work patterns all seem to push it another way. Management works best when it goes with the grain of its surrounding culture, not with the dictates of logic. We should, therefore, expect to see a different balance of gods in different countries and in different occupations, and we should not necessarily expect to be able to replicate Japanese ways in Britain or the practices of business in a church.

We do, as it happens, know something about national differences in management style, we have some clues as to the nature of successful Japanese organisations and successful American businesses, and we are beginning to understand the essential differences of, for instance, schools and voluntary groups as organisations. In this chapter, we say a little about each to emphasise that the theory of cultural propriety must take account of the setting of the organisation as well as the work to be done. It is also important to understand that the gods, and the cultures they represent, apply in their different ways to all organisations, not just to those of business or of Britain.

National differences

Geert Hofstede* spent six years trying to pin down the essential differences between national cultures. He looked at and compared

* G. Hofstede *Culture's Consequences – International Differences in Work-related Values*, London, 1980.

all the other studies (thirteen of them) which had tried to do the
same thing, but he also hit on a neat idea; he persuaded IBM to let
him interview some of their personnel in forty different countries.
Since they all worked for the same corporation in similar jobs, any
differences in their cultural attitudes would most likely be due to
their national differences, not to their occupation. He is, of course,
dealing with norms and generalisations – not all Mexicans are alike,
but they may, most of them, have certain characteristics in
common.

He came up with four distinguishing features:

Power
Some nationalities like and approve of hierarchies, others want
everyone to be as equal as possible. Some want everyone to be
independent, but others accept that most should be dependent on
others. He measured people on their preference for Power
Distance.

Uncertainty
Some societies are more worried by uncertainty and risk than
others. They like rules, stable careers, fixed patterns to life. They
accept that there are experts and they listen to them. Hofstede
classified cultures on an Uncertainty Avoidance Scale.

Individualism
Some societies favour a loose social framework, in which individuals are supposed to look after themselves. Other societies want
more collectivism, tighter, closer families, organisations that look
after you and in return expect your loyalty. Hofstede's scale ran
from Individualism at one end to Collectivism at the other.

Masculinity
Some countries are more 'masculine' in their attitudes, valuing
assertiveness, the acquisition of money and things, and not caring
for the quality of life or other people. Other nationalities were the
opposite, veering towards more 'feminine' values. Interestingly,
the more 'masculine' a society was as a whole, the wider the gap
between the way the men and the women in it thought.

When Hofstede groups the nationalities together it is clear he is
on to something. It is also clear that there are implications for the
mix of gods. For instance:

South-East Asia is happy with hierarchy and power and able to live with uncertainty. Singapore, Hong Kong, India and the Philippines by these measures are lands fit for Zeus, and the entrepreneurial organisations of this region seem to bear that out.

The Anglo-Saxons and the Scandinavians do not mind uncertainty, but they are far more democratic than South-East Asia, suggesting more of a penchant for Athena, a suggestion supported by the scores compiled by British executives in answering the questionnaire at the end of Chapter 2. Athena is the personal choice of most of them, even though few find that their organisations' scores correspond.

The Anglo-Saxons are also, however, strongly individualist (Dionysian), a fact which will become important in the future, as the next chapter will emphasise, whereas the Scandinavians are more collectivist, which can be a polite word for conformist.

The Japanese are very different. They dislike uncertainty and are very collectivist, as opposed to individualist, masculine rather than feminine and rather neutral about power. It is a culture made for families and Apollo – exactly what we find in practice. They are likely to be efficient but not entrepreneurial, to be conformist and materialistic, not eccentric.

France likes power and hierarchy, is individualist but not risk-taking; Zeus sitting on top of Apollo, and in the middle. Management will be full of rules interrupted by crises.

Countries like Austria and Germany, which dislike uncertainty, want equality but not individualism and espouse masculine and material values, are asking for Apollonian institutions tempered by formal democratic procedures, which is what they have. They will be hard-working, efficient and egalitarian, but also conformist and, with notable exceptions, unadventurous and even unexciting.

MANAGING BY OBJECTIVES, CROSS-CULTURALLY

Management by objectives has been a favourite Anglo-American tool of management. It does, however, as Hofstede points out, depend upon certain assumptions which may not work outside the Anglo-Saxon countries.

* G. Hofstede, 'Managing Differences in the Multicultural Organization', *Organizational Dynamics*, Summer 1980.

MBO assumes that subordinate and superior can negotiate (not power-conscious). It also assumes that results are important (masculinity) and that some risks are worth taking (uncertainty) which are the individual's responsibility (individualism). MBO is made for Athenians.

In France, its equivalent, DPPO (Direction Participation par Objectife), never caught on. The French are accustomed to arbitrary and personal leadership, which creates dependent behaviour and an unwillingness to take individual risks. Apollo studded with Zeus is no place for negotiated contracts.

In Germany, MBO has been formalised and transplanted into Management by Joint Goal-Setting – a democratised Apollonian revision of the original.

These cultural stereotypes can, of course, be taken too far. Not every German or every Briton fits the pattern. There are many entrepreneurial German firms, while Japan, as we shall see, is dependent not only on its large organisations but on a host of small independent businesses. The other factors, size, life-cycles and work patterns, also emphasise the choice of gods and their mix. Nevertheless, the surrounding culture is important. As we shall see in the next chapter, the crisis facing organisations in Britain and other Anglo-Saxon countries is caused by the conflict between the kinds of organisations which reason and logic would give us and those which the cultures of democracy and individualism are prepared to live with.

TRUST IS BETTER THAN CONTRACTS

The overseas Chinese businessman – typically a Zeus at heart – prefers to deal without written contracts. If you need a contract, he argues, to keep a man to his obligations then you should not be doing business with him in the first place.

It follows that overseas Chinese businessmen cannot afford to try to squeeze all they can get from customers or contractors, because there is no enforceable contract to fall back on. Instead, they have to try to negotiate deals where both parties benefit, so that it is in nobody's interest to default or delay.

That sort of trust comes slowly. The overseas Chinese starts with small orders and small contracts when he does not know you. If the trust is demonstrated, the orders grow.

The idea, however, that success means a deal where each side wins is not always understood in Western cultures.

The gods in Japan

The best test of cultural differences between nations comes if you try to apply Japanese management practices to American organisations. If the surrounding setting *does* matter, then what works in Japan may well not work in America, and vice versa. The principles of management may not be as universal as some would like. The differences between Japanese and American organisations are great, which does not mean, of course, that they cannot learn something from each other. 'Quality Circles', after all, were invented in America before being taken up and developed to their full potential in Japan and then re-exported to America.

A Japanese organisation is built upon a fundamental contract of trust between the individual and the organisation. The individual trusts the organisation to employ him (very seldom her) for life, to reward him better as he grows older and more senior, and to use him and his talents appropriately. In return, he puts the immediate requirements of the organisation before his own, being prepared to change jobs, locations and even careers if the organisation requires it. It has to be a contract of trust, because formal contracts for longer than one year are actually forbidden by law.

Because of this blend of security and flexibility the organisation can operate a proper Apollonian culture, a culture in which the individual fits into the role and the system which logic would require. In Western eyes, this can make the Japanese sound like human robots, replaceable human parts, but it does not feel like that if the organisation is viewed as a caring family where, because your long-term interests are guaranteed, it is no sacrifice but rather a privilege and a pleasure to do your duty in that role to which it has pleased the organisation to call you. The Apollonian contract, in its present form, is not one in which the organisation *uses* the individual, but one where there is a long-term identity of interest between the organisation and all the individuals within it.

THE JAPANESE ASSEMBLY ROOM

William Ouchi* describes the experience of an American electronics firm which opened a manufacturing plant in Japan. In the final assembly area of the plant, young Japanese women wired together electronic products on a piece-rate system: the more you wired, the more you got paid. About two months after opening, the head foreladies approached the plant manager. 'Honourable plant manager,' they said humbly as they bowed, 'we are embarrassed to be so forward, but we must speak to you, because all the girls have threatened to quit work this Friday.' 'Why', they wanted to know, 'can't our plant have the same compensation system as other Japanese companies? When you hire a new girl, her starting salary should be fixed by her age. An eighteen-year-old should be paid more than a sixteen-year-old. Every year on her birthday she should receive an automatic increase in her pay. The idea that any one of us can be more productive than another must be wrong, because none of us in final assembly could make a thing unless all the other people in the plant had done their jobs right first. To single out one person as being more productive is wrong and is also personally humiliating to us.'

The company changed its compensation system.

The Japanese, it is true, run a very sophisticated version of Apollo in order to keep it family-like and human. Roles, for instance, are deliberately kept ambiguous and overlapping. There are few of the detailed job descriptions in which Western Apollonian organisations abound; instead, the responsibility for any task is spread across a number of roles and it is understood that responsibility for all the tasks is shared by all the roles in a group. This only works if the individual bits of the organisation are kept small enough; but the sense of collective responsibility which results is a guarantee against the negative power in which Apollo cultures abound. But the groups which result in Japanese organisations are subtly different from the Athenian groups of Western institutions. These are not the problem-solving task forces of skilled individuals, but collections of roles doing prescribed tasks. The 'role-family' which results is the basic building-block of Japanese organisations

* W. Ouchi, *Theory Z*, Addison-Wesley, 1981.

and much care, time and trouble goes into the nurture and main-tenance of these organisation families. Asked his job, a Japanese will name his group rather than his particular job and will spend maybe two hours a week after hours socialising with his work group. Apollonian temples built of role-families are very human places *if* you are happy to give over part of your identity to such a family and such a temple. Japanese organisations are 'total' organisations and 'total' organisations, as William Ouchi points out, are equated in the West with prisons, hospitals, military establishments and such-like. They are not, in other words, the preferred cultures of the West. Apollonian temples of the excellence seen in Japan can only be built in a land where security is more important than individua-lism and where organisational success counts for more than personal advancement – the kind of values thrown up in Japan by Hofstede's research.

The Japanese organisations do, however, go to great lengths to reinforce their side of the Apollonian contract. They consciously build up the image and the tradition of the corporation, admittedly using Apollonian devices, like the company song, company training schools and company slogans. They reinforce the image, not only with the promise of a secure career but with a compensation system which pays approximately half of each person's total remuneration as a six-monthly bonus tied to the results of the total organisation and each person's basic salary. It is the corporation's success, not one's own, which counts, and this is outwardly symbolised by the fact that everyone wears the same uniform, that no one has a reserved parking place or a special place to eat. The individual should see himself as part of a group and as a proud member of a great corporation, one which serves him as well as being served by him.

The organisation also serves the individual by providing him with a career. It is not usually a specialist career but one which moves the individual from role to role and place to place. That breeds more versatile, flexible and rounded people, but also, of course, people who will find it less easy to leave the corporation, which matters not at all *if* you trust the organisation with your career. The career system is, therefore, a powerful bonding device. So is the decision-making system.

Decisions in Japanese organisations are not taken by the top man

or by a special group. Instead, quite logically, all the roles involved
have their say; not, however, in a committee, where many have to
be silent so that one can speak, but through the 'nemawashi' and
'ringi' systems. 'Nemawashi' requires the informal contribution of
everyone interested and involved at the discussion phase. 'Ringi'
requires that every decision is first circulated to all relevant roles for
their approval or comment, and re-circulated if, in the process, an
alternative comes up. It is time-consuming, but by bonding every
role into the decision it is another way of pre-empting any possible
use of blocking or negative power. In the end, while the Japanese
take an age to decide anything, once decided, it can be implemented
immediately.

The Japanese may be devout and very sensible followers of
Apollo, but they do not ignore the other gods. Richard Pascale and
Anthony Athos in their book on Japanese management* provide a
detailed description of Matsushita (producer of National Panasonic
and Technics brands), and make it quite clear that the founder,
Konosuke Matsushita, was a Zeus when he started the business in
his living-room in 1918 and remained a Zeus over sixty years later
when, although nominally retired, he intervened to appoint a new
chief executive because he deemed it to be necessary. Matsushita,
perhaps because of their Zeus-like history, have an original way of
allocating overheads to the ancillary divisions. They don't. Instead
they require each division to pay a tax of 60 per cent of their gross
profits to the centre but allow them to keep the remaining 40 per
cent to reinvest in their own future. The 60 per cent tax not only is
expected to cover overheads but to finance the centre's venture
capital fund. It is a system which provides room for Zeus figures
within a tight Apollonian framework. Japan also has its product
development groups and its planners and researchers, who fit into
the Athenian problem-solving mode, as do its renowned and much-
imitated quality circles – Athena on the shop floor.

A JAPANESE SPEAKING

'*One thing you notice rather quickly is that everyone who comes here
[Toyota] with any experience soon leaves . . . . Sometimes I wonder*

---

* R. Pascale and A. G. Athos, *The Art of Japanese Management*, Penguin, 1981.

if those who quit are normal and human, while we who remain are the abnormal ones. Those who stay seem to lack self-respect. If you want to think and act independently, you can't stay.' (Quoted by S. Kamate in *Japan in the Passing Crowd*, Allen & Unwin, 1983.) *Dionysians do not fit.*

If you want a lesson in how to run an Apollonian system without falling foul of the perils of impersonality, blocking tactics, inertia and lack of creativity, go to Japan. But the extremes to which the Japanese go would not be possible unless the surrounding culture was also Apollonian, one in which the individual was content, even proud, to be but a small part of a large whole, and prepared to make present sacrifices for future security. NSK, which set up a plant in the northeast of Britain to manufacture ball-bearings for Europe under Japanese management, but with a British workforce, overlaid the strong Apollonian culture with an Athenian task culture, which set store by the professional engineers and encouraged problem-solving groups at all levels. This may have been a response to the requirements of an evolving technology and a difficult market, but it would undoubtedly help to make the dominant Apollonian ethos more tolerable to the more individualist Britishers.

EDUCATING FOR APOLLO

Life can be tough for a child in Japan. To get into one of the great organisations, it is almost essential to graduate well from one of the Imperial universities, which are all free, so that rich and poor can compete alike. But the courses at all high schools are identical in content, using similar texts from only three textbook publishing houses. The pressure, therefore, on formal examinations is enormous – there is no other criterion available for success.

Parents therefore go to great lengths to coach their children to get into the best nursery school, so that they may from there get into a good primary school, because only then will they have a chance of entering one of the top high schools and thence university – or, best of all, the University of Tokyo. At four years of age, reports William Ouchi,* many children of ambitious parents will be going to special

* W. Ouchi, *Theory Z*, Reading, Mass.: Addison-Wesley, 1981.

*summer schools, eight hours a day, to get special coaching just to take
the entrance exam for that one nursery school.*

*Education, too, is Apollonian, leaving little room for individual
differences or deviations from the system.*

The gods in America

American organisations are different. In America, the Apollonian
organisation has been made viable not by turning its parts into
role-families but by infiltrating it wherever possible with Athenians
and aspirers after Zeus. It is true that some corporations, notably
perhaps IBM, have sought to emulate the Japanese and to become
'total organisations' in their own way, and many have been successful, but it has not been the usual American way.

Listen to some of Peters and Waterman's recipes for excellence,
arrived at after studying America's most successful companies:*

A bias for action. 'When we've got a big problem here, we grab ten
senior guys and stick them in a room for a week. They come up with
an answer and implement it.'
(Athenians?)

'The action-oriented bits and pieces come under many labels –
champions, teams, task forces, czars, projects centres, skunk works
and quality circles.'
(Zeus and Athena?)

Autonomy and entrepreneurship. '3M . . . seems not a large corporation but rather a loose network of laboratories and cubbyholes
populated by feverish inventors and dauntless entrepreneurs.'
(Zeus and Dionysians?)

'They don't try to hold everyone on so short a rein that he can't be
creative. They encourage practical risk-taking and support good
tries.'
(Zeus?)

Productivity through people. 'The excellent companies have a
deeply ingrained philosophy that says, in effect, "Respect the individual", "Make people winners", "Let them stand out", "Treat
people as adults".

* T. H. Peters and R. H. Waterman Jr. *In Search of Excellence*, New York: Harper
& Row, 1982.

(Everyone a Dionysian or a Zeus?)

Simple Form, Lean Staff. 'The . . . structural form should be based on "three pillars", each one of which responds to one of three basic needs. To respond to the need for efficiency around the basics, there is a stability pillar. To respond to the need for regular innovation, there is an entrepreneurial pillar. And to respond to the need for avoiding calcification, there is a habit-breaking pillar.'

(Apollo balanced by Zeus and Athena?)

This last quotation emphasises that the good American companies are not all Zeus, Athena and Dionysus. Apollo is essential, for stability and control. So are other things, as Peters and Waterman emphasise. Successful businesses know their markets, they keep to what they do well, and they emphasise their corporate values, so that everyone should, as in Japan, feel proud to be on board. The point is that they do not try to run an enlightened all-Apollonian organisation, but keep it alive, kicking and changing by a liberal infusion of the other gods, who are more in tune with the American character.

Other studies agree. Rosabeth Moss Kanter* also looked at leading American corporations to see how they coped with innovation. She found clear differences between what she called 'segmentalised' companies, which put everything into separate bits or divisions, had tall hierarchies and an abundance of formal systems, and the more 'integrative' companies, which are flatter and more open in their structure, who don't rest on the laurels of past achievement but adopt the future as a challenge and meet it with teams and entrepreneurs. She described one of the best of them below:

CHIPCO

'*Employees portrayed Chipco (a pseudonym for a real and very successful company) with a variety of vivid images: a family, a competing guild, a society on a Pacific island, a group of people with an organisation chart hung around it, a gypsy society, a university, a theocracy, twenty-five different companies, and a company with ten thousand entrepreneurs. Organisation charts drawn by Chipco people often resembled plates of spaghetti more than a conventional*

* R. M. Kanter, *The Change Masters*, Allen & Unwin, 1983.

set of boxes. Such imagery described many of the striking features of Chipco: its large number of enterprising employees, their interdependence in a complex matrix organisation, the emphasis on knowledge and teamwork, continuing vibrant growth and change, and Chipco's sense of its own uniqueness as a market pioneer with a culture of creativity. Its youthful exuberance was aided by a workforce with a mean age under thirty.'

A place made for Athenians and Dionysians, with the odd Zeus.

Where Apollonian organisations tried to innovate by doing it the Apollonian way – splitting the task up between the appropriate roles and divisions – nothing much happened. Apollo is necessary but, in America at least, the energy and the charge come from the other gods.

There are, it seems, many more ways than one to run a successful organisation. The gods can be balanced in different ways, and that balance can and should be affected by the surrounding culture. This, as we shall see, is an increasing problem in Western societies, where Apollo is not the most popular of gods but is still the preferred god of many organisations.

The gods in schools

Because of their setting, schools, and other academic institutions, are faced with a tug of war between Dionysus and Apollo, with Zeus as umpire. Their staff, the teachers or professors, are by training and inclination the members of a profession. They have, most of them, taken on board those professional values which are to do with service to the client, commitment to the profession and the right to use their discretion in their job. Once admitted to a profession, the new professional is his or her own boss. Management, as we saw in Chapter 1, is the servant, not the master, of professionals, who are the true Dionysians.

To a teacher, the point of the work is the time spent with the students, usually on one's own, teaching them and working with them in one's own way, although within an agreed curriculum and timetable. If the classroom is no longer alluring, the job has lost its point. Teachers are therefore, by profession, likely to be Dionysian in their attitudes to management and organisation. On the other hand, set in the classroom in front of twenty-five or more students, there is great incentive to turn from Dionysus to Zeus, when all is, more or less, under your control. On the other hand, again, teachers are realistic enough to appreciate that they are working in an institution which has to be formally managed. There have to be institutional rules and procedures, meetings to go to, forms to be filled in, superiors and subordinates as well as colleagues. Apollo in other words has to be acknowledged as a part of the institutional reality, however much it interferes with professional freedom and discretion.

Teachers, like most Dionysians who find themselves inside organisations, are, on the whole, ready to compromise by turning Athenian where individual talents are harnessed to an institutional task by the group. Unfortunately, most schools, colleges or universities are not in fact organised on Athenian lines, with the exception of some small nursery or primary schools and some special schools. The result is, inevitably, a clash of gods, as Zeus and Apollo seek to manage Dionysus.

The clash is all the greater because schools tend not to be organised as professional institutions, in which management is the servant, but as producing organisations, like business, where management directs and controls. In Britain, it is one of the senior teachers who is appointed head and in that capacity is seen as the manager of the school, not the servant of its professionals. The secondary school, in Britain, is forced to operate against the grain of its culture, to be run like a factory rather than a professional office.

WHO OR WHAT ARE THE CHILDREN?

Mingling in the staff room before I started the formal interviews of my research into school organisation, I would ask the teachers I met how many people there were in the organisation. Almost always I was given answers like 70 or 82 or 57. These were large comprehensive secondary schools with 1200 or more students, but the teachers, when asked about the size of the organisation, *had instinctively left out the children. This did not mean they did not care about the children – most of them cared passionately – but they did not see them as fellow-members of the organisation; as clients, maybe, or as products?*

It is the same in hospitals, I reflected, and in prisons. The temporary population of patients or prisoners are not seen as members of the organisation, but as something else. It makes a huge difference. If they are clients, their wants as well as their needs will be important. They will be seen as the judges of the performance of the institution and often of its individuals. They will be listened to as well as cared for. If, however, they are the products of the organisation, they will be processed rather than served and have things done to them rather than for them. If the client image dominates, it is the institution's fault if the examination is failed or the disease uncured; if the product model is dominant, the child is judged to be at fault, the patient is too ill to be treated successfully, or the prisoner unrepentant.

Dionysians have clients. Apollonians prefer products.

The children in primary schools have it better. In Britain they sit around tables, not in rows. They work on both individual and group tasks, talk among themselves, help each other, use each other. They stay for most of the day in the same place, going away from it only for specialist activities, like physical education. They have the same teacher, or 'boss', for most of the week. It is like working in the real world.

Secondary schools are different. At their most traditional the student will work for ten bosses in one week in ten different locations, with perhaps three or more different work groups. He or she will have no workplace to call their own, will be forbidden to help others or to accept help, will be discouraged from talking, asked to memorise data rather than look it up, and will eventually be tested by a procedure which will ensure that only a certain percentage passes. It is like a workplace only if the student is seen as a product going through a factory, with a rigorous quality control procedure, not as a worker in that factory.

Not all schools are like that, of course. More and more are finding ways to allow students to learn by working together on tasks, to use colleagues and resources and to see the teacher as counsellor and coach rather than as controller.

The dilemma for schools is that, whilst they are quite properly staffed by Dionysian-leaning professionals, the size and complexity of their job drives them towards an Apollo-type structure, which is the logical route to efficiency. Carried too far the Apollonian culture turns the school into a processing machine, with the kids as its products. The tendency then is to top it all off with a Zeus-like head who institutes, controls and directs the Apollo structure – in a very un-Japanese way. You can hardly blame the head, whose only experience of managing others is likely to have been in a classroom, where Zeus behaviour is not out of place and comes naturally to many Dionysians. The end result, however, can be a cultural mix-up which does little good to anyone.

Primary schools have evolved differently. Smaller sizes, less segmented tasks and simpler structures have made it possible for the teachers to work together as one group whilst still retaining their individual areas of expertise. Some seem to operate as simple Athenian task cultures. Others are small enough to allow the head to operate very effectively as Zeus, forming the teachers and the children into a club around himself or herself. Given a good Zeus, who allows others to develop their own strengths, this is a perfectly viable model; but not every Zeus, alas, is a good Zeus.

To be culturally compatible, the secondary school has to think of itself as more like a professional partnership than a factory. Professional partnerships group individuals in teams; the Apollo element is essential but subservient; the organisation is flat (there are often only three steps to the top status level), is led rather than managed with a maximum of consultation, and leaves as much room as possible for individual discretion. American schools, in separating off the administrative element under a non-teacher, have gone some way down this path. British schools need to do something similar, as well as dividing themselves up into mini-schools in order to get the size element reduced.

Interestingly, as we shall see, the cultural dilemma of the school turns out to be no different from that faced by other organisations – the crisis of Apollo. Conceivably, the answers will be the same.

The gods among the volunteers

Voluntary organisations, be they churches, relief organisations, campaigning groups or mutual-help bodies, will always stoutly maintain that they are different from the organisations of business and government and have nothing to learn from them about management – a word which they dislike because of its overtones of direction and control, of manipulation and profit-making. The truth is that they dislike the Apollonian culture, which they see as typical of business and government, preferring an often anarchic blend of Zeus and Dionysus, gathered together by Athenian groups sitting as committees or task-groups.

At first sight, voluntary organisations are composed of Dionysians, people who are there, as volunteers, because they want to be there making their contribution and doing their thing. The organisation has no power or hold over them and therefore has to see its role as facilitating them and servicing their activities. The paid staff are presumably there to support, co-ordinate and assist the volunteers, as it would be in a professional partnership.

It is not, however, as simple as that. While the volunteers may indeed look for a Dionysian culture they are not usually educated and licensed to act independently – like an architect or a doctor. Sometimes they are, as in the organisations which provide professional but voluntary counselling and advice, but in many organisations the volunteers are the fund-raisers and the leaflet-folders, the unpaid hired help, with the true professionals being the salaried staff of the agency. It would not be, or feel, appropriate for the professional salaried staff to behave as the facilitators of the voluntary help – in a Dionysian way – yet it is also inappropriate to regard the volunteers as if they were normal employees of an Apollonian role culture.

It is even more complicated when one considers the congregation of a church. Are the members of that congregation part of the organisation, or its customers? Can they be organised or are they there to be ministered to? Clearly they are not employees, so that Apollonian procedures would be inappropriate, but what are they? It is the same with campaigning organisations – be they for peace, against famine or in support of conservation. How are the volunteers to be classified? Are they workers, or just followers?

It is because many voluntary organisations are unclear about these relationships that they have difficulty in knowing what sort of organisational model they should use. How should they manage themselves? If Apollo is inappropriate, which god should they follow?

Voluntary organisations can be of three types, each needing a different blend of the gods. It is when the types get confused or combined that the problems arise, although it needs to be emphasised that voluntary groups are always harder to run well than more ordinary organisations. The three types are *fellowship, service* and *campaigning.*

Fellowship organisations are those which gather people together for mutual support, encouragement and enjoyment. They include mutual-help groups, like single-parent families, as well as church congregations, social groups and youth clubs. Such organisations welcome all who qualify and wish to be members. There is no selection – all single parents are welcome to a single-parent group, not just the best or the more competent, and all who 'profess and call themselves Christians' are welcomed to their local church or chapel. The organising required – no one would dream of calling it management – is to do with the provision of facilities and the structure of the occasions which are the focus of the fellowship. Much of the organising is done by volunteer helpers, who see themselves as helpers or arrangers, not as managers or as persons in authority. Fellowship organisations, in fact, are quite Dionysian in the way they look at organising: it is something done to facilitate the work of others.

Many voluntary organisations start life in the fellowship mode but move into a *service* mode when they realise that more needs to be done for their membership than providing opportunities to meet together. There are normally specific needs to be met and specific forms of assistance or advice to be given. Service organisations do, however, have to be particular about whom they use to provide the advice or give the service – anyone who volunteers is not necessarily good enough. As they become more service-oriented, they tend to employ more paid staff and to insist on the proper selection and training of staff and volunteers. Professional standards have, after all, to be applied. Goodwill is not enough. Service organisations, therefore, are the source of the apparent paradox, that the biggest and best of voluntary and charitable organisations are staffed by paid and professional staff. The volunteer element is found in the supervisory board, or management committee, which represents the constituency being served, and often in the fund-raising effort which sustains the organisation, although many such service organisations draw the bulk of their support from government or local authorities. Service organisations, therefore, are much more like other organisations: they need to be managed, directed and controlled. They understand budgets, procedures and defined roles as well as the nature of formal authority. They need Apollo as well as a bit of Zeus and Athena. The problem comes when the fellowship traditions and the service needs clash.

Thirdly, a voluntary organisation can be a *campaigning* organisation, seeking to raise support for a cause, to combat injustice, poverty or racialism, to fight for peace, individual rights or better housing. Such organisations are different again. They will welcome any adherents to their cause, will be led rather than managed, although they also need an effective administrative back-up to do research, organise meetings or arrange recruitment drives. At their head there will usually be a Zeus figure, for such organisations require a very personal and forceful form of leadership, a person who can represent and articulate what the movement stands for; and it is a movement rather than a formal organisation.

Most voluntary organisations end up as a mix of the three, although they may have started off at either the fellowship or the campaigning end. That is perhaps a natural and understandable progression, but it leaves the resulting organisation with three conflicting cultures. The theory of cultural propriety can end up as a battle-ground for the gods in many a voluntary headquarters, as Apollo seeks to apply some order to a Dionysian tradition infiltrated by Zeus. Athena is often seen as the way out, with her emphasis on the group rather than on hierarchy, and on professionalism in the pursuit of a solution. But Athenian organisations, as we have seen, are unstable cultures, hard to manage effectively, and they can be expensive. They easily drift into more committees, more project groups, who connive to perpetuate themselves, more independent cells doing their own thing. Athena, undisciplined, reverts to Apollo or Zeus, and so it often is with the voluntary world.

THE CONFUSIONS OF A VOLUNTARY ORGANISATION

The organisation was founded nearly 100 years ago. Its aims were clear – to provide a meeting-place for lonely strangers in our big cities.

That was easy enough, but the organisation felt that more needed to be done for particular groups. Some needed help with accommodation, others wanted advice on jobs, or counselling, legal assistance or just money. Gradually, the organisation set up separate agencies to provide each of these services. What had started as a fellowship organisation run by volunteers had evolved into a service agency, staffed by professionals and funded by volunteers, but the old fellowship ethos remained, which said that anyone who was a stranger could belong, and every volunteer had the right to help.

It went further than that, as the organisation began to perceive that it might be more effective to campaign to get rid of injustices rather than patching up the after-effects. A campaigning wing was added to the organisation, taking a radical stand for individual rights and becoming politically active under a forceful leader.

The new director wanted to bring order to the situation. She set out to introduce some management discipline, with objectives, budgets, performance reviews and personnel appraisals. The fellowship strand, which still permeated the organisation and was well represented on its many committees, was outraged. Such techniques, they said, were quite inappropriate to the 'open house, everyone welcome, contribute what you can' philosophy for which the organisation stood. 'Not so,' said the service agency groups. 'We are nowadays in competition with many other organisations who offer similar services. We need to be more efficient, tougher and more discriminating.' The campaigning arm took no notice – there were more important causes and the leader had his own band of enthusiasts who welcomed any adherent to their cause. It seemed, reflected the director, as if there were really three quite different organisations jostled together under one roof, making living together quite difficult.

Or three gods in one setting.

THE GODS IN CHURCH

Many a church congregation has, in the best Christian tradition, proclaimed its task to be the threefold one of worship, ministry and prophecy. All three are necessary to provide proper witness to a Christian presence in that place. What the congregation often fails to realise is that each task implies a different (Greek) god. Worship is akin to fellowship, ministry to services and prophecy to campaigning. There are really three different organisations needed, all under one umbrella. It can be done. The gods can learn to live together, as Chapter 3 demonstrated, but often it is one god who triumphs over the rest, so that in the end only one of the tasks is properly done. It is perhaps unfortunate that the servant tradition is taken so literally to heart by many churches, because that fits best the Dionysian tradition and the fellowship model, meaning that the tasks of ministry and prophecy are inadequately done. Organisationally, it is probable that many congregations will end up as little more than holy huddles.

57 varieties

Japan and America, schools and charities – these are but four of many possible settings. Hospitals and prisons, armies and parliaments, Mexico and Nigeria – they all demand different cultural blends in their organisations. The theory of cultural propriety has to take account of the surroundings. It would, however, be unfortunate if every setting felt that it had to work out its own unique theory of management, unheeding of what the rest may be up to. Wheels come in different sizes, materials and colours, but the principle need not be reinvented each time.

Organisations can and should learn from each other, which is not the same as saying that they should copy each other. The gods can be blended in different ways, but they each represent continuing traditions which seem to apply across a range of contexts and settings. The Japanese may find it easier, culturally, to run Apollo organisations, but they put a lot of effort and ingenuity into the task as well. We can learn from that, just as we can learn from the best of American businesses and the best of schools and charities.

PART TWO

The Apollonian Crisis

Negative Power

Chapter 5

THE DILEMMA OF APOLLO

The first part of this book may have made things look easy. They are not, of course. It has always been easier to describe principles than to follow them, which is why grandparents, who no longer have to practise what they preach, have such a good time. Management, it should by now have become clear, is the art of combining opposites, of blending the cultures or of managing paradox. One set of pressures drives one towards tight control, central monitoring, keep it all at one's fingertips, whilst at the very same time there are many instincts, and very valid reasons, for doing just the opposite, decentralising, delegating and letting go. Management is the art of compromise.

Part Two explores the ways in which the pull of opposites has come to a head in Western organisations. The pressures to become more Apollonian, to make organisations tidier and more formal, are pressing and convincing, but so are the opposing pressures to recognise the individuals who make up those organisations and the need to give them more scope, more rights and more independence. I will argue in this second part that these more individualist, or Dionysian, pressures, which spring from a freer and richer society, are inexorable. Apollo will have to compromise. The result will be new kinds of organisations, new structures and new ways of relating individuals to organisations. It adds up to an organisational revolution which will affect not only the way we manage our institutions but the way we live and plan our lives. Nor is it that far off. There are signs enough to suggest that the year 2000 will see the waning of the employment society as we have known it.

The drift to Apollo

If you are sitting near the top of an organisation, responsible in

129

whole or in part for its continued success, or at least survival, there is a strong urge to want to make it *bigger* and more *internally consistent*. There are good reasons for each of these tendencies, which need owe nothing to the supposed egos, lust for power or dictatorial ambitions of those in authority.

First, bigness. The bigger you are, the more able you are to influence your own destiny. A small organisation has to ask others for money: banks, other lenders, the stock market, the government. The more money you, as manager,* can generate internally, the less you are dependent on others, and if and when you need their money, the more likely they are to believe your estimates of your future. The bigger, therefore, the easier.

And bigness brings clout: clout in the market-place, enabling one to offer comprehensive ranges or services, to launch sales drives, price offensives or massive advertising campaigns; clout in the research laboratories, allowing adequate finance for adequate research and development, all of which is insurance against the future (93 per cent of the research in Britain happens in large – over 3,000 – firms); clout in recruitment, offering scope for varied careers within the protection of one organisation.

And finally, bigness brings flexibility and a built-in insurance. A loss in one area can be offset against unusual profits elsewhere. Resources can be taken from one use and given to another without the need for anyone outside to know or be concerned. It is no accident that the big corporations are private universes, revealing only the tips of their icebergs to their shareholders in their balance sheets or to their employees in their internal communications. Privacy carries its freedoms and as the custodians of the organisation's future, its managers and directors understandably want as much discretion as they can retain, and bigness to provide that discretion.

---

* Of course, pure capitalist theory would have all surplus earnings returned to the owners, who would then decide where it was appropriate to reinvest. But this 'city-state' view of the capitalist notion implies a more perfect market, better information and speedier decision processes than could in practice exist, so the managerial prerogative has become enlarged until managers have acquired the right to reinvest their earnings in the continuation of the business. Due payment must be made, in dividends or interest, for the *use* of the capital, but the capital itself is seldom returned voluntarily to the owners.

WHY DO FIRMS GROW?

An analysis of the evolution of giant firms in Britain was made by S. J. Prais.*

He pointed out that the share of net output contributed by the 100 largest manufacturing firms in Britain rose from 16 per cent in 1900 to 22 per cent in 1949 and to 41 per cent in 1970. But whilst the size of the firms increased, the size of plants remained relatively static. Prais argues that it is economics in marketing, transport and the likelihood of cheaper finance that encourage growth, not economies of scale at the plant level.

Does it work?

Leslie Hannah and John Kay** agree that, while firms grow, plants remain small, but found little evidence that the new giants performed better. The giants certainly export less, and have higher labour costs than the overall average.

In search of the 'clout' of size, have we lost efficiency?

WHY HAVE LARGE SCHOOLS?

Schools with 2,000 pupils seem excessively large to some. Why were they designed like that? Well, it is logical, really. Suppose you want to offer a minimum choice of twelve subjects to be taught at sixth-form level, with an average of ten students per class. If each student does three subjects, that gives you a sixth-form of 360 students and 180 in each of the two years of the sixth-form. If half of each class leaves at sixteen, the end of compulsory schooling, you will need an average class size of 360 to produce your sixth form. If they join the school at eleven, there will be five years of 360 students and two of 180, which works out at 2,160. 2,000 then seems a rather modest target.

The logic is impeccable, given the assumptions. But are the assumptions inevitable? Should schools cover an age range from 11-18? If they split at sixteeen, the arguments break down. If they started at thirteen, the school would be significantly smaller. If a higher percentage stayed on, the school size could be proportionately reduced. And so on.

---

* S. J. Prais, *The Evolution of Giant Firms in Britain*, Cambridge University Press, 1977.
** L. Hannah and J. Kay, *Concentration in Modern Industry*, Macmillan, 1977.

Given the logic, however, and the assumptions, size is inevitable and so, therefore, is Apollo.

The second urge is towards *consistency*. Consistency is desirable to a manager in two ways. If the future is consistent with one's expectations of it, then planning can be tighter and all the provisions for that future taken care of – in that way things will happen as they were expected to happen. A catering firm once claimed that the *predictability* of its operations was such that it could forecast to within two dozen the number of eggs that would be consumed by its 250 London outlets in any given day. This consistency over time allowed it to run a more cost-effective purchasing and delivery system than its competitors.

Most organisations seek to achieve the *consistency of predictability* by choosing the kind of future they want and then setting out to achieve it. That is not quite the way they put it, of course. They talk instead of forecasts, long-term plans and corporate objectives, but essentially these plans are intended to be self-fulfilling prophecies. J. K. Galbraith, the American economist, has found alarming portents in the ability of large corporations to create self-fulfilling prophecies, seeing this as a corruption of democracy. Others have deplored the way the consumer becomes just a part of the corporation's plans, the patient an 'input' to the hospital's operations. We need not, at this stage, take sides on the rights and wrongs of this managerial urge for predictability, but only take the plaints as evidence of its existence.

Managerially, consistency over time, or predictability, is highly desirable. The longer one can guarantee predictability, the more scope there is for tightening up the operational side of the organisation. Consistency over time is an entirely normal and appropriate instinct for those seeking managerial comfort.

UNPREDICTABILITY AT HOME

Have you ever stayed in an unpredictable household?

> '*Is there anything for supper?*'
> '*How should I know, have a look. There may be if the children haven't eaten it all. There isn't anything? Well, don't blame me, I've had other things to do.*'

'Where's Alan, we've got to leave now?'
'He's gone off on his bike.'
'Did he say when he'd be back?'
'No idea.'

'I need the car today, dear.'
'You can't have it, I'm afraid, I'm driving to Gateshead.'
'Well, then, how do I get to mother's?'

For a time, the feeling of spontaneity carries its own brand of charm. On a holiday, the charm can linger for days, even weeks. But slowly the irritation mounts, and its costs. It is impossible to plan in these conditions. Time is wasted as people stand around. Activities cannot be co-ordinated or days organised in advance. Every joint venture becomes a major event. Instead of everyone doing his or her own thing, everyone begins to feel thwarted by the others. Tempers flare. Stress mounts.
Organisations demand predictability.

Consistency across activities, *comparability*, is also highly desirable. In any case, it is being pressed upon us in organisations whether we desire it or not.

Comparability is desirable, even essential, for the *dovetailing* that lies at the heart of most organisational activities. One task depends on another and contributes to another. Seen at its most obvious in the automated assembly-line, the principle of dovetailing applies to the accounts department and the despatch warehouse as much as to the factory.

Comparability is necessary for *control* from the top. Without a proper basis for comparison, control becomes arbitrary, governed more by whims and impulses than by rationality.

Comparability is imperative in certain *work-flows*, particularly the copy or flow types. The arrival of new expensive technology which demands high throughput to justify its existence drives organisations to flow or copy work-patterns, and the consistency or comparability which these demand. The high technology of process industries is one example of a technology demanding a precise standard of consistency between inputs in order to operate efficiently. More commonly, the computer, with its insatiable appetite for input data, has imposed copy conditions across organisations which did not need them or want them.

Consistency is also forced upon organisations from outside. The spate of legislation, of government regulations, of union bargaining mechanisms, all encourage consistency, a comparability across activities. In some organisations, this consistency is achieved initially through *centralisation*: by, for instance, establishing a central negotiating office to deal with union negotiations. But centralisation is only one way, and can be the most costly, to achieve the consistency which is often the driving force behind the apparent need to centralise.

There are, then, these twin pressures towards *bigness* and *consistency*. They are not only understandable, but, viewed from the standpoint of operational efficiency, much to be desired. In the original sense of the word, things are more 'manageable' if they are under our control. Bigness and consistency both increase control. Unsurprisingly, ambitious managers concentrate their attention on opportunities for growth and on improved systems of control.

However, both bigness and consistency imply an *Apollonian culture*. Size, as we have already shown in an earlier chapter, brings formality, impersonality and rules and procedures in its train. There is no way out of it. When a man cannot rule by glance of eye and word of mouth because there are just too many people, he has to lean on formal systems of hierarchy, information and control. Similarly, consistency implies budgets, forms, standardised methods, fixed reporting periods, common documents and the whole barrage of bureaucracy. The ineluctable logic of efficiency drives organisations towards Apollo and the role culture.

APOLLO TRIUMPHANT

It has been suggested that, by the end of the century, fewer than 200 companies will control more than 70 per cent of private sector activity in the Western democracies. In Britain, the 100 largest manufacturing companies accounted for 22 per cent of total net output in 1949, but 41 per cent in 1970.

The consistent trend in organisational reform in the British public sector has been towards amalgamation and standardisation. The comprehensive schools have typically been created by a merger of one 'grammar' school with one 'secondary modern'. The reform of the National Health service amalgamated into one regional organisation the remedial, preventive and service activities that had previously run their own separate affairs. The Maud reforms of local authorities created larger and more all-embracing units. The Water Authorities have decreased in number but increased in scope.

Research by John Child of Aston University shows that in the faster-growing and more profitable large companies, as total size increases so do certain types of systems and procedures: sophisticated financial controls applied to a wide range of activities, a precise definition of operative tasks by management, the application of work study and methods, the use of labour turnover statistics, the planning of recruitment, and the regular updating of company forms and documents.

Apollo thrives on size.

The resistance to Apollo

Unfortunately, logic no longer reigns supreme. Psychology also counts, and these Apollonian systems are managed and worked by humans. And from these humans comes an increasing resistance to the inexorable advance of the Apollonian culture. One strand of this resistance suggests that we are creating systems that are simply too complex to be managed by humans, that logic has outdistanced psychological capacity.

A second strand argues that the extreme specialisation of the work role is alienating, that it deprives man of control over his destiny and splits his work off from his other lives: family, recreation, community.

A third strand says that, rightly or wrongly, the new norms and values of society expressed through our schools and traditions of child-rearing do not encourage the kind of obedience and subordination to imposed methods which are required by Apollonian organisations.

THE FIRST STRAND OF RESISTANCE

Size brings complexity, and it may well be that we cannot humanly handle the complex decisions of the mammoth corporations within the time available. Professor Elliott Jaques believes that individuals of immense conceptual span are needed, and that there are too few of these around in any generation. The evidence of mergers has been that bigness on its own does not lead to increased efficiency but rather the reverse, as we import more administrative 'slack' to handle the increased complexity. Computers have immeasurably increased our capacity to handle information and complexity, but they have also added hugely to the information that we have to handle. Some multi-nationals, looking at the incredible complexity of trying to manage a wide range of national subsidiaries in a constantly shifting environment, have, in a sense, abandoned the pursuit of 'the one best' solution and left their subsidiaries to go their own way. Most managers would agree that the apparent logical pull of bigness and consistency does not seem to make their job any easier.

A cultural analysis according to patron gods would suggest why. The Apollonian culture demanded by bigness and consistency will work as long as the work is routine, the environment stable and change infrequent. Unfortunately, as an organisation gets larger, it *imports* uncertainty when it begins to get involved with more and more outside groups, and becomes exposed to a wider range of forces. Ironically, as an organisation gets larger, it *ought* to attempt to make do with *less* of Apollo's culture rather than more. This is the first glance at the Apollonian paradox: the tendency for Apollo to self-destruct. For just as size creates an *internal* need for Apollonian methods, so the very increase in that culture tends to make the total organisation less responsive to its environment, less capable of changing, more dinosaur-like than ever – impressive but out of touch, and often out of control.

The first consequence of the excessive complexity of large Apollonian systems is what Derek Sheane of ICI has called the 'symptomology of bureaucratic breakdown'.* His list of symptoms includes:

1. The invisible decision: no one knows how or where decisions are taken.

---

* In his stimulating booklet, *Beyond Bureaucracy*, 1976, available from Management Research.

2. Unfinished business: too many tasks get started but not finished.
3. Co-ordination paralysis: nothing can be done without checking with a host of other interconnected units.
4. Nothing new: bureaucracies polish but do not invent. This applies to both processes and products.
5. Pseudo problems: bureaucracies seem to magnify some issues until they become an internal organisational epidemic, for no apparent reason.
6. Embattled centre: the conflicts between the centre and the local or regional units increase as the centre battles for consistency.
7. Negative deadlines: the dates for reports and historical explanations become more important than doing the work. He who carries bad news gets priority over good news.
8. In-tray domination: individuals react to their inputs rather than impose their own initiatives.

THE COSTS OF WAITING

Specialisation ought to make things change, but the costs of co-ordinating specialised activities can hugely outweigh the savings.

Take batch production.

The component to be manufactured is split down to a set of operations on machine tools. There may be as many as twenty separate operations. Each operation will involve a different tool, or at least a different setting of the same tool. In between operations, the component has to wait. It has been calculated* that, out of the average 100 days it takes a component to go through a normal efficient factory, it will spend 99 days just waiting. The cost in work-in-progress can be huge if the material of the component is expensive.

In the name of consistency, we specialise, then we co-ordinate, and so we pay.

The second consequence of excessive complexity is that the burden of holding the thing together now falls upon the manager – typically

---

* By D. T. N. Williamson in 'The Anachronistic Factory', *Personnel Review*, 1973.

the middle manager. In a straightforward Apollonian role culture, he would be an ordinary man in a straightforward routine administrative job. Instead, today, in the oversized organisation, he receives all the imported *uncertainty*, yet is equipped only with the (Apollonian) methods for dealing with *certainty*. Lashed in by the rules and procedures dictated by the pressures for consistency, he has to find a way of coping with the inconsistent. He can only do it, Zeus-like, by ignoring the rules and procedures, by playing organisational politics, by taking organisational risks, and by working enormously hard. Many succeed in doing this, but the costs can be high, both to themselves and to their organisations. It is understandable if they feel themselves under-rewarded in a society that depends on the organisations which they seem to be carrying on their shoulders.

The cost of coping with imported uncertainty in an Apollonian system designed for certainty is overload. When the overload gets too much, ways of coping with it have to be evolved. All of these 'coping mechanisms' in effect create 'slack' or inefficiency in the organisation.

COPING WITH OVERLOAD

Think of yourself when tired, when there is more to do than you can easily cope with.

Do you ever:

Polarise – *push problems into extremes of black or white, good or bad? Do you find yourself saying to a subordinate, 'I don't want to know that there are pros and cons, I want to know is it viable or not?' (It is easier to decide between black and white than shades of grey.)*

Shorten time-horizons – *put off to tomorrow that which does not have to be done today, leave the five-year plan till the week after next, think about the growing apathy over the Christmas holidays. (Postponement of longer-term decisions is one way to lessen the load.)*

Search for routines – *say, 'What did we do last time?', or, 'PO requirement', even if the situation doesn't neatly fit that box? (Finding a routine avoids a decision.)*

Delight in trivia – *when baffled, turn your attention to an easy problem or delve into some issue of minor importance? (Taking the easy things first does at least reduce the load.)*

React, not proact – *deal with the in-tray before going out to change the world, cope with events as they arrive rather than seek to influence them before they arrive. (Reactivity reduces the list of things to be done, proactivity adds to it.)*

Flare up – *show irritation, anger, emotion over matters of relatively minor importance, often to illustrate that you are still around and matter. (Emotion acts as a relief valve.)*

Withdraw – *either physically or emotionally, take yourself away from the centre of action – shut yourself in your office, go on a trip, claim that 'it's all unimportant anyway'. (Withdrawal puts the load into a reduced perspective.)*

Hammer away – *do what you normally do, only more of it. Work longer and harder, write more reports, hold more committees, make more visits. (More effort will reduce the load.)*

Escape – *into excess behaviour, often accompanied by unnecessary humour, drink, drugs, etc. (These are forms of sublimation.)*

Breakdown – *collapse, usually into hospital. (An extreme form of enforced withdrawal.)*

All of these mechanisms do cope with the overload, for you. But they either export it to someone else, or they reduce the ultimate efficiency or success of the operation. Some of them (Escape *and* Breakdown) *have unwanted consequences for oneself.*

THE SECOND STRAND OF RESISTANCE

The second strand of resistance to Apollo arises from the emphasis that the Apollonian culture of management gives to the 'role' as distinct from the 'individual'. Here lie the ideas of 'organisational sin' and 'corporate slavery'.

We have already glancingly noted that traditionally 'sin' meant 'denying oneself', being false, in word or deed or thought, to one's true beliefs and true self. The concept of sin has these days been so downgraded to a list of mere peccadilloes that it is even socially respectable to boast, 'I am a confirmed sinner'; but one would still be unlikely to *boast*, 'I do not believe in what I do, nor does my behaviour reveal the kind of man I am.' That is simply not a boast. Instead it is a kind of bleat, and it is heard often enough. A man's job or official role can become his private crucifixion, as he finds himself forced to act and speak in ways which do not reflect his real beliefs, in order to do his job.

George Orwell has described how once, as a minor colonial official in Burma, he found himself, an apostle of non-violence and a lover of living things, raising a gun to kill a harmless elephant because he lacked the will, or perhaps the courage, to deny the demands of what others called his 'duty'. It is a moving description of a private shame, or sin.

For many people, organisations seem to reek of this kind of private sin. It is not that employees are forced to cheat, or bribe, or lie – although such dishonesties are not unknown in organisations – but in smaller ways they feel pushed to submerge their identity in the job, to argue cases of whose merit they are not convinced, give priority to rituals they know to be charades, be charming to those they despise, appear fierce when they feel sympathy, and act committed when unconvinced. Perhaps it is not profit that makes youth shy away from organisations – but sin?

The idea that organisations deprive individuals of the right to express their values and their personalities in their work has a long and distinguished pedigree. William Morris and D. H. Lawrence in England, Thoreau and Marcuse in America, Brecht in Germany, Simone Weil and André Malraux in France, and, of course, Karl Marx, have all sung this song. The IBM young men are but the latest exponents of the idea, which is embedded in many Western cultures.

THREE QUOTATIONS

Karl Marx:

> *'In his work, therefore, [the worker] does not affirm himself but denies himself . . . does not develop freely his physical and mental energy but mortifies his body and ruins his mind . . . His labour is . . . not voluntary but coerced; it is forced labour. It is therefore not the satisfaction of a need: it is merely a means to satisfy needs external to it.'*

Frederick Taylor:

> *(originator of 'Scientific Management'): 'One of the very first requirements for a man who is fit to handle pig iron as a regular occupation is that he shall be so*

> *stupid and so phlegmatic that he more nearly resembles an ox than any other type.'*

Adam Smith:

> *'The man whose life is spent in performing simple operations . . . has no occasion to exert his understanding . . . He generally becomes as stupid and ignorant as it is possible for a human creature to become'.*

RUNAWAY SLAVES

In 1970, IBM France had a new experience – they lost a team of softwear specialists, who decided to leave to found a business of their own. The manager of Computer Services, the new company, said, 'Never has man owed more to a private business enterprise. Without IBM, the economic level of our planet would not be what it is today. Why, then, did we quit? To perform more interesting work, and above all for moral reasons. Tomorrow, the real power will belong to those who master software. Whereas this firm has dominated the world's information-processing market, the French engineers participating in IBM's activities have by no means been involved with decision-making. They are in some ways nothing but "golden slaves".'

All these people see Apollonian organisations as inevitably alienating places. Alan Fox has demonstrated that low levels of discretion lead to low levels of trust. Apollonian organisations cannot tolerate much discretion – it would violate their consistency. They will not, cannot, be high-trust organisations. One can redesign jobs to allow marginally greater discretion, introduce flexitime or autonomous groups, create works councils, but these all remain placebos, temporary pills to relieve the pain and alleviate the inherent incompatibility between man and this type of work. Today, they point out, more than 90 per cent of the working population are in organisations and many of them – the majority, probably – in a bureaucracy of one sort or another. One hundred years ago, fewer than 30 per cent worked in any form of organisation, and very few of those institutions that did exist would have been classified as bureaucratic, even if they had other flaws and faults. The bureaucratic phenomenon is, then, of fairly recent origin. Only today, they would argue, are we becoming aware of the extent of the malaise. When it afflicted only a minority it could be ignored, or the minority could be regarded as volunteers, prepared to suffer the so-called indignities of organisational work because they wanted the money, the security or the promise of higher status in time to come. Now that it is the majority that is involved, 'sin' is no longer a voluntary option but a built-in requirement of life. In Apollonian organisations, the individual is a *role* more than a *person*; initiative comes from above, not from within; and creativity too often is counted as disruption.

RULES FOR STIFLING INITIATIVE

Rosabeth Kanter took these ten rules for stifling initiative from her observations of 'segmentalist' (Apollonian) companies in America. *

1. *Regard any new idea from below with suspicion – because it is new, and because it is from below.*
2. *Insist that people who need your approval to act first go through several other levels of management to get their signatures.*
3. *Ask departments or individuals to challenge and criticise each other's proposals. (That saves you the job of deciding: you just pick the survivor.)*
4. *Express your criticisms freely, and withhold your praise. (That keeps people on their toes.) Let them know they can be fired at any time.*
5. *Treat problems as signs of failure, to discourage people from letting you know when something in their area isn't working.*
6. *Control everything carefully, make sure people count anything that can be counted, frequently.*
7. *Make decisions to reorganise or change policies in secret and spring them on people unexpectedly. (That also keeps people on their toes.)*
8. *Make sure that any request for information is fully justified and that it isn't distributed too freely. (You don't want data to fall into the wrong hands.)*

---

* R. M. Kanter, *The Change Masters: Corporate Entrepreneurs at Work*, Allen & Unwin, 1983

9.   *Assign to lower-level managers, in the name of delegation and participation, responsibility for figuring out how to cut back, lay off or move people around.*

10.   *Above all, never forget that you, the higher-ups, already know everything important about this business.*

THE THIRD STRAND OF RESISTANCE

This problem is not concerned so much with rights and wrongs, as with the way things are. A new generation has grown up in the Western democracies, a generation that is less frightened (it has experienced no major wars), is less hungry, less insecure, and perhaps less greedy than preceding generations. But not only have external conditions changed (improved?) for the new youth, so have the ways of rearing and educating children. Education is as much about the nature of authority as it is about information and skills. When the parents of the young currently in their twenties went to school, most of them sat in rows and copied down what the teacher said, only to write it back to him in due course as a test or examination. Whether or not this was an efficient method of learning, it certainly conveyed the message that the younger, or more junior, or less clever, did what their elders and betters said. The message from the home matched that of the school, obedience and conformity to those in charge were a prerequisite of life. Today, it is different. My young children sit in groups in their school. They work on projects. They think of themselves as learning rather than being taught. They are encouraged to express their own personalities in stories, poems and paintings, instead of memorising or imitating those of the great. And again, for better or worse, the home mirrors the school. From an early age, due partly to the exigencies of small houses and communal living, the young are treated as equals in the family, with a right to their own views and attitudes. In adolescence, the new affluence, the increased ability to earn marginal income, allows the growing men and women to be rapidly independent of their elders. The result is predictable, and is summed up by David Yankelovitch's survey, summarised below.

'AUTHORITY' TO THE YOUNG

David Yankelovitch carried out a survey for the IDR Third Fund to investigate the changing views of American student youth.* Amongst many other facets of their attitudes, he looked at the increasing resistance to authority:

> *In 1968, six out of ten students (59 per cent) found that they could easily accept the power and influence of the police. In 1971, that number had been reduced to 45 per cent. Many fewer students than formerly (15 per cent) find it easy to accept outward conformity for the sake of career advancement, and to abide by laws with which they do not agree.*

> *The greatest single erosion of relationship to authority is in the 'boss' relationship and the work situation. In 1968, over half of all students (56 per cent) did not mind the future prospect of being bossed around on the job. This number fell to 49 per cent in 1969, 43 per cent in 1970 and down to 36 per cent in 1971. The result: today, two out of three students do not easily see themselves submitting to the authority of the 'boss'.*

> *A student's relationship to authority of all kinds – including the boss – is at best one of grudging but not easy acceptance. Students see the major barrier standing in the way of securing desirable work to be their attitude to authority. No obstacle comes even close to this one, including political views, style of dress, or unwillingness to conform.*

> *This random concatenation of words and phrases captures as well as any formal definition the things which students do not want in their world:*

> *Professional . . . . system . . . . planning for the future . . . . conceptual framework . . . . experiment . . . . organisation . . . . detachment . . . . management . . . . verification . . . . facts . . . . technology . . . . cost-effectiveness . . . . theory . . . . rationalisation . . . . efficiency . . . . measurement . . . . statistical controls . . . . manipulate . . . . mechanisation . . . . institutions . . . . power . . . . determinism . . . . intelligence testing . . . . abstract thought . . . . programming . . . . calculate . . . . objectivity . . . . behaviourism . . . . modification of the human*

---

* D. Yankelovitch Inc., *The Changing Values on Campus*, New York: Washington Square Press, 1972.

environment . . . . *literal* . . . . *moulded to specification* . . . .
genetic planning . . . . *achievement.*
Dionysians all?

BRITISH VIEWS OF WORK

A survey by the Guardian *newspaper in 1982 tapped the satisfactions
that people in work wanted from their job.*

Top of the list came – personal freedom, the respect of people one
worked with, learning something new, challenge and completing a
project. *(Athenians all, with a touch of Dionysus).*

Security *came seventeenth in the list,* working conditions *twenty-
first, with* money, organisation *and* social status *bringing up the rear.
(Apollonians were much in the minority, although it might have been
very different if the questions were put to people* not *in work but
wanting it!)*

Gordon Rattray Taylor, in his book *Rethink*, has drawn attention to
the difference between what he terms patrism and matrism in our
society. The values and attitudes of patrism might be called traditional, or tough, as opposed to radical, or tender. Patrism believes
in order and discipline, wishes to maintain the traditions of the past
and respect for authority; it values self-control and rational behaviour, distinguishes male and female roles, puts more faith in
experience and age than in youth. Matrism, on the other hand, is
optimistic about the future, decries the past, believes in openness
and likes emotions, makes little distinction between the sexes,
wants discussion rather than orders, places reliance on expertise
rather than experience, values youth and imagination more than
age. Rattray Taylor is convinced that there is a marked swing
towards matrism in our society.

In my cultural terms, we are bringing up the young in a Dionysian
tradition – individuality and personal expression – with Athenian
overtones – groups, projects and shared values. It is not surprising
that they then reject the Apollonian culture when they begin to
meet it at work, or that they look increasingly to the established
professions for their careers (the schools of law and medicine are
those in most demand in universities everywhere), or to the new
professions in the media, in writing or design or fashion. These are

the Dionysian occupations, and today they are overcrowded.

In some countries, Japan perhaps most obviously, the educational and family systems are still Apollonian. There the bureaucratic organisation is more readily accepted, even welcomed as a natural and necessary part of life. In Germany, France, Switzerland and parts of Italy, the Apollonian tradition in schools and homes is still strong but weakening. In these countries, the Apollonian culture is still viable and cost-effective, but perhaps not for very much longer.

There is, in other words, a growing clash in Western society between organisational logic and the feelings of the individual. The argument that efficiency justifies the subordination of individualism to the organisation may no longer carry so much weight in societies where efficiency and (relative) abundance are taken for granted. Japan has demonstrated that there are ways of running Apollonian cultures which make them more tolerable to the individual as well as efficient but, as we shall see in later chapters, this is achieved for only a minority of the working population and at some cost to the remainder. We have also noted that what works in Japan may not work so well in countries where the underlying culture gives a higher priority to individualism and to risk, or to personal power or feminism. The growing crisis of the Apollonian organisation is likely to be most pressing in Anglo-Saxon countries, but its pressures are likely to be felt everywhere, even in Japan, as more and more groups react against the overweening control of the organisation. To help them in that reaction they have one powerful weapon – the organisational hijack.

THE FRUITS OF ORGANISATION

To celebrate the Queen's Silver Jubilee in 1977, Readers Digest compared conditions then with those at the start of her reign.

In 1952, the small family car cost the equivalent of 62½ weeks' work by the average industrial worker. Twenty-five years later, it needed only 32½ weeks, even though wages had more than doubled in the meantime.

Barcelona, by scheduled flight from London, cost 4¾ weeks' work at the beginning of the period, only 1½ at the end of it.

22 minutes' work in 1977 was enough to earn a dozen eggs, compared with 57 minutes in 1952; 23 minutes for a pound of butter, instead of 32 minutes; and 11 minutes a packet of cornflakes, instead of 17½ minutes.

Even a bottle of Scotch, loaded with ever-increasing taxes, cost only 2¾ hours' work in Silver Jubilee year, compared with 7¼ in 1952.

The fruits of Apollo? Could it have happened otherwise? Will it continue if Apollo is weakened?

Organisational hijacks

This is how it works. Organisations get designed logically, according to the precepts of Apollo. As in a clock, each wheel fits the next in a hierarchical dovetailing of systems. One part depends on another and in its own turn is essential to the proper functioning of its neighbour. But take one cog out of a large clock and the whole apparatus is halted. Clocks are not designed with alternative relief systems, that would be an expensive and seldom utilised form of *slack* for a mechanism that can count on its cogs always being there. But it is not so with organisations. The cogs cannot be relied upon. Indeed, the power to stop or remove a cog is actually given to the cog itself. In organisational terms, the cog is a work-group, a sub-assembly unit, a department. Should the members of these groups decide to withhold their labour, skill or talent, they can bring a tightly designed organisation to a halt.

In many organisations, this hijack capacity has been unwittingly handed to the very people who are most likely to be resistant to the Apollonian tradition. They may feel bruised as individuals, but into their hands has been thrust a weapon with which to hold their enemy to ransom. Increasingly they will use it, indulging in a walk-out or a spontaneous strike, often in support of some quite trivial incident.

The incident itself can be merely the product, the symptom of a deeper discontent. The mini-strike or walk-out will often fail to win the support of the union (which can perceive the longer-term consequences of supporting hijackers), or even of fellow-workers whose earnings can cease if the whole system grinds to a halt. But, in the short term, it will usually pay the organisation to bribe the group

back to work, even though the longer-term precedents are likely to
be punitive in terms of higher rates across the board.

The monolithic over-tight design of our organisations is an invitation to hijack and a major contributory cause to wage inflation.
We have given what is called *negative power* in huge amounts to
those people most likely to use it. Apollonian cultures come
equipped with this time-bomb, which will destroy the whole temple
if it is not defused.

NEGATIVE POWER

*In 1974, a Turkish Airline DC-10 crashed north of Paris, killing over
300 people. A ground mechanic had failed to close the door of a
luggage compartment in the appointed manner. He was probably the
lowest-paid member of the ground staff. Reputedly, he was illiterate.
Yet he had the power to destroy one of the most sophisticated and best
cared-for of man's creations. He had little or no positive power, but
immense negative power. In this case, he used it unintentionally. It
can always be used intentionally.*

*All members of interlocking systems can find some negative power
to use. Its conscious use, often by lower officials in bureaucracies, is a
way of reminding themselves, and the organisation, that they do exist
and do matter. Negative power is therefore fertilised by unhappiness,
low morale or a feeling of powerlessness.*

*Travelling in India, I needed to hire a bed-roll for an overnight
train journey. This is a complicated procedure at the best of times,
involving filling in a document with seven separate copies, so I
allowed plenty of time. Nevertheless, on arrival at the desk of the key
functionary responsible for the hire of bedding, I was informed that
he was closing the office for one hour for his statutory meal-time
allowance. I pointed out that by the time he reopened, my train would
have departed. He expressed regrets, but assured me there would be a
later train. I begged him – yes, begged him – to deal with my request
before he closed the office, but he was adamant. His time was already
overdue. Had he no assistant? 'Not today, he is absent attending his
sister's wedding.' 'Can I talk to your superior?' 'He is not, alas,
available until tomorrow morning.' 'Would this [showing some
money] help?' 'Ah, no, sir, I'm not that sort of man, sir.' By this time,
we had used up more time than the actual issue of the bedding could*

*conceivably have required. The desire to exercise his negative power,
for whatever reason, prevailed over logic, economics and human
charity. I spent a very uncomfortable night.*

Less perceived, less dramatic but more pervasive than the active use
of negative power to hijack organisations is the stealthy threat of
absenteeism. So stealthy is this threat that figures are hard to collect,
even in statistics-conscious Britain. Some estimates, however,
suggest that absence due to sickness, family need, or just unex-
plained, is as much as *100 times* greater in the UK than days lost
through strikes. This silent stilling of the clock is the real threat to
Apollonian cultures. It is countered by over-employment, by sufficient over-manning to cope with any anticipated absenteeism, by
manpower slack. But this remedy exacerbates the disease. If it is
obvious that you are not needed, you may the more easily be
absent. And the cost? Immense. Here is the 'concealed unemployment' in industry, here the true nature of the 'English Disease'.
Maybe it is not after all, a disinclination to work, but a silent
expression of negative power in reaction against the Apollonian
cultures of organisations, that saps the energy of Britain's productive machines. And the disease is not confined to Britain. It is
estimated that the *net* average working day (after sickness, absenteeism and holiday) of the Italian worker is only four hours (instead
of the formal eight), while Swedes each take an average of 24 days a
year sick leave.

NATIONAL NEGATIVE POWER

Mancur Olson* wrote a book with the impressive title, The Rise and
Decline of Nations. *It is an important but depressing book. In it, he
argues that a society which has stayed politically stable for many
years with unchanged boundaries (Britain? America?) tends to accu-
mulate all sorts of collective organisations and informal collusions.
The most effective of these will be small groups with narrow but
identical interests. These coalitions find that they have more to gain
by diverting more of the nation's resources to themselves or their*

* M. Olson, *The Rise and Decline of Nations*, New Haven: Yale University Press,
1982.

causes, than by trying to increase the total of all the resources. Distribution not creation is the name of their game. They are exclusive, new members mean less for the old members, they resist innovation in order to protect their own markets or constituencies, they slow down change and make political life more divisive. Trade unions are one of these coalitions, but more important are cartels, trade associations and professional bodies.

Wars, revolutions and changed boundaries disrupt these conditions. Turbulence, therefore, with the prospect of a more stable future, is the likeliest predictor of economic success – because it destroys, for a time, the possibility of negative power.

Overcoming the resistance

If the efficiency of Apollo is to triumph, the resistance to it must be overcome. We have identified three strands to this resistance, and now we must examine counters to each. How effective these counters may be is a question to which we must continually return while we consider them.

The first strand had to do with the unmanageability of the complexity of large Apollonian structures. But perhaps we should not accept defeat: cannot we increase the comprehension span of selected individuals and equip them with further computational aids? Already the computer is in the boardroom. There are programmes which will evaluate the likely outcomes of any combination of strategic decisions, and flash them almost instantaneously on to screens in front of the decision-makers. Cannot this kind of facility be taken farther? Using another approach, is not management education the solution to the comprehension span problem?

Certainly the computer's ability to explore the effects of changing assumptions is potentially of great assistance to management. Just as the effect of different economic options open to government can be checked out on a computerised model of the total economy, so, notionally, could all options open to a manager. There is much work in progress attempting to find a generally applicable way of modelling the flows of information, of goods, activities or money within organisations. No doubt in time these models may become close enough to the reality to be more useful than the oversimplifications of the present. Whether they will ever be able to replicate the emotions, needs and beliefs of human beings which lie behind the equations in the models is another matter. The essence of being human lies in our ability to override our own predictions. This 'essential humanness' may be the unbridgeable gap in the modelling approach to management.

So far, the attempt to educate for conceptual span has been another of those searches for the elusive Holy Grail. Techniques can be taught, information transferred, skills acquired, by practice and coaching. But the ability to embrace complexity, or the cathedral mentality (to envision or start something whose completion you will not live to see), are rarer things. Some will maintain that they have to be inherited, or at least acquired, in those precious first years. Others argue that one can learn to think conceptually, that the study of history, economics, business case-studies and even literature can bring out whatever latent abilities there are to see patterns in things, and to look beyond the particular to the general. Yet there is little evidence for this. And if the ability can be acquired at a mature age, then assuredly it requires more time and attention than the four-week course which is the most that any practising manager would feel justified in devoting to it.

We must conclude that, *at present*, neither computers nor education offer a likely or a quick way out of the Apollonian impasse.

DOES EDUCATION HELP?

To most people, education means learning useful things, be they facts or techniques. In that sense, most further or higher education has an effective usefulness of about ten years maximum. After that, either the knowledge is outdated by advancing technology and new discoveries, or the individual has moved to a level or an occupation where he no longer needs it. How many 40-year-olds are still using anything they learned at school or college?

But it may be that higher education creates or improves the ability to cope with complexity, to deal with issues rather than facts, and the abstract as well as the particular. Watch what people talk about. Can they reason? Do they deal only with facts, turn opinion into fact, shun logical discussion? Is this related to their educational background?

Dunning, in a study* of the relative profitability of US subsidiaries in Britain, writes, 'Table 13 . . . reveals quite decisively that US and UK firms in which executives possess degrees or equivalent formal qualifications earn considerably higher profits than those who do not. It is noteworthy too that, whilst this relationship is broadly the same for both the US and the UK firms in the sample, a much higher proportion of executives in US firms possessed university degrees or equivalent formal qualifications.'

The cross-cultural comparison does not apply only to the US. Fewer executives have degrees in Britain than in any other western European country or Japan.

Does this mean anything in terms of relative managerial ability, or is it only a reflection of different cultural fashions?

The second strand of resistance had to do with the essential 'sin' of the Apollonian culture, which makes it an alienating place for the individual. The counter to this strand is not a denial, but an acknowledgement that in any society and in any organisation there must be a lot of boring jobs. Roles have to take priority over individuals. Work, for most people, is something that has to be done in order that the rest of life may be enjoyed. There are, of course, those fortunate few whose work is their hobby. Was not happiness once defined as 'being paid for your hobby'? For the rest, it is obviously important that work be made as painless as possible, that the physical conditions of work are congenial (but how can you make a foundry congenial?), and that the contractual side of employment is fair. And most importantly, the rewards of harder work, whether they be in money or increased leisure time, must be seen to be adequate. Here, it is argued, is the modern rub. The equation is not clear, more money is not linked closely enough to more work when clever negotiating or hijacking tactics can win the money without the work. Even when increased rewards do flow from increased productivity, penal personal taxation robs the individual of most of the fruit of his labour. If today the game of work is no longer worth the candle, the fault lies in the candle, not in the game.

There is, however, a fatal flaw creeping into this age-old argument. One man's rewards are too often now another man's

* J. H. Dunning, '*U.S. Subsidiaries in Britain and their U.K. Competitors*', Business Ratios, June 1968, p. 16.

grudge. Fred Hirsch, in an important book called *The Social Limits to Growth*, calls this dilemma the false promise of the affluent society.

It works like this: as long as you don't mind everyone else having what you've got, then you can offer the same carrot all round and it works as a universal incentive. So far so good. Plentiful food, better heating, more leisure – these are things that all men might want all others to have as well as themselves. But there are a whole lot of things we want which, *by definition*, all others cannot have because they depend on *comparative* advantage. Private education is one of them in Britain – give it to everyone and it ceases to be desirable. Servants used to be another, but we cannot all be masters, for who then would serve? A house with an unspoilt view? If all had them, we would end up looking at each other in that view. Once we move from universal goods to comparative goods, we come up against the endless paradox – 'When you've got what you want, you don't want what you've got, because everyone else has got it, too.' The majority cannot enjoy a minority right.

When people are hungry, incentives work universally. When they work for comparative advantage, then increasing the incentives for some will only make others discontented. As they catch up, the effort from the first group will fall away. It is like walking up the down escalator. Apart from anything else, it is a built-in inflationary pressure.

'Let them go hungry, then.' Indeed, a dose of massive deflation, unemployment and siege economy conditions would soon bring back the universal incentive side of money. The counter-argument to the second strand of resistance to Apollo would then be justified. But to use hunger as the lever to organisational efficiency is not politically acceptable today. We should be glad.

DOES MONEY MATTER?

Studies in both British and American organisations have shown that a substantial pay rise (over 10 per cent in net pay) does produce increased effort, energy and enthusiasm – for an average period of six weeks. Thereafter, the new pay becomes the new base line.

Questioned by Nancy Morse and Robert Weiss in America, 80 per

*cent of 401 employed men said that they would continue working
even if they did not need the money.**

In a study of British managers undertaken by Harry Hansen,** *the
personal objective 'to earn a substantial amount of money' ranked
well below the other objectives:*

>'Have freedom to carry out your own ideas, a chance for
>originality and initiative;'
>'Belong to a growing, successful organisation;'
>'Work with associates whom you personally like.'

The third strand concerned the changing values and norms of society
as revealed in our educational methods and our child-rearing
habits. The attention given to personal expression, to the development of one's own talents, to group activities, to influence through
persuasion and a search for common purposes – Dionysian and
Athenian attitudes – is antithetical to the impersonality, conformity
and obedience required in Apollonian systems. The counter to this
strand might be to revert to more traditional ways of bringing up our
young. In Britain, as in France, the Netherlands, the US and parts
of Germany, education was in the forefront of public attention
following the student unrest of 1968. In all these countries, there are
many who argue for a return to former ways, and their arguments
are based as much on the need to re-establish the traditional
patterns of authority as on the efficiency of the learning methods.
They maintain that the young, the less extrovert, the ordinary
majority of working folk, need and appreciate structure and discipline in their lives. Too much, it is claimed, has been given and
promised to the young. The pendulum must swing back and the
disappearance of the 'youth bulge' in the population statistics of all
countries will help to push youth back in their place as a minority
apprentice group in society.

To a degree, they must be correct in their predictions. In 1965,
over half of the population of the United States was under 25.
Twenty years later, over half are over 40. Society will be middle-
aged, youth will be in a minority, middle-aged values of stability and
security will prevail. There are even some worries that in the 1990s

---

* N. Morse and R. Weiss, 'The Function and Meaning of Work and Job,' *American
Sociological Review*, 1955.
** H. Hansen, *The British Manager*, Boston: Harvard University Press, 1976.

there may not be a large enough working population to fill the available jobs.

Nonetheless, there does seem to have been a radical shift in society's attitude to the individual – a shift of which our educational philosophy is only a mirror, even if a slightly distorting one. If that is so, then organisations cannot ever again expect to rely on an obedient, complacent, dependent workforce. Democracy has worked its way through to the workplace, but Apollo prefers to ignore the democratic process. The clock cannot be turned back, even if its rate of change is slowed down, even if it is halted for a time. Our organisations are increasingly going to be populated by people who are Dionysians and Athenians at heart, with the occasional Zeus to flavour the mix. Necessity will make Apollonians out of many of them – at least on the surface. Many of them will not have the talent or abilities to sustain a Dionysian or Athenian job, inside or outside the organisation. Hunger will breed conformity in some, but it will be a reluctant conformity, one that fertilises negative power, absenteeism and hijacks. And though some there will be who are true Apollonians – the tidy-minded, those prepared to subordinate self to system – they will not be enough to staff the mega-bureaucracies pushed on us by the pressures for bigness and consistency.

The conclusion begins to seem inescapable. The three strands, or tendencies, that frustrate the Apollonian logic of the large organisation will neither fade away nor be overcome in today's world. The visible result is expense – the expense of buying off hijacks, of staffing up for absenteeism, of compensating for the incapacity of the humans at the top: *slack*. For a time, in monopoly or quasi-monopoly situations, when your competitors are in a similar state, the extra expense can be concealed by higher prices. In some few cases, a technological breakthrough, or a giant step up the economies of scale, will so lower the cost of production or service that the expense of the Apollonian system is absorbed – for a time. But there is no end to the possible costs of Apollo. In the end, the inflationary pressures of over-pricing force themselves into the wider society. In competitive situations, the collapse comes sooner and is confined to the individual enterprise.

The railways can offset their reduced numbers of passengers for a time with increased fares, but society in the end will repudiate the sight and the cost of endless empty carriages whistling through the stations.

This, then, is the crossroads for the organisation, particularly for the mega-bureaucracies of government and industry. Do they commit themselves to the ultimate victory of bigness and consistency, heads down as they go, believing that the resistances are little local difficulties? Or do they change course? Although the resulting decisions will be hugely important for the 90 per cent who work in organisations, and therefore crucial decisions for society, the issue is not a political one, or an ideological one, but a practical question of the design and management of organisations. It is not that the mega-bureaucracies are irresponsible, corporations taking over from the state: the truth is that they may be too expensive because they have become, literally, unmanageable.

Today's dilemma was foreseen, of course. Keynes, the economist, perceived that his theories of economics were the economics of scarcity. Once scarcity had been eliminated, the central theories might lose their validity.

KEYNES THE POST-KEYNESIAN

In 1930, John Maynard Keynes looked foward in an essay to the 'Economic Possibilities for our Grandchildren'.* He prophesied that his grandchildren (who would be adults today) would discover that the 'economic problem is not the permanent problem of the human race'. He went on, 'If the economic problem is solved, mankind will be deprived of its traditional purposes. Will this be a benefit? If one believes at all in the real values of life, the prospect at least opens up the possibility of benefit, yet I think with dread of the readjustments of the habits and instincts of the ordinary man, bred into him for countless generations, which he may be asked to discard within a few decades. . . .

'The strenuous purposeful moneymakers may carry all of us along with them into the lap of economic abundance . . . but the rest of us will no longer be under any obligation to applaud and encourage

* Published in *Essays in Persuasion*, New York: The Norton Library, 1963, and quoted by Professor Gurth Higgin in his inaugural address (1975) at Loughborough University of Technology, entitled 'Scarcity, Abundance and Depletion'.

them for we shall enquire more curiously than is safe today into the true character of this purposiveness . . . for purposiveness means that we are more concerned with the remote future results of our actions than with their own quality or their immediate effects on our environments.'

Gurth Higgin has argued convincingly that, since the Middle Ages, the whole thrust of society has been towards the elimination of scarcity. Now that this is potentially a solved problem in the industrialised world, society is searching for a new thrust, and old values and systems and codes of behaviour come into question. When scarcity was the enemy, then much could be tolerated in the name of efficiency. The organisation was the instrument of society and men, machines and money the instruments of the organisation. When scarcity is no longer a common enemy, except in time of war or natural disaster, the costs of efficiency begin to seem high.

Never will so many Owe So Much to so Few

Chapter 6

REACTIONS

The Apollonian dilemma is not new. We have all been aware for a long time that the disciplines which efficiency seems to require are not always palatable to free men. Marx may or may not have exaggerated in comparing industrial organisations with the institutions of slavery, but he has always had many sympathisers, many of them vehement. For a long time society could afford to ignore the dilemma. The results of efficiency in terms of more to eat and spend, of years lived and comforts enjoyed, were so obviously worth the costs of organisational discipline for society as a whole. Of course, the benefits were not always as well distributed as they might have been, but political pressures could be relied upon to put that right in the end. But that cost-benefit equation is no longer so obvious today, when there appear to be diminishing returns to the individual from increased efficiency. The game is no longer worth so much candle, and the dilemma of Apollo gets more urgent as a result.

We can detect in society various attitudes and responses to the dilemma. None of them seem to me to be adequate. Some of them even compound the problem. Yet we need to examine them, if only to dismiss them, because they, between them, make up the conventional wisdom in this field. Let me describe them briefly.

One attitude relies on a staunch belief in the inexorable logic of efficiency. More growth will once again make the game worthwhile. In effect, if the theory of cultural propriety succeeded in eliminating slack, we should once again be swallowed up in a common objective of material growth. Others, however, would accept that we should need impossible rates of growth to keep us all profitably employed. To them the solution lies in the creation of a sort of industrial meritocracy who would create wealth that the rest of us might live. The preconditions of their view are that the meritocracy be properly rewarded and that the rest of us be educated for leisure, or life without employment. Both of these views have, of course, a lot of popular support, but I will argue that they do not present us with a long-term solution to the need to blend efficiency with individualism for the whole of society.

Then there are those who see organisations as inevitable, and as inevitably diminishing to the individual. The pressures of efficiency need, as they see it, to be balanced by pressures for individual rights in organisations. Democracy must apply within work as well as in the wider society. Many of these democratic enthusiasts would have their cake as well as eat it, by maintaining that increased democracy would bring increased efficiency. Others are more realistic, recognising that democracy has never been known for efficiency, but maintaining that it is a necessary precondition of human relationships in a civilised society (cost what it may, they might add). There is finally, a lower key variant of full democracy which argues for practical participation and organisation on a human scale. I would have more sympathy with this last approach if I felt that it was genuinely concerned with the dilemma of human dignity at work, and not merely tinkering with the distorting effects of excessive alienation.

The arguments between the exponents of these different viewpoints are often violent. The diverging perspectives of the 'industrial meritocracy' view and that of the 'full democracy' stance do in fact colour the whole of our political debate. To call it a debate is to dignify it, for usually the advocates of each view cannot understand or even hear what the others are saying. Society sometimes seems to be tearing itself apart over this Apollonian dilemma. The debates go on in private, too, as the following example demonstrates.

WHEN AUNTIE CAME TO DINNER

My aunt by marriage is a splendid character, but from a bygone age. Her father never worked, nor his father before him, nor, of course, had she ever earned a penny in her life. Their capital worked for them, and they managed their capital. Work was done by workers. She sees all governments today as insanely prejudiced against capital, all workers as inherently greedy and lazy, and most managements as incompetent. No wonder the world is in a mess and she getting poorer every day.

Tony is a friend from work. His father was a postman. He started life as a draughtsman in a large engineering firm. He grew up believing that inherited capital was socially wrong. He had never met any man who did not or had not worked for his living.

They met, by chance, at my house over a meal. It started quietly, politely. Then she inquired what he did. It transpired that he had recently joined his staff union. Auntie had never met a union member.

'Good heavens, how could you?' she said.

'It makes very good sense', said Tony, 'to protect your rights.'

'What rights? What poppycock is this? If people like you spent more time at their work and less looking after their own interests, this country wouldn't be in its present mess.'

'Don't you', said Tony, 'spend your time looking after your rights?'

'Of course,' she said, 'but then, I've got rights. I provide the money that makes it possible for people like you to live.'

'I provide the labour that keeps your money alive, although why I should work to preserve the capital of rich people whom I've never met is something that puzzles me.'

'You talk like a Communist, young man, although you dress quite respectably. Do you know what you're saying?'

'You don't have to be a Communist to question the legitimacy of inherited wealth.'

My aunt turned to me.

'You see why I'm worried about this country?' she said.

Each regarded the other as an example of an unnatural species. Given their opposed 'core beliefs', no proper argument or dialogue was possible, only an exchange of slogans or abuse. It is a score which is replicated at negotiating tables as well as dinner tables.

Let us now examine these unavailing responses in a little more detail.

The first response

The first line of response to the Apollonian crisis sees organisations as the instruments of an efficient and effective society. We could not get richer without them, nor could we be looked after when ill, be educated, protected or serviced in the ways we are accustomed to. It is therefore a citizen's duty and responsibility to put up with the disciplines of work in return for the benefits of belonging to society.

'Responsibility' is the key word in this approach. It is irresponsible to negotiate high pay increases when these would hamper the efficiency of the organisation or force it to put others out of work. People need to be educated to understand where their responsibilities and their best long-term interests lie, and they need to be disciplined by an efficient labour market, which keeps wages and salaries competitive and allows organisations to get rid of inefficient workers.

Apollonian organisations, in this view of things, may not be fun palaces for everyone but they are justified, in the end, by the greater benefit they produce for all. The end, in this case, justifies the means. One has only to look at places like Hong Kong, in its heyday of the late 1970s and early 1980s. Work was work, but it was abundantly justified by the results.

THE ANTI-INDUSTRIAL ENGLISH

Matin Wiener, who teaches history at Rice University in Texas, produced a devastating analysis of the British attitudes to industry.* He argued that almost as soon as Britain began to industrialise she surrounded the social change in a cultural cocoon which muffled industrialism and prevented its full effects.

The idea of an English gentleman, and a gentlemanly attitude of disdain for trade, played a big part. Successful industrialists wanted their sons to become educated gentlemen and country squires, not to succeed them at 'the works'. The English dream was of the countryside, stability and an 'epoch of rest', as William Morris called it.

Education preferred 'science' to 'engineering' and the arts to both. Agriculture and the ownership of land was preferable to business and the ownership of machinery. The professions, including the armed forces, were socially superior to industry.

* M. Wiener, *English Culture and the Decline of the Industrial Spirit, 1850-1890*, Cambridge University Press, 1981.

Could it change? Could schools and the media make industry fashionable? Some hope so, others doubt it.

When advocacy fails, and the wolf cries of newspapers get ignored, this response falls back on the discipline of the economic pendulum to return people to their (Apollonian) senses.

It may be, they will say, that in the short term one must envisage the progressive over-pricing of our outputs because of the cost of large Apollonian systems operating amid current popular values. This over-pricing can be sustained artificially for a time by lowering the exchange rate, by large external borrowings, by import controls, by selective earnings. In the end, however, we shall run out of mechanisms, and the threat of scarcity will no longer be a threat but a perceived reality. Efficiency in the face of this common enemy will then once again be seen to be worth its costs, in terms of lost individualism. We shall no longer take things for granted but will start to instil the virtues of discipline, conformity and obedience into our children. In return, the organisation will on its part revert to the obligations it used to have to provide work and careers for life. Look at Japan. For a time after the war, they embraced American ideas of individualism and American practices of management in their organisations. After a period of vicious inflation and political immobility, they returned to an organisational contract that exchanged protection for commitment, supported it with more traditional educational systems, and arranged for their own form of participation at work, the unique concept of 'Groupism'. It could happen here in the West, but only if we get hungry enough. Maybe, the travellers on this road would argue, things will have to get worse in every country before they get better. The Apollonians who argue this way believe it is the country, the people who make up the country, who are out of step, not them. Time, with some pain, will bring them back to their rightful culture.

Alas, the pendulum swings both ways. Maybe hunger would make us Apollonian once more, but as soon as efficiency returned us to abundance, would not the problems recur? Is this not a route to a generational stop-go cycle of a more traumatic kind than the minor economic ones of the past twenty years? There are signs already of a return to individualism in Japanese society.

The second danger is that, as they seek to delay the sweep of the pendulum and the ultimately inevitable hunger, governments may make changes that will be more fundamental and more long-lasting than any mere import controls or rationing procedures. It is doubtful, for instance, whether any stock exchange would be willing or able to provide the desired quantities of new investment in the desired areas under the conditions of over-pricing in the first part of this scenario. Government would then be forced to step in, first as banker of last resort and ultimately as the prime source of new investment. This is the economic road to totalitarian rule, with the increased bureaucracy that would inevitably accompany it – compounding Apollo everywhere. Governments, furthermore, in an attempt to hold back the damaging costs of organisational hijacks, will be forced to collude with any who can guarantee labour peace, even at the long-term cost of over-manning. This temporary by-passing of the democratic process may leave permanent damage behind it by down-grading the whole notion of electoral democracy. Thus, by a process of successive expedients, without conscious aim, a nation can be forced into government by edict. And once the economic and political mechanisms of a more responsive democracy have been allowed to wither, they may not bloom again for a long time. Democracy might be the price one has to pay for under-writing Apollo as the principal god of the organised society. Is our hunger great enough?

The second response

The second response to the Apollonian crisis would make organisational work not a duty, but a privilege. Employment in a large organisation would be for the minority, not the majority. The organisations, slimmed down and properly automated, would need to employ only two classes of people – core professionals and flexible labour, both kept to a minimum and well paid. The rest could be contracted out. Where it is a privilege to belong to the organisation, the drills and disciplines of the organisation will be readily accepted and adhered to. Apollo will be honoured.

The organisation would only employ those whom it absolutely had to – the managers, experts and skilled technicians who together possess the organisational knowledge which makes the organisation special and unique (the core professionals), and a labour force, mostly semi-skilled, to carry out any tasks which cannot be automated. Everything else can either be contracted out to people or groups who provide similar services to other organisations, or automated, if more money and technology is invested.

Organisations, in other words, would be sought-after places because of the security they offered, or the money, or sometimes both. Money would compensate for anti-social hours, one-sided contracts, or uncongenial work. Key people would be promised careers and a variety of perks. The extra cost involved would be paid for by increased productivity, which is another way of saying that there would be fewer people in the organisations or around them. Employment would be rationed and therefore privileged. In return for the privilege the disciplines of Apollo could be enforced. The dilemma of Apollo would thereby be, in effect, bought out.

HIGH PAY FOR LOW WORK?

There was an interesting exchange of letters in one of the national newspapers not so long ago.

The head of one of Britain's newer universities wrote to complain about the low numbers and poor quality of the students applying to enter his university.

'It is, perhaps,' he said, 'hardly to be wondered at. After all, the salary which they are likely to receive on leaving will probably be less than that earned by a new or unskilled recruit to an assembly line in a car plant.'

Four days later, the paper printed a reply from a shop steward in a car plant.

'No doubt,' said the letter, 'the vice-chancellor has never worked on an assembly line. If he had, he would not wish his graduates to find their employment there. As a result of their education at his university, they will find jobs in pleasant surroundings, with an opportunity to use their talents and influence events around them. Is it not fair that my lads, deprived of these things, should get more money by way of compensation?'

A recent calculation showed that already, today, in Britain if one man decided to become an academic and eventually a professor, whilst his brother remained as an engineering fitter, the professor would be 54 before his accumulated life-time earnings would over-take those of his brother.

Fair or unfair?

It would be going the Japanese way, for work in Japan is not all that it is reported to be _ at least not for everybody. Lifetime employment is not for all workers but only for those who work for the big corporations, perhaps 30 per cent of the labour force at most, for Japan's corporations contract out as much of their work, and their labour requirements, as possible. For that minority, life is secure and predictable but for the rest it can often be precarious and impoverished.

WORKING IN JAPAN

The big Japanese corporation floats on a raft of sub-contractors. A typical car-maker, like Toyota, would have 36,000 sub-contractors, of whom 35,000 would be small businesses with less than 100 employees.

Life-time employment only applies to the 30 per cent of workers who are employed by the large corporation, and it ends at 55. The individual is then, hopefully but not necessarily, picked up by one of the sub-contracting firms, when his organisational knowledge can be important.

Self-employment is big stuff in Japan. There are, according to O.E.C.D. statistics, 19 per cent self-employed in Japan, compared with 9 per cent in Britain, and there is a further 10 per cent categorised as 'unpaid domestic workers'. Self-employed people cannot, by logic or by law, be unemployed, although they may be poor. Part of Japan's concealed unemployment may be in this category, as well as in the 'seat-warmers' of the large corporations.

Perhaps it is not so surprising that the inhabitants of Japan's Apollonian temples are so happy to conform with their ways. Maybe in Britain the feeling of privilege would outweigh the irritations of the Apollonian disciplines.

It is a possible future but it is one fraught with social peril. It was a talented young woman who said to me, 'There will always be jobs for people like me, and I think that we should be prepared to pay extra taxes so that the rest can live in reasonable comfort and even go to the Costa Brava for a fortnight.' She meant it well, but she was describing a society split in two, one in which the 'working-class', by an ironic twitch of fate, had become the privileged ones and the 'leisure class' were now the deprived. The last time that happened was in Imperial Rome and the precedent is not encouraging. Hi-tech alternatives to the bread and circuses of those days may be no more satisfying than the originals were. Dependency, it seems, pleases neither the giver, particularly if the giving is compulsory, nor the getter.

Secure careers and high wages for a few may help to make Apollo both smaller and more bearable but it must be questionable whether the price is worth it or whether it is a sustainable solution where there are likely to be so many left on the outside. Slimmed down professional organisations are, we shall argue, part of a viable future, but they will be ones in which Apollo is really the servant not the master. Turning Apollonian organisations into a meritocracy may be tempting to those inside, but it is a recipe – in Europe, at least – for a divided and divisive society.

In any case, there is some evidence that the privilege is not enough to convert Athenians and Dionysians into willing Apollonians. It could be that the employment organisation, left in its Apollonian state, might end up as the waste-bin of the organised society, left with all those who could not cope outside (see below).

PROS AND ANTIS IN AMERICAN COMPANIES

An American study* investigated pro-company and anti-company attitudes among organisation employees. The pro-company people turned out to be competent, self-assured and independent. The 'antis' despised and condemned the firm they worked for, although not many ever left it. The disgruntled anti-company workers were found to be personality types who needed a lot of sympathy and support from others. When support did not come from the company, they turned to unions and professional associations.

Ironically, it seems to be the Dionysians, or at least the Athenians, who are at ease, not the Apollonians. Who would lose out in the meritocratic organisation? Would they let it happen?

The third response

The third response to the Apollonian dilemma goes beyond the

* Reported in the *Sunday Times*, 6 March 1977.

ideas of duty or privilege to democracy. The organisation, it agrees, is central to an effective society. It ought, therefore, to be a better reflection of that society, because it is in fact one of the principal *communities* of that society.

Already we can see how the state uses the work organisation as its favoured administrative community. Wherever possible, taxes are collected through the work organisation, not the local authority. Legislation on incomes, on equality of opportunity and of treatment, on the treatment of the disabled or the underprivileged, is all enforced through the work organisation. Naturally, because this is where most of the people spend most of their time.

If, then, the organisation is the new community, it is appropriate that the rights of the individual be extended into that community. What does this mean? What are these rights? The normal citizenship rights in a democracy include the following:

The right of tenure *(or protection against eviction without due process of law). In organisational terms, it is the right to a job.*
The right of appeal, *if decisions affecting an individual are disputed.*
The right to information, *if that information has any impact on oneself.*
The right of free speech, *as long as neither treason nor libel is involved.*
The right to elect one's own rulers, *and, occasionally, the right, in referenda, to tell them what to do.*

Increasingly, it is pointed out, we see these rights being brought into the organisation. In the smaller organisations, they can and have happened informally. It is because they have not happened often enough in enough places that they are not imposed by legislation. It is a recognition of what the EEC in a Green Paper calls 'the democratic imperative'.

These rights are not, this third approach might claim, anything to be unduly alarmed about. They are merely a recognition, in legal terms, of something that has been readily accepted by many managers for a long time: that an organisation is as responsible to those who provide its labour as to those who provide its capital, its shareholders. Indeed, since increasingly the capital comes from retained earnings (i.e. from the labour), the responsibility to the workforce must far outweigh that to the original owners.

Now that scarcity is potentially a solved problem, we are really talking about comparative degrees of abundance. The organisation, therefore, is no longer an instrument of society, it is much more than that, it is part of the main body of society, a fact which has to be reflected in the way it is run. A community is a collection of individuals who must be allowed their individual rights. Life, Liberty and the Pursuit of Justice are not to be valid only in the home or the sports arena – they must be carried into the factory, the office, the hospital, the field, everywhere that man works.

There are even, it is argued, long-term economic grounds for this legislation for individual rights. The large organisations are essential to maintain our societies in that precarious state of modern abundance which we have now achieved. The collapse of these organisations would return us to that scarcity from which we have only recently managed to haul ourselves. Yet these organisations are now so powerful, so dominating and often so alienating that people will not work in them, will not join them, or contemplate joining them, unless they can be assured of some countervailing power, of the protection of the law and of the state. There are already quite enough incentives for those who rule these corporations to be efficient. Let there be some pressures for individualism.

We would be foolish, however, or at least naive, to think that a better Charter of Individual Rights will be enough to redeem Apollo. Necessary it may be, sufficient it will seldom prove to be. Indeed, the first effect will be to compound Apollo, creating yet more bureaucratic hurdles, more 'no entry' signs in front of possible decision paths, more tribunals, arbitrations and lawyers' tangles. It is right that an individual at work should have the same protections and the same opportunities as a citizen at large, but while it may mean that the worst abuses of organisations are prevented it won't make them any less complex or any more fun or free for the individual. It may be an understandable, even inevitable, response to the growing crisis of Apollo, but it will not solve that crisis. We have to go beyond a Bill of Rights.

There are some (see below) who think differently. Apollo made secure will, they believe, be Apollo welcomed. They see the organisation as being there for those who work in it. Markets must be expanded, profits increased, to provide more work and better guarantees of what work there already is. They have some evidence to prove them right, but they are few and while they are big enough to influence their destinies and to ride out the storms, they may yet prove to be running against a tide of values.

JOB TENURE PAYS OFF

In December 1982, the workforce at Delta Airlines gave their employer a £30m gift of a Boeing 767. It was, in a way, a form of thank you to the firm for its policy of no lay-offs. Delta has not made anyone redundant since 1956. IBM has an even longer record, going back to 1954. Some other firms are starting to follow their example, including Hewlett-Packard, Avon Products and Bank of America, in the belief that such a policy builds loyalty, confidence and trust in management, less resistance to technical change, lower staff turnover and better employee relations. They put the trust back into Apollo, Japanese style.

Such policies, however, bring problems. Firms must hold back on government business, which comes in chunks which may not always be renewed; they cannot be too aggressive in looking for more market share, in case it could not be maintained; they must reduce pressure on earnings in lean times by keeping their debt low and their dividends small, and they must be prepared to build up stock rather than lay off workers.

Not surprisingly, therefore, Foulkes and Whitman* found only thirty American companies following such policies, and they were all big ones in relatively stable industries.

Call it what you will – industrial democracy, participation, the protection of individual rights – this road to the future must be a Dionysian charter. Even its advocates might admit that the enforcement of these rights, however necessary, will hamper short-term efficiency. It may do more than that. It may tilt the balance of power so much toward the individual that the management of large organ-

* F. K. Foulkes & A. Whitman, *Full Employment, product/marketing strategies*, Human Resources Policy Institute, Boston University, 1984.

isations will become impossible. The emerging Bill of Rights will be seen as a license to use negative power if there is not the opposing draw of commitment, dedication, service. Yet to create these conditions in a large formal organisation is perhaps to ask too much of any leaders. Warren Bennis, then head of one of those huge American multi-versities, has written of the 'politics of multiple advocacies' in which pressure groups spring up (he had to contend with over 500 in his university alone) to 'represent people who are fed up with being ignored, neglected, excluded, denied, subordinated. No longer, however, do they march on cities, or bureaus, or on organisations. . . . Now they file suit. The law has suddenly emerged as the court of first resort.' He asks, 'Where have all the leaders gone? They are all scared,' he concludes, 'and who can blame them?'

This formal enfranchisement of the individual, this organisational Bill of Rights, is, when one thinks of it, an Apollonian response to individualism. 'Codify it, formalise it, institute procedures,' is the Apollonian way. Such a response may do no more than acknowledge the *legitimacy* of individualism in organisations. It will not be enough to contain it. 'Industrial Democracy' which turns out to be a modest attempt to introduce formal representative democracy into the central government of organisations, may well turn out to be as full of false promise as representative democracy traditionally has been in the wider society. It may, as it spreads, signal the complaint rather than cure it – like coloured ointments on a boil – leaving the true disease to fester underneath. In 1977 in Britain, the Bullock Committee on Industrial Democracy published its proposals for the formal representation at board level of the employees of large industrial organisations. The general reaction was that the problem (of industrial democracy) is much bigger than the proposed solutions (of formal representation), and that the detailed proposals may actually cause more problems than they resolve.

There is, however, a more pragmatic variant of the democratic imperative. Organisations are communities, true, say such people. But the only communities which mean anything are small ones, communities which have to do with the individual and his personal hopes, fears, activities and friendships. In the organisation, that community must be the immediate work group, the ten or a dozen or twenty people that converge on a particular task. If participation is to mean anything, it is at this level where it matters. If individualism must be expressed, then it is here that it would be most appropriate.

Volvo led the way in a redesign of the engine shop which allowed the group to organise their own work. Why did they do it? Because the workforce which they had traditionally used on the traditional assembly line had to return home. They were Finns, working as aliens in Sweden for the higher wages of that country: hungry, or greedy, people tolerating Apollonian restrictions for the money. Swedes, however, are less hungry or more greedy (depending on how you look at it) and they were less prepared to accept the alienating procedures for that sort of money. So the work was redesigned.

There are now innumerable examples of firms handing over more responsibility to work groups, breaking down assembly lines, increasing job cycles so that each worker does more than one operation. The results nearly always include a lower rate of absenteeism and of sickness, better overall morale, and, often, better quality. In the IBM typewriter plant in West Berlin, for instance, typewriters used to be assembled on two lines, each 150 metres long; individual employees had a repetitive job cycle of six minutes each. It was boring work, with social contact limited to the people on either side. The line was then replaced with six shorter lines, each worked by a team. The teams developed a system of 'mutual obligations', which allowed people to take time off for sickness or refreshment. They increased the job cycle to 24 minutes and were allowed to choose their own teams. Morale, turnover, quality all improved.

Often, however, these ideas are sparked by the general thesis that smallness is not only beautiful but also economically efficient. The difficulties in organising larger complex organisations (referred to in an earlier chapter as the first strand of resistance) can be very expensive. H. G. Van Beck, of the Phillips plant at Eindhoven, in Holland, has described how he split up the 104-man assembly line into five groups with buffer stocks between each group. As a result, the waiting time caused by lack of material fell by 45 per cent, and the workers experienced the higher morale and lower absenteeism that could have been expected.

SMALL IS EFFICIENT

In the period 1971-3, time lost through industrial disputes increased with the size of the plant from 15 days per 1,000 employees in small organisations (fewer than 25 workers), to more than 2,000 days per 1,000 employees in large organisations (over 1,000 workers).

Evidence collected in Wales and England on farm performance* suggests that very small farms are inefficient but that once the three-man unit has been reached further improvements in performance are small or non-existent.

For most firms, the maximum efficient size seems to be when it controls 10 per cent of the market. After that, for all but a handful of companies, the ratio between profit and size does not change, however large it grows, although the danger of fluctuations in profit is reduced in a large operation.

When Serck Audio Valves pioneered the idea of manufacturing 'cells' in their factory (effectively, these were self-contained manufacturing units, or 'villages'), their sales went up 32 per cent, their stocks (the slack in an Apollo system) went down 44 per cent and the output per employee increased 60 per cent in the first five years.**

There is now a whole movement, grandiosely entitled 'The Quality of Working Life', which seeks to promote, through research and dissemination of results, this approach to the design of the more boring jobs. No one can deny that it is sensible. We know quite a lot about boring, repetitive work, or the micro-division of labour, as it has been called:

- The micro-division of labour induces fatigue, boredom, distractions, accidents and anxieties. The indirect costs of these things are reflected in spoilage, absenteeism and high staff turnover.
- The true costs of monotony come in very high wages for low skill level, high rates of strikes and wastage.
- Men, unlike machines, work more efficiently at a variable than at a constant rate.

* Quoted in E. Johns, 'Where Smallness Pays', *Management Today*, July 1976.
** Quoted in D. T. N. Williamson, 'The Anachronistic Factory', *Personnel Review*, Autumn 1973.

- Moderately complicated tasks resist interruptions and generate psychological impulses towards their own completion.
- Excessive specialisation reduces the opportunity for social contact or team-work. Long periods of unrelieved isolation are hard for individuals to tolerate.

It is not then just good sense to put some variety into the job? Are we really dealing with the individual's need to express himself at work? Many of the studies of job redesign show a gradual return to the old norms of morale and absenteeism, once the changes have become adopted as the new routine. A 24-minute job cycle is much more interesting than a three-minute one, but given the tolerance to which it has to be done, the eventual anonymity of the product and the remoteness of the end-use, is it really such a big deal? In one study it was discovered that the workers in small towns and factories responded well to the redesign of their work. The workers in large cities showed no response or reaction at all. The research called them 'anomic', rendered insensitive by large-city life. Perhaps they were not duped. It would take more than an enlarged job cycle to get them to put their identities into their work.

A MIRAGE OF DIONYSUS?

The autonomous work group is the nearest that most large, formal organisations have got to recognising the pressures of individualism.

The idea of an autonomous group is that a work group becomes responsible for organising its own system of working, job rotation, quality inspection, leave roster, etc. The foreman becomes a liaison man with other groups, a provider of information, but not a boss. The following example from Denmark shows how it works, but there are now very many examples from all the industrialised countries.

In a factory producing measuring instruments, the assembly section was re-organised into autonomous groups. All groups are made up of skilled and unskilled workers (both men and women). The groups themselves divide the work. The groups co-operate intensively with the quality control section, and now other groups and the control section discuss each batch together. The workers state that they find it more meaningful to work with a whole apparatus rather than a part, as one has no idea what the parts are. Several find that they are more concerned with each other under the work group, and that they learn more. Productivity rose 25 per cent.

No one can quarrel with this way of organising work, but is it enough? The workers' final comments speak for themselves.

'The firm is a profit-orientated enterprise, and we only come here for the sake of the money, but that does not keep us from making our daily work as pleasant as possible.'

Autonomous groups offer only a mirage of Dionysus. The real thing will have to be much more significant.

It is possible that organisations adopting this approach can hold Dionysus at bay for a time. But today's change so quickly becomes tomorrow's routine. The Dionysian cult is not to do with monotony at work but with the whole relationship between organisation, individual and society. This approach does nothing to change that relationship. It is not therefore likely to be the true road to the future.

Growth, of course, we need, and the efficiency that produces it. But at what price, and paid for by whom? Do any of the views discussed contain the true solution? Confirmed Apollonians will stick to their guns, modifying their ways, perhaps, to accommodate the 'autonomy' of the last approach as long as it can be demonstrated to improve efficiency. The meritocrats will continue to work towards their ideal of the slimmed-down organisation, properly rewarded. The more modest and humble will settle for a Bill of Rights: some, behind it, will play their game of economic brinkmanship with the managers and directors; others will settle for a quiet life, keeping their individualism for the garden.

In modern industrialised societies, we can see progress down all three approaches. None of them leads, on its own, to a future which we can want. A three-way split is painful as well as unproductive. If these ways will not work, what might? That is the theme of the next chapter.

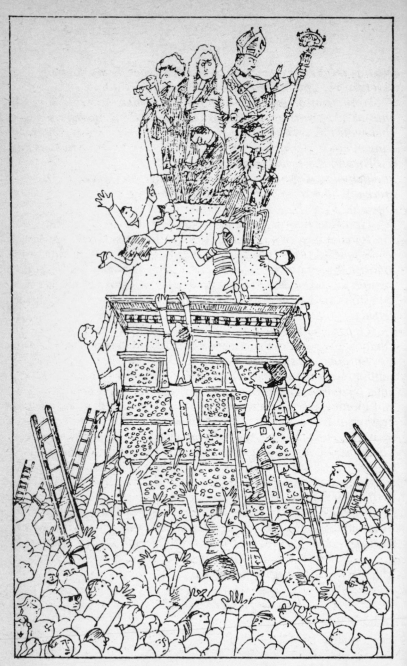

The New Professionals

Chapter 7

THE GODS IN NEW ORDER

We have argued in the last two chapters that the *organisational* imperatives (for increased size and greater consistency) in our present society are locked into an inevitable battle with the *individual* imperatives (for greater opportunity for personal expression and choice). It is a conflict that will not disappear. Nor, in my view, is it a conflict that Apollo can win. If our organisations are to survive, they must adapt their managerial philosophy to one which is better suited to the needs, aspirations and attitudes of *individuals*. In the new mix of the gods which will result, Apollo will be less dominant and less inhuman. This will mean, however, a massive re-organisation of the structure of organisations and of their work.

We might describe the kind of change that is needed as a switch from the employment organisation to something more like a combination of a professional partnership, a contractual organisation and a federal state. Treating people as individuals rather than human resources requires a culture and structure more like that of a professional organisation, where each individual is qualified and certificated, where there are few levels of authority and where the place is run by consent rather than decree. Professionals, however, have tenure and cannot easily be laid off; nor do they readily do the more mundane and boring jobs. To keep their flexibility, therefore, organisations will need to combine a professional core with a contractual element, on the basis that there is no need to employ people to do what others can do for you, often more cheaply. Finally, to prevent the individual being swamped by the size of the operation (and the Apollonian structures which come with size), organisations will need to keep their separate bits as small and as autonomous as they can, without at the same time losing all the advantages of bigness. Federalism, which is, at its best, a way of combining independence with interdependence, ought increasingly to be a model to be followed. Good organisations, like the best of our cities, will be made up of villages, where people can be individuals and yet part of a greater whole.

We need to look, therefore, at the implications of the professional organisation and the contractual organisation to understand the ways in which the theory of cultural propriety is effected, or the gods re-balanced, which will entail a return to the village and the adoption of federalist notions.

The professional organisation

The best way of looking at the pressures of individualism is to think of work as becoming increasingly professionalised. It is an ironic consequence of the specialisation so beloved of Apollonian systems that everyone is now a specialist of some sort, and most jobs are skilled jobs, or are so termed. And every specialist, as we know, looks for the personal prerogatives and advantages of specialisation – professionalism.

Professionalism brings with it some advantages and some consequences. The advantages include a protected entry to the profession, agreed fee scales and effective 'tenure'. Moved down a slot in the social scale, these become the closed shop, differentials and guaranteed job security – all items in the managerial news these days. Only the managers seem to be left as unorganised professionals, as they have recently begun to realise. This emphasis on the terms and conditions of work is normal, even when scarcity and bread for one's family is no longer the critical issue, because to a professional his work is the major source of his identity. If you cease to describe yourself in terms of where you live or who your father was, but in terms of your trade, skill or occupation, then the nature and style of that occupation are of great symbolic and real importance. Work is no longer a means of paying for the groceries, it is central to personal identity.

Similarly with earnings. A professional, like a craftsman, is paid for his skill, not for his length of service or his loyalty. Differentials are important, for symbolic as well as economic reasons. The professional worker will be concerned to ply his skill to his maximum advantage, for his commitment will be to his profession before his organisation, and we should not expect it to be otherwise. Professionals, therefore, will be mobile, with a reference group which spreads across organisations. They will move, and be able to move, when they want to. Organisations have to handle their good professionals gently or they will disappear. The good professionals have effective tenure and may be expected to exploit this.

And professionalism means freedom, the freedom to express oneself and to be true to oneself (the Dionysian virtues). A professional puts his or her mark on the job – his is not an anonymous act, even though it conforms to a set of standards common to the profession. Freedom also implies that you are owned by no man, and by no organisation, even though you may lend it your skills. This freedom of the personal-service professions is greatly sought after today. It is the personal-service professions of law and medicine whose schools have the highest application rates, not the impersonalised professions of the civil engineer or the industrial chemist, whose talents, on the other hand, may be in even greater demand. It is this freedom of the personal-service professions which the new specialisms envy and would claim for their own.

Professionalism, of course, carries responsibilities, but they are responsibilities to the practice of one's trade, craft or skill, not to an organisation. Professions are likely, as a consequence, to be jealous of their traditional territories, to resist new developments not initiated by them, and to be generally conservative in many of their attitudes. Demarcation disputes are found in medicine and law, as well as in engineering, even if they go under other names. Today, in Britain, the legal profession is fighting to continue its monopoly in property transfers.

To be a recognised professional today, at any level of society, is to substitute the protection and the status of a trade for that of an organisation. Work has become professionalised, and all men want to be treated as Dionysians or Athenians, whatever bit of the organisation they work in, or whatever the cultural demands of their work.

This spread of professsionalism colours all the cults. Even the true believer in order, predictability and system, the Apollonian, will be influenced by the wish to be treated as a recognised expert in the tradition of Athena, if not of Dionysus. It is this spread of professionalism which in the medium term will *force* us to change our ways of managing, for professionalism has added the teeth to the forces resisting Apollo listed in Chapter 5. We may have been able to get away with lip service to cries for more individualism. We shall have to do more in the face of organised professionalism.

Our starting models for the new ways of managing must be among the existing professional organisations.

'Universities,' I said, 'are the prototypes of the organisations of tomorrow.'

'If that be so,' said a professor standing near, 'then God help us all.'

Behind my remark was the suggestion that universities, rather like professional partnerships, mountain climbing teams, and theatrical groups or orchestras, have to be managed to be effective, but have to be managed by consent.

What is meant by an *organisation of consent?* In these organisations, the 'psychological contract' between individual and organisation is implicit, and has a particular slant. In traditional, more Apollonian, organisations, the contract runs something like this: 'The individual is here because he has a particular talent or skill or aptitude or just a pair of hands; he is lending this resource to the organisation in return for some mixture of money, facilities, excitement or companionship, and he cedes to the organisation the right to deploy this resource, himself, as it sees fit, within reasonable limits, often formally defined and negotiated.' If the organisation violates this implicit contract – if, for instance, it offers increased excitement or job satisfaction, when all the individual wants is money – then it runs into difficulties.

In the organisation of consent, the contract goes beyond this. For one thing, it has a very individual slant. A person sees himself as a valuable *person*, whom the organisation ought to cherish, not just a resource to deploy. He is very much an individual, with a personality, with individual desires and rights which the organisation must respect. The contract also includes some deep beliefs about the way people should relate to each other. Hierarchy is bad. Argument is good. All men and women are on an equal footing.

We are talking, it is clear, about Athenian and Dionysian attitudes.

The manager in an organisation of consent is meant to manage, to take decisions, set up information systems, to plan and to organise. Each individual believes that he has his own proper and valuable role to play and nobody wants to do anyone else's work for him. But the important decisions, the right to institute procedures, start things, stop things or change major things, must be exposed to possible disagreement before implementation. The individuals may not want to be involved, but they do want to be consulted. They want to be unfettered but not unnoticed. The minority report may never be implemented, it must be listened to.

MANAGEMENT BY CONSENT

Once, I had to manage one part of an organisation by consent. I was trying to discuss why my instructions had not been carried out by a colleague whom I thought of as my subordinate.

'You cannot tell *me to do something,' he explained gently, 'you can only* ask *me.'*

'On the other hand,' he went on, rubbing salt into the wound, 'I don't ask *you if I'm going to do something, I* tell *you.'*

Similarly, a friend, moving into an organisation of consent from a traditional hierarchical business, was dismayed to find that his circular memoranda and his published requirements of his associates produced absolutely no result at all, not even rebellion. Just silence. 'Would you believe it?' he said, 'I've had to go along and make an individual personal contact with each of them?'

He got into further difficulties when he assumed that, since his associates rejected his assumption of the right to decide, they wanted to take all decisions themselves. Not so. 'That's your job,' they said. 'We have other and better things to do than help you take your decisions. But we need to be consulted about those decisions before they go into effect.'

It was not authority in itself that they were objecting to, but his assumption of that authority before it had been given him. The distinction is tricky – but important.

Professional organisations are flat organisations; most have only four steps to the top layer of status, and anyone with talent and application would expect to be a full partner, professor or board member by the age of forty. That results in a long list of names at the top. The list, however, is not the top line of the organisation chart, for no one could run anything that way. The list is a recognition of professional status, but the work is organised in groups, teams, sections or faculties – Athenian structures for Dionysians.

The contractual organisation

Professionals are expensive and permanent; or, to be more precise, they have to be treated as if they were permanent if they are employed. Few organisations therefore use their own professionals for things that other people can do equally well. They keep their professionals for the core tasks of the organisation, including management. The remaining work they contract out, to outside sources (called, in the jargon, outsourcing) or to various categories of temporary help. The professional organisation, to be viable economically, has to be accompanied by the contractual organisation.

The contractual organisation works on the basis of paying *fees* rather than *wages*. Fees are paid for work done whereas wages are paid for time spent. The fee payer is concerned that the work performed or delivered is up to standard, on time and in the right quantity. It is not his concern to motivate, control or organise the time of the worker, to see to his or her conditions of work or pension requirements; he does not have to house them, feed them or counsel them while they work, but he also has less control over them.

There have always been organisations of contract. Independent professionals have always charged fees, and so have craftsmen, artists and artisans. Publishers do not employ their authors or, indeed, their printers. They work entirely on the basis of contracts and fees, their role being that of the fixer in the middle. Architects, although responsible for the design and the construction of a building, do not employ all the talents necessary to do that – it would never occur to them that it was necessary or desirable to own and run a building firm. Advertising agencies do not employ the people who actually make the advertisements.

It used to be felt, in the days of the grand Apollonian organisations, that to control anything you had to own it and employ all the people in it. That way you could make things happen your way. But it got expensive when the cleaners, caterers, drivers and maintenance people all had to be offered the same terms and conditions, and even the same sort of career expectations, as the essential professionals. Increasingly, organisations started to get outsiders to clean buildings, cook food, arrange travel and drive vehicles. There was less direct control but also less cost. Almost all organisations today have a contractual fringe, called outsourcing, privatisation (if in the public sector) or sub-contracting. Contracting takes other and grander forms. One can sub-contract the manufacture, as architects do, but also as Marks & Spencer do in Britain, or as all manufacturers do for some or all of their components, so that any manufacturer is more truthfully called an assembler. Selling can be subcontracted to agents, debt collection can be sub-contracted for a price, or the whole operation can be franchised, with the originator keeping only the design or the formula as his own.

The contractual organisation, in other words, is very familiar to us, although we do not always think of it that way. It should not, therefore, be very difficult to extend the concept to other parts of the activity, or to institutions like schools and hospitals, where it is less familiar, and to apply it to individuals as well as groups.

A halfway house is the short-term employment contract, where people are paid wages, yes, but wages for a particular job for a particular length of time. At present this is seen most obviously at the top and bottom of organisations. At the top, a chief executive is nowadays hired on a term contract, to do a particular job, and can even have a fee element attached, related to performance and traditionally paid by stock options or bonus, but on occasion, as with Ian MacGregor at British Steel, by decision of a review committee. At the bottom, the specific employment contract applies to short-term part-time work, where people are hired to cover peak loadings – in the summer, on farms and vineyards, or on Saturdays in supermarkets, over Christmas in retail stores. There is no longterm commitment by the organisation. It is really a fee for a specific piece of work, paid as a wage.

The contractual organisation allows individuals or groups to have a relationship with a large organisation whilst still maintaining their independence. It is a way of linking Dionysians and Athenians into the Apollonian centre. It is, of course, only too easy for the organisation, in some cases, to use its superior bargaining power to exploit the individual or the group. Outworkers have been notoriously exploited in many industries and trades. That is a problem which we shall have to examine when we look at the consequences for society. Dionysus does not always spell riches.

NETWORKING

In the early 1980s, Rank Xerox in the UK needed urgently to cut the cost of its headquarters staff, without losing too much valued expertise.

They came up with a proposal to turn many of their experts into independent professionals and to buy back some of their services for a fixed period of years. Both parties benefited. The organisation was able to reduce its employment at senior levels quite significantly, saving on space, pension contributions and other related costs. After all, at that time, it was costing £25,000 p.a. to provide space, food, service and transport for a senior executive in central London. They were however, able to buy back much of the expertise they had lost by paying a fee. The individual got a chance to establish himself or herself as an independent, with a guaranteed chunk of business to start with, and a benevolent patron at his back.

The organisation, however, took great care to make sure that the individuals to whom it offered this opportunity had the personal qualities, enough self-reliance and technical skill, to make a success of independence.

Not everyone is born a Dionysian.

Quality control is the key to the success of the contractual organisation. Payment of a fee for work done means that the work done has to be the focus of any control. Jaguar Cars pulled itself back to reputation and profitability largely by an attack on the quality of its components, made by sub-contractors. The best of the American companies are obsessed by quality, both of their own end product and of their sub-contracted components. McDonalds' beef has to be first-rate if their hamburgers are to taste first-rate and McDonalds do not make the beef.

Quality control, inspections and examinations sound hierarchical, Apollonian and antithetical to the Dionysian, Athenian and Zeus-like values which the contractual organisation seeks to satisfy, but they should not be. Checking on results leaves the individual free to decide on the methods. Control the ends and you can trust others to take care of the means. The Apollonian role culture, contrariwise, prefers to control the methods, believing that, logically, this will guarantee the results. It is cheaper, and more liberating, to control the results. The contractual organisation has to be a results-oriented organisation, which suits Zeus, Athena and Dionysus very well indeed.

NASA – A CONTRACTUAL ORGANISATION

In the 1960s, NASA, then in its heyday of the Apollo Project, interacted with 20,000 different organisations. 90 per cent of the total workforce were outsiders, employed in basic research, launching and tracking spacecraft and a whole host of support activities.

But a critical amount of designing, testing, planning and operating was conducted by NASA personnel. NASA believed that outsiders could not be successfully stimulated, managed or co-ordinated without a technologically sophisticated internal organisation.

The contractual organisation needs a professional and managerial core of high quality.

THE DOCTRINE OF SUBSIDIARITY

Contractual organisations believe in subsidiarity, although they may not realise it. The principle of subsidiarity has long been advocated by the Roman Catholic Church. It holds it to be immoral not to push responsibility as far down and out as it will go.

It was restated by Pope Pius XI in Quadragesimo Anno in 1941 as follows:
  'It is an injustice, a grave evil and a disturbance of right order for a large and higher organisation to arrogate to itself functions which can be performed efficiently by smaller and lower bodies.'
  It sounds like a condemnation of Apollo.

The implications for the managerial gods

THE EROSION OF MANAGEMENT

Professionals, self-styled or real, do not like to be 'managed', with all that the word today implies of control, manipulation and direction. They would prefer to use the word 'manage' in its colloquial or nineteenth-century meaning, where it is equivalent to 'coping', as in 'How did you manage today?', or, 'Did you manage to . . .?' It is interesting that our old-established institutions or professions do not use the word at all for their *high*-status roles, preferring governors, presidents, directors, senior lecturers, deans, commanders, or even (in the British civil service) secretaries. Managers, when the word does occur in such institutions, refer to the office managers or warehouse managers – the necessary 'coping' roles. Management, in other words, seems to be an Apollonian term. Management began to be a high-status occupation with the rise of the Apollonian corporation, some two generations ago.

The first major implication of the new professionalism in organisations, and its Athenian overtones, will undoubtedly be a tendency for 'management' to revert to its earlier meaning. In other words, the Apollonian, bureaucratic, administrative part of organisations will become culturally subordinate to the professional parts. Managers will no longer automatically be the high-status people in these organisations.

What, then, must one say about all the planning, organising and controlling that is supposed to be of the essence of management and upon which the organisation traditionally depends for its survival? These must still continue. We must remember, however, that only in the role cultures is there a particular person for every task or role. It is not some equation inherent in nature that a task equals a person. There are many jobs that can be done by temporary groups, and it is a feature of the organisations of consent that the professional members wear a variety of hats, sitting in the morning, perhaps, as the planning group and in the afternoon as the adjudicators on standards – the quality control function. The design and use of the planning, organising and control systems will be in the hands of the people whose work is being planned, organised and controlled, although the actual administration of the systems, the collection and processing of data, could well be done by others. To an Apollonian it sounds illogical to put the control devices in the hands of those being controlled. To an Athenian or Dionysian, it is insulting and degrading to have it any other way: it would be to treat them as children, deviants or incapable and would start them on the 'spiral of distrust'.

ADHOCRACIES

One word that has been used to describe the new kind of organisation is adhocracy.* Mintzberg describes it this way: 'Highly organic structure, with little formalisation of behaviour, high horizontal job specialisation, based on formal training; a tendency to group the specialists in functional units for housekeeping purposes, but to deploy them in small market-based project teams to do their work.' He goes on: 'Of all the configurations, Adhocracy shows the least reverence for the classical principles of management, especially unity of command.'

NETWORKS

Nancy Foy** sees networks as the key to the new organisations and postulates some laws for their proper management:
1. *The effectiveness of a network is inversely proportioned to its goal.*
2. *A network needs a focus, not a goal.*
3. *A network needs a spider at the centre, not a chairman.*
4. *A network needs a note or a newsletter, not a journal.*
5. *A network needs a good list of members more than a set of bylaws.*
6. *A network needs groups, not committees.*
7. *A network needs a phone number, not a building.*

Both are Athenian structures for Dionysians run by Zeus.

THE NEED FOR LEADERSHIP

But whilst Dionysians and Athenians may be happy to sit in various groups wearing their different hats from time to time, when they are not exercising their professional skills in groups and individually, they are not usually culturally self-sufficient. In practice, they need a Zeus to lead them and Apollonians to serve them.

An examination of the variety of co-operative organisations

---

* A. Toffler, *Future Shock*, Pan, 1971. H. Mintzberg, *Structure in Firms*, Cliffs: Englewood Prentice Hall, 1983.
** N. Foy, *The Yin and Yang of Organisations*, Grant McIntyre, 1981.

operating in the UK, which range from co-operatives of craftsmen, local community redevelopment schemes and welfare organisations to chemical manufacturing and motor-cycle makers, reveals that the successful ones are always *led* by some kind of charismatic energising figure. He tends to be an unusual Zeus, in that his power seldom stems from ownership, but from personality, ideas and initiatives – the kind of Zeus that Athenians and Dionysians can accept because his power justifies itself in action, so that he is continually re-authenticating himself in their eyes. Organisations of consent, in other words, have to be led – not managed. Indeed, if one wanted a criticism of our contemporary organised society, it is that it is currently *over-managed and under-led*. The Zeus of the organisation of consent is therefore a critical feature, but he must be one of the gang, different only in his personality, his attitudes and the way he works, operating with power granted implicitly to him as leader, but depending always on his colleagues for their consent.

THE STEADY-STATE VILLAGE

The organisations of consent and contract still need an administrative steady-state: jobs which have to be so prescribed that individuality has to be squeezed out, where any problem-solving has been done at the design stage and is, it is hoped, no longer required – Apollo's section.

Goods and money have to be counted, products and services checked for quality, offices cleaned, computers fed, and machines emptied and filled again. Trains must still run on time and cannot be left to the individual entrepreneural instinct of the drivers. How are the steady-state sections of our organisations to be run (managed?) under this new cultural revolution?

Apollo, it must now be emphasised, does not disappear in this confrontation of the gods, he only retreats. Individualism and professionalism, with their Athenian or Dionysian attitudes, are widespread, but they *mix* through the other cults and *overlay* them – they do not *displace* them. Just as Zeus, infected by Dionysus, is a more personal Zeus, so Apollo, when infected by Dionysus, becomes a human Apollo. Lots of people, in other words, whilst wanting individual recognition, still have the propensity for order, the liking for discipline and routine in work, and the tidiness of predictability.

The new Apollo has a human face.

How is this achieved? Essentially, by reducing the *size* of the Greek temples of each steady-state so that those who work there have names, not just roles, and names that are known to the rest of the organisation, and where the duties attached to each role have meaning, because everyone can see the end result and can understand how his role contributed to the outcome.

Small, in this context, is not so much beautiful as essential. Without the appropriate scale, Apollo loses his human face, our Dionysian instincts are denied and the old symptoms of the resistance to Apollo emerge. When Dionysus is denied, his claims and pressures dominate. Once placated, our other cultural instincts can come to the fore. Apollonians, treated as individuals, can devote themselves to predictability, Athenians to planning, knowing that each is necessary to the other.

It is at this point that we need to change the model to reflect the changing face of Apollo in the organisations of consent. The *village*, with its villagers, must replace the Greek temple as the centrepiece of the organisation. Villages are small and personal, their people have names, and characters and personalities. What more appropriate concept on which to base our institutions of the future than the ancient organic social unit whose flexibility and strength sustained human society through millennia?

How big, then, might these villages be? It is hard to say, but let us at a guess give the organisational village a *maximum* of 500 working individuals. Above that number, it is no longer possible to know everyone – anonymity sets in. It is clear that society has long ago outgrown the village as far as most of its inhabitants are concerned. And so have many organisations. But it is time to return to it, if we can. Psychologists speak of 'environmental disorientation', which can occur when distance or size or complexity gets too great, so that the individual withdraws from his environment or rebels against it. It is possible that aeroplanes or ships may become, or have become, so big that people no longer feel safe in them. It is known that some buildings, some conurbations, some institutions, are simply so large that they are repugnant. 80 per cent of Britons in a recent poll said that they would prefer to live in a village or small town, rather than in a large city.

Sir Frederick Catherwood, then head of the British Institute of

Management, said once that the new challenge to management was to find a way of running our organisations with 'no more than 500 heads under one roof'. It was a call for the organisational village to replace the temples of Apollo.

THE RE-ORGANISATION OF WORK

The realignment of the managerial gods, however, cannot happen in isolation. We have just seen the implications for the size of any steady-state activity. The implications go further than that.

TOO BIG AT 65?

The Urban Church Project in Poplar, London, has been investigating the odd phenomenon that, whatever the size of parish, the average core church congregation levelled out over time at 65. They also noted that the numbers who turned up for their annual meetings were of the order 55-65, and that the average staff of secondary schools had drawn back from 100 to between 60 and 70. They began to read and think.

It is widely held, they discovered, that the primary group saturates at 12, after which it is difficult to know everybody well. Within a group of 12 there are 66 possible relationships, and within a group of 66 there are 2,145 relationships, which is very close to the point where any further increase becomes meaningless, a community becomes a crowd with whom one cannot identify.

They began to find that if congregations grew over 65, they broke up into separate groups.

THE HARNESSING OF TECHNOLOGY

In the Apollonian era which is ending, man is the servant of technology. Men are hired to operate, service or often just to watch increasingly sophisticated equipment, working in an increasingly advanced technology. The equipment is often so expensive that man must march to its tune, adjust his working day and his habits to it, learn its language and be in many senses its servant.

The relationship must be reversed if the Dionysian urges of our new workforce are to be satisfied. Technology must once again become the servant of man. Ideology and preaching won't bring this about, of course. But economics will. The cost of providing servants for dominant technologies will, through the exercise of negative power and the hijack, outweigh the economics of scale which originally justified the creation of the technology.

Wherever the professional or craftsman attitude has been dominant – in photography, fashion, science or farming, for instance – technology has been developed to *extend man's capacities*. The resulting equipment has remained essentially in the control of one man and his assistant. In Apollonian cultures, the technology, e.g. the computer or the assembly line, was developed to *do as much of the work as possible,* leaving man to service the machine and do those bits that the technology could not handle. Craftsmen (Dionysians) need tools, Apollonians need machines. The distinction seems semantic or philosophical – it is not. It is of crucial importance in the future design of the work of our organisations.

The design of technology to extend the capacities of one man or one man and his *small group* of colleagues calls for an advanced rather than a simplified technology. It is easier to design a series of specific machines with men to bring the work to them and to service them, than it is to design some all-purpose, robot-like machine-tool for the individual craftsman machinist. It is easier to design a large chemical process plant than a small one. Only when the costs of staffing the large one become intolerable will there be *economic* incentives to design the smaller one. Only when it becomes prohibitively expensive to man an assembly line will we look for ways to automate the line completely and give it to one man to run, or find ways of doing without it.

Economic forces follow human forces as often as not. It is the lag that brings the pains. Wise men anticipate economics, others react. Which shall we choose?

FLEXIBILITY OF WORK

The organisations of consent and contract prefer that money is paid for work done rather than time spent. This allows the individual to control his own allocation of time and effort within overall deadlines. The attempts by Apollonian organisations to pay piece-rates have always foundered because they confused piece-rates with time spent. To couple the two, to determine norms of work for periods of time, must be self-defeating for it is seen as prescription, control, manipulation, with all the connected overtones disliked by people who might respond to the challenge of fees rather than wages. Any return to contract or piece-work must be uncoupled from time spent. There is no inherent reason in many industries why this should not be done. Even in such an Apollonian world as that of life insurance the salesmen are essentially on contract to be paid, by commission, for work delivered, leaving them free to allocate their own time.

Organisations of consent and contract find it hard to insist that all work is done on their premises. The old tradition of out-work remains with artists, writers, designers, teachers, and is carried over to many consultants, research scientists and many managers who find it easier and more productive to do some of their work at home or in a place remote from the main organisation.

Flexitime is but a small and partial step down these roads. Those organisations who have experimented gingerly with flexible working week arrangements (a set number of hours to be worked in flexible patterns agreed between the individual and his working group) have found no ill-effects, but the experiments still deal in minutes or hours rather than days or weeks.

The trend will need to go much farther to satisfy the Athenian and Dionysian needs of the new professionalism. There will have to be far more scope for *part-time work*. Individuals will work for more than one organisation *simultaneously*. Work will be done at home to be brought in at regular intervals, or communicated electronically to a central point.

Once again, economics will be the spur. For certain specific (professional) tasks it will be cheaper to use part-time rather than full-time employees, even after allowing for the extra co-ordinating time. The possibilities of more part-time or contract work will tap new sources of talent – including the under-employed housewife. The increasing cost of transport to work (reflected ultimately in wages) will make outwork more economically attractive to both individual and organisation. The increasing availability of real-time on-line communication links will make it both unnecessary and expensive to have people in one building in order to co-ordinate them. If people wish to be rewarded with discretionary time (university teachers traditionally have 20 per cent of their time for their own pursuits) instead of money, it may pay the organisation to accommodate them, instead of binding them full-time to the organisation with disproportionate amounts of money.

Existing Athenian organisations (consultancies, laboratories, universities) find that flexibility suits their work-flows, which are seldom copy or flow ones. Other work-flows will have to begin to adapt as Apollo retreats, We shall find ourselves investing in the *breakdown* of flow technologies such as assembly-lines, but the investment will be justified by economics, not ideology, as the costs of manning those flow technologies become prohibitive.

TYPISTS INTRAPRENEURIAL

Norman Macrae of The Economist *is an advocate of more entrepreneurship within organisations – what he calls 'intrapreneurship'.**
He illustrates it thus:

'If you need a typing pool . . . it might be best to set up several competing groups of Typists Intrapreneurial. You would offer an index-linked contract to the group for a set period, specifying the services you wanted in return for a lump-sum monthly payment. The typists would apportion the work amongst themselves, devise their own flexitime, choose their own life-styles, decide whether to replace a leaver by a full-timer or part-timer, or whether to do her work and keep more money per head. They could also decide whether to tender for extra paid work from outside.'

A contractual organisation at work – with Dionysians led by Zeus?

SELF-CONTAINED UNITS

The specialisation of work will get reversed in the organisations of consent and contract. Specialisation involves the fragmentation of activities and the consequent need for more co-ordination, systematisation and centralisation. With Apollo in retreat, each unit will want increasingly to be given the means of solving its own problems, instead of hitching on to some central procedure. Instead of a

* N. Macrae, 'Intrapreneurial Now', *The Economist,* 17 April 1982.

central maintenance function, each operating group will want its own maintenance man, to give it more flexibility and self-control. The accounting and sales staff, which have progressively been pulled back into central offices, will begin to be pushed out again. Groups will increasingly be judged by results rather than by methods. To use the phrase of Norman Macrae, organisations will be *re-competitioned*. That is to say, organisations will have more than one unit doing the same kind of work. Those who do it better will provide the models for the others, for competition of this sort sets standards more cheaply and more acceptably than any central set of rules and checks. Large combines of railways, mines, steel firms, hospitals and local government will increasingly be divided up again, and, whilst their *areas* of operation might be defined to prevent wasteful competition, they will increasingly be allowed the means to secure their own ends. Organisations will then have to continue to resist the urge to *impose* the means that succeed in one unit on to all the rest, or to think that a rationalisation of activities will bring the economies it seems to promise.

The truth is that the economies of scale do not follow a constant graph, with economies steadily following scale. Logic and industrial engineering would have it so, but the resistance to Apollo means that, after a spurt of economies, increased scale produces dis-economies and the graph flattens out, till eventually the cost per unit will actually rise as the cost of operating the *controlling* systems spirals. Unfortunately, this rise is today concealed by inflation and, in any case, the alternatives are by now lost in history and not comparable – so that, too often, no one notices.

An economist in the Hungarian government once explained to me that, on principle, even in their small country, they liked to have at least *two* of every type of plant, even if this principle went against the apparent logic of economics. 'It is easier, and cheaper, to let them set standards for each other than for us to try to fix and monitor those standards from the centre.'

THE SUCCESSFUL CABINET MAKER

The cabinet maker had been very successful. He now had 110 people working for him and had just won a contract with a big chain of retail stores which would more than double his output for the next five years. He saw that he would have to give up his rather informal 'village' atmosphere and regroup his people into divisions and hier- archies. Whilst the consultants he had called in were working on the problem, a delegation of his workers came to him. 'We like it the way it is,' they said. 'We don't want this factory to grow any bigger. If you want to grow, why don't you start another factory for this new business?'

And so was the group philosophy born. No factory had more than 110 workers. A new factory opened every year, then every five or six months. 25 per cent growth was sustained overall. Each factory made its own line of products and ran itself, asking the man at the centre only for new capital.

But eventually he had 23 factories. How long could this go on? The pressures for rationalisation were getting stronger. His factories were beginning to compete with each other for business and cutting their margins (his margins) to beat each other. The demands for funds were getting progressively larger – he needed more control over cash inflows if he was to provide cash outflows. The economics of cen- tralised purchasing of services such as accounting and advertising were becoming more and more obvious.

And he still wanted to grow. That was his thrill. The old problem was here again. What should he do? If he rationalised, he might ruin the whole spirit of the factories, offend his workers and feed oppor- tunity to the unions, build up an unwieldy and unwanted central organisation. But could he resist his own need and the apparent logic of greater consistency and control?

In the end, he divided his empire. He no longer has his fingertips on each enterprise, only on three lieutenants. He has lost something, perhaps, but his organisation retains its vigour and its enterprise – and its inconsistency.

The self-contained unit philosophy will have to spread to the service units of organisations. Organisations will increasingly find it cheaper to contract out much of their central services, such as their management services, computer bureaux, training departments and consultancy divisions in engineering, finance, advertising, etc. The desire of top management to have all these activities under their own control conflicts with the needs of the service groups to be independent, and eventually conflicts with the intolerable overhead

costs of maintaining them as a free good for the operating units.
There is no reason why these service groups should not be *owned* by
the central organisation, but not controlled by it, except in terms of
results. Organisations will then find themselves sprouting small
entrepreneurs, giving to them freedom under an economic
umbrella, ruling by selection and trust rather than procedures and
control. Zeus will outrank Apollo.

ORGANISATIONAL FEDERALISM

As Apollo is pushed into retreat and into the 'village', the apparent
organisational imperatives of increased size and greater consistency
will tend to be ignored, and indeed reversed: workflows will be
broken up, units made smaller and more independent, and
employees will be working on contract out of sight and hearing. It
would, however, be sad to see all the economies of scale and
consistency disappear before the march of professionalism. Small
may be beautiful, and even efficient on its own, but a lot of small,
self-centred villages do not necessarily create a great nation. Organisations will rightly try to retain the advantages of co-ordination and
central planning, of copy techniques and specialised inputs,
wherever these can be compatible with the new cultural mix of
management philosophies.

It would be logical, therefore, to extend the village concept into a
form of *federalism*.

Federalism is not just a new word for centralisation. Colin Ward
(of whom more anon) talks of 'topless federations' and points to one
of the most successful federal operations in the world: the international postal service, whereby it is possible to post your letter in
Germany and have it delivered in China. Where, one might ask, is
the building of the International Postal Authority? It does not exist.
Or who, to take another example, can point to the International
Railway Building? It, too, does not exist, yet your ticket can carry
you across Europe. Federations can be merely agreements for
co-operation.

Yet most federations are more than this. Autonomous entities,
usually states or countries, decide to cede certain of their rights to a
central federal authority the better to serve their joint interest.
Organisational federalism will probably come about in reverse, by

devolution rather than by acts of union, but the net result will need to be the same, a separation of rights and powers between the centre and the 'villages'. The centre may retain the ancient rights of shareholders vis-à-vis the villages – that is, the right to a dividend, to the appointment of strategic figures, and to the provision of new strategic finance. There may also be grouped at the centre the ancillary services, operating as self-contained units with their own entrepreneurial freedom. No doubt there will, too, be some 'federal laws' and a law-enforcing mechanism to ensure a degree of homogeneity amongst the villages, perhaps on some industrial relations matters, on accounting formulae, on quality procedures. But these would have to be negotiated to ensure that they did not infringe the independence of the villages, nor the requisite variety needed for the long-term survival of the federal organisation. Theoretically, the federal centre *serves* the states.

THE CONDITIONS OF FEDERALISM

Derek Sheane, of ICI in London, has spelt out some of the conditions for 'industrial federalism' by comparing the workings of successful federal countries (e.g. the USA or Switzerland) with those of more centralised systems, such as the UK and France.

   Federalism succeeds best when:
● *There is a common external threat.*
● *There is a 'web of interdependence', so that one state cannot dominate the rest, but each needs the others for some resources.*
● *There is diversity, whereby each state has separate needs and can look after its own internal affairs.*
   Federalism works as long as:
● *There is a separation of power.*
● *There is a clear definition of the role of these powers.*
● *There is an inverse relation between the amount of power you give those in authority, and their tenure of office.*
● *The individual is assumed to belong to multiple groups, with a variety of interests.*
Federal Chambers of Parliament are usually horseshoe shaped and there is no 'leader of the opposition'. The simpler 'them and us' polarity has no place in federalism, because life is seen as too complex a business to be dealt with in one dimension.

Villages in a federation would tend to have freedom to control the means and to negotiate the ends. This is quite contrary to Apollonian logic, which calculates which means are necessary to its desired ends, and then controls those means. In a federation of villages, if one village prefers a three-day week with twelve-hour days, and another a six-hour, six-day week, both would have freedom to do it their way as long as output over a period was the same. For villages are private territory. Even the landlord cannot enter, except by permission or if there is evidence of abuse. As long as the rent is paid and the federal laws obeyed, independence in a federation is guaranteed.

To permit local idiosyncrasy appears, to an Apollonian, to be lending indulgence to inefficiency. This need not be so. Federalism, unlike corporatism, can exploit the productive spur of competition. In the corporate state, in which *functions* are co-ordinated, each function must co-operate for the whole to work – an invitation to hijack. Concessions to one branch must be matched by concessions to another, which is ruinous competition. Under federalism, the system can be uncoupled. If one village does not co-operate, the whole is not ruined: there will be other villages who, in return for favours promised or anticipated, will move into the breach. It is a bargaining, not a conflict, situation.

Indeed, if organisations are to avoid the increasing costs of hijack, they will need to uncouple their corporations as quickly as they can; though unions who have got used to exploiting the hijack may be expected to resist the spread of federalism, for it must weaken their power.

The professional urges for an individual to leave *his* imprint on *his* work, to make a difference, personally, and to work at his own pace and discretion, can all be accommodated within a village – by judicious design of the work, because of the flexibility that is possible if all the factors are within one's control. When nothing can be altered without discussion with other units, nothing is altered. That way discretion disappears. Zeus organisations stay flexible if they remain independent and small. Gangs came before factories. Factories which are sheds for gangs are more tolerable than those factories which are sheds for machines.

GANGS IN THE FACTORY – ATHENIAN VILLAGES

In the early 1950s, Standard manufactured the Ferguson tractor in Coventry under licence, as well as their own cars, using a gang system. An American professor, Seymour Melman, has described the process.* 'In this firm . . . thousands of workers operated virtually without supervision as conventionally understood, and at high productivity: the highest wage in British industry was paid; high-quality products were produced at acceptable prices in highly mechanised plants; the management conducted its affairs at unusually low costs; also, organised workers had a substantial role in production decision-making. In production, the management has been prepared to pay a high wage and to organise production via the gang system, which requires the management to deal with a grouped workforce, rather than with single workers, or with small groups . . . . The operation of integrated plants employing 10,000 production workers did not require the elaborate and costly hallmark of business management.'

In the car factory, fifteen gangs ranged in size from fifty to five hundred people, and the tractor factory was organised as one huge gang.

'The gang system sets men's minds free from many worries and enables them to concentrate on the job. It provides a natural frame of security, it gives confidence, shares money equally, uses all degrees of skill without distinction and enables jobs to be allocated to the man or woman best suited to them, the allocation frequently being made by the workers themselves.'

Alas, Standard got swallowed up in British Leyland in pursuit of market clout, and Apollo took over from Athena in the factory.

FEDERAL ORGANISATIONS IN ACTION

Johnson and Johnson is a $5 billion company broken up into 150 independent divisions. The divisions are each called 'companies' and each is headed by a 'chairman of the board'. The central staff is small, with no specialists travelling among the subsidiaries. There are over 55 consumer product divisions, each responsible for its own marketing, distribution and research.

* Reported by Colin Ward in *Anarchy in Action*, Allen & Unwin, 1973.

Britain's GEC encourages its 130 businesses to retain their own identity. In industrial relations, each business makes its own agreements. Shop stewards, as well as managers, are jealous of their independence and encouraged to be so. When GEC took over from AEI, the headquarters' staff was reduced from over 5,000 to under 500.

When I rang a community school and asked for 'the Head', the receptionist asked, 'which Head?'

Tube Investment advertised itself as a collection of independent businesses where 'we made it big by keeping it small'.

Dana's 90 state managers in the US, contrary to economic logic, each do their own purchasing, have their own cost-accounting system and control virtually all aspects of personnel policy.

Implications for the task of management

No doubt it will be called government, or direction, or anything other than management, but both the centre and the villages need to be 'run' in these organisations of consent and contract.

THE CENTRE

The centre will be dominated by planning, by the need to prepare plans, reach agreement on plans, disseminate the plans and co-ordinate the village efforts to implement the plans. The centre's aim must be to emphasise the interdependence of the villages, the common threat or purpose of the federation, whilst recognising the individual needs of the different villages (Derek Sheane's preconditions for federalism).

The resulting 'plan' is not the rational exercise beloved of corporate planners. It is the balance of forces, the 'possible compromise'. The expectations of the villages and the projects of the centre have both to be allowed for, and incorporated in the ultimate jigsaw.

The process therefore is one of bargaining, adaptation, persuasion and compromise. Vision and imagination are required, but so are sensitivity, the ability to understand other points of view, patience, tact, the skill to weld groups and fuse perceptions. It is a job meet for Athenians, often led by a Zeus with a dream, a mission or a vision.

Derek Sheane's mechanisms of federalism will be required to implement the plans. There must be a separation of powers. Those who execute policy must not be exactly the same as those who legislate policy, for this would be to give too much power to one group. In federal organisations, it will be increasingly common to find the two-tier board of policy-makers (elected or appointed by various constituencies, e.g. the shareholders, the employers, the consumers) sitting above the management team. This is the solution increasingly favoured by West Germany (a federal country) and, in principle, advocated by the minority group of industrial leaders in Britain's Bullock Report on industrial democracy. Power must be inversely related to tenure of office in a federal constitution, claims Sheane, and policy-makers and senior managers will serve for defined terms (the fixed-term contract). Management then is a task for a time, not a career – quite proper to the organisations of consent and contract. There is a clear definition of roles and power. Good fences make good neighbours, and a clear understanding of 'boundaries' in work makes it easier to negotiate, plan and compromise, because expectations become more explicit. Those organisations which depend on contract labour, as in the construction industry, are *very* specific about expectations of quantity, quality, elapsed time, payment due, etc. – about the *ends* required, but not the *means*. Federal organisations based on villages of consent and contract will need to be equally specific about roles and responsibilities if they are to survive.

Finally, it will be accepted and recognised that an individual has a variety of interests and can belong to multiple groups. He may be both an accountant and a person with a passion for his region or for a product. He may be a devoted citizen of the organisation half the week, and a part-time priest the other half. No group, no organisation, should feel able to claim the whole of a man, of his time, his energy and his interests. Nobody can claim a monopoly of other men's loyalty. Again, this federal principle of multiple interests fits neatly into the ideas of consent and contract and the notions of individual freedom.

It will, then, not be an easy place to manage, the centre of these mini-societies. The problems will be constantly changing, and so will the composition of the groups to deal with them. The balance of power and of priorities will shift according to the problem and the degree of interest of the various constituencies. Authority will wax and wane for each individual, depending as it will on expertise for the task in hand, access to information or to sources of power. Decisions will emerge rather than be made, and it will often be hard to discover where or how they start or finish. A sensitivity for the possible will be more important than an understanding of the ideal. Conflict will be endemic, but if it can be focused on problems and issues rather than on factions or groups of people, it will be managed productively. It is not a place where many would choose or be chosen to work for the whole of their career. People will tend to move in and out of the federal government, staying for perhaps five or ten years at most. Careers at the centre are out. Jobs and roles are in. For a qualified Athenian none of this is frightening or unusual. It all fits his needs for variety, flexibility and mobility, for the politics of persuasion and the art of compromise.

THE TRUNCATED PYRAMID

Dr Irving Borwick has described the organisation, ITT Europe, as a set of truncated pyramids with a multigon sitting on top of a traditional set of hierarchical organisations. The multigon is made up of the product groups, business groups, functions and associated organisations, which all overlap and interact with each other and sit above and apart from the national ITT companies.

He points out that the nature of authority, influence, power and

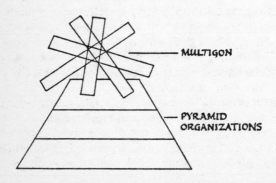

MULTIGON

PYRAMID
ORGANIZATIONS

conflict changes when you move from pyramid to multigon. In the pyramid, authority depends on position in the hierarchy, influence stems from formal authority, decisions are made at prescribed levels, conflicts become established between departments. In the multigon, authority is derived from information and acknowledged expertise. Roles change frequently; decisions are managed rather than made, and emerge from groups rather than individuals; conflict is about problems or situations rather than between the departments.

All this, he points out, makes life very confusing if you are moving between pyramid and multigon, as many do. The multigon is a confusing, untidy political world to those from the pyramid.

The multigon seems very much akin to the federal centre I am proposing, even if the pyramids are not yet the villages. It is a world for Athenians, not Apollonians.

But what about the federal bureaucracy? Will that not loom large? It should loom, but not large. There is need of an auditing function, an information-collecting mechanism, an accounting and financing operation, and an administrative support to the planning procedures. But they are there to inform, not to control; to serve, not to master.

Detailed assessment and appraisal systems should not be required, for the centre will not be responsible for the manning requirements of any community save itself. Financial controls need be minimal, recording only the outcomes not the details of the methods of each operation. Information will often be particular to a problem or project, rather than routine. It is essential that the bureaucracy sees itself as subordinate to, and assisting in, the planning operation. Apollo must be subservient and as small as possible.

THE VILLAGES

Common purpose, informality, leadership, individuality, honesty, initiative. All good motherhood words. Words that indicate art rather than science. They are the materials of management in the village.

There are jobs to be done in the organisation village, and roles. But the place is too small for careers. To lead is not to manipulate, to bribe, cajole or threaten, with promises or fears of future happenings. Effort must come from the desire to play one's part in a common task, to be seen to be doing one's thing and doing it well. Dismissal or layoffs will be exceptional, promotions rare. It has to be management by consent and by inspiration. The villages are the heart of the organisations of consent.

There is a check-list for the would-be leaders of these villages – they need leaders, not managers – which goes as follows:

1. *Recognise the Right to Disagree: in consent organisations, John Stuart Mill's dictum that truth proceeds from argument is widely held. To be invited to disagree is everyone's privilege, but this does not imply that everyone has the right to take the decision. That right belongs to the one on whom the responsibility has been conferred by popular consent. Distinguish discussion from decision wherever possible.*

2. *Control by Planning, not by Checking: it is legitimate to plan and to replan and to change plans. It is not legitimate to check what others are doing, unless their specific agreement has been obtained. Information for planning is willingly vouchsafed, information for monitoring less willingly. The manager therefore has to work with a variety of planning cycles, and to be clearly seen to use past information as a basis for future planning.*

3. *Manage by Reciprocal Trust: trust and control displace each other. If you are seen to control someone you are seen not to trust them. If you cannot control him, you must trust him. Similarly, he must trust you. Reciprocal trust is hard to establish and it is not self-maintaining. It is easier to trust those whom you have chosen than those you are landed with. Since firing will become impossible with tenure, hiring will become a vital decision in these organisations.*

4. *Manage by Platoons: individuals find it easier to identify with smaller groups. They also perceive themselves to have greater influence, the smaller their primary group. Trust is easier to create, the smaller the group. The concept of platoons (the ten-group, in Antony Jay's phrase), has served the Army well and must be one of the buttresses in an organisation of consent. The platoon concept should be allowed to override other ways of organising work, which may look more rational but involve larger primary groups. Individuals may be individuals, but they need a group to identify with. Everyone should therefore be a member of at least one platoon.*

5. *Be Yourself: organisations of consent are personal rather than impersonal. You cannot trust a façade. Openness, frankness and sincerity are valued. To act a role is to disappear as a person. Whatever your idiosyncracies or habits or values, let them be visible. Your own sense of identity and purpose gives identity and purpose to your part of the organisation. It will be tolerant of unimportant differences, but it places great emphasis on the concept of 'mission' or 'purpose'.*

6. *Husband your Energy: leadership in these organisations is exhausting. To treat individuals as individuals, to welcome disagreement, to tolerate dissent, to listen more than talk, to be true to oneself as well as to others – all these require a deal of energy. When energy fails, we fall back on routines and general principles; we listen less and dictate more. Fatigue should not be a battle honour, it should be a crime. Protect what Toffler calls 'stability zones', the places of retreat, the times of withdrawal, and you will protect your colleagues.*

7. *Think Conceptually: the ability to find patterns in things, to connect the apparently unconnected, to make the words that shape the vision – this is what distinguishes the statesman from the politician.*

8. *Emphasise the common task, purpose or output – not the separate roles or functions. Tedium, unpleasant effort, even pain, are acceptable in pursuit of a tangible outcome. A job is a job is a bore, unless you can see how it matters to the end product. Roles detached from the end result are soulless. Means need to be attached to ends, and the end should be a common purpose signalled by a* common *language.*

It is a check-list for Zeus, a Zeus with wisdom as well as charisma. There will be Apollonians in the villages, looking for security, predictability and tidiness. There will be Athenians, solving problems with their colleagues. There will be the Dionysian craftsmen and professionals. All will be imbued with the cult of professionalism. They need a Zeus to lead them, to give them common purpose, to recognise their interdependence and their differences.

In conclusion

We have argued that the tide of resistance to Apollo and bureaucratic corporatism cannot be halted. In an economy of plenty, individualism will flourish. To tamper with the organisations of Apollo through job redesign, or to soften the blow with promises of job security and participation, will not make these corporate prisons any easier for the individualist. Apollo must retreat. We must find ways of designing and running organisations in which the other gods predominate and in which Apollo is encouraged to have a human and a smiling face. If bigness and consistency force an inhuman Apollo upon us, then bigness and consistency must be reduced.

Will it happen?

It is happening. In Britain, three-quarters of the member firms of the Confederation of British Industries employ fewer than 200 people. In Germany, the proportion is higher still. It is not in these organisations that the strikes and absenteeism occur. The British Donovan Commission on Industrial Relations in 1966 found that, even in unionised small firms, only 25 per cent of the managers had ever experienced a strike, compared with 43 per cent in large plants.

In most countries, the construction industry provides an interesting example of an existing federation of villages at work. It is a structure that has grown out of the nature of their work and their technology. Each job has to be treated differently – so that consistency must be left to the lowest common denominators. Sub-contracting is an accepted principle of the work. Groups of 'professionals' (artisans, experts or specialists) work together on site under the *leadership* of someone who, to be successful, has to be an accepted Zeus figure. The functions of the centre are perforce limited to obtaining new projects, selecting key staff, counting and collecting the money and providing a few advisory services. Attempts to rationalise the construction industry, make it more Apollonian and predictable through 'industrialised building' techniques, failed to have their expected impact. The nature of the work does not suit Apollo. The list of sub-contractors posted on a building site is the 'organigram' of an organisation of contract.

Federations of villages and the accompanying managerial cultures were thrust upon the construction industry. Its companies were, in a sense, fortunate. Other industries and other organisations will have to follow by deliberate decision in place of instinctive reaction. We shall have to change our workflows for we cannot wait for them to change us.

There is, however, a certain inevitability about all this. Large, non-federalised Apollonian systems are likely to self-destruct after a time if they do not change. But all will not then disappear. The work will remain, it is the bureaucracy surrounding it that will go. Phoenix-like, new villages will emerge from the ashes of the Greek temples. Society will go on, but after trauma and confusion. It would be pleasant to avoid them both by conscious thought and deliberate action.

In Germany, Scandinavia and France, the trend towards larger organisations has slowed down and in some cases has reversed. In Britain, size and consistency still seduce. Britain is thus being forced to confront the Apollonian dilemma more urgently and more dramatically than others. The developments of the next ten years will be watched with great interest by other countries. No doubt, with their puritan zeal, the British will publicise the traumas and not the successes, but there are bound to be some of both.

It is a conflict that has been long heralded by some, even if ignored by most. In 1951, Lord Radcliffe, the eminent British jurist, gave the annual series of BBC Reith Lectures. He said, 'The British have formed the habit of praising their institutions, which are sometimes inept, and of ignoring their character, which is sometimes superb. In the end, they will be in danger of losing their character altogether and being left with their institutions – a result disastrous indeed.'

VILLAGES RULE OK

Britain's industrial organisations may not have performed as well as they should in the past, but Britain is famous for many things: for the excellence of her theatre, television programmes and journalism; for agriculture, consulting and financial services; for university education and research; for exploration and mountain climbing. When you think about it, all these activities are based around small groups, professionals and strong leaders: Athena, Dionysus and Zeus.

Italy has now a thriving textile industry. One of its governments exempted firms with less than twenty workers from all bureaucratic controls. As a result, of the 15,000 textile factories in Tuscany, 13,000 have fewer than ten employees. The industry has now just about the highest textile wages in the world. Textile villages.

'Keep it simple, stupid' (Kiss) has long been a watchword of American business. Today it is 'keep it small and simple', with all organisational observers advocating a return to small comprehensive units which can influence their own destiny and therefore that of the corporation as a whole. Change and innovation, they observe, come from villages led by Zeus.

The Affluent Outworker

Chapter 8

THE CONSEQUENCES

The gods are changing. Organisations are restructuring and re-balancing to stay alive. It is happening, let us be clear, out of self-interest and a survival instinct, not because there is some grand vision for society or even some new theory of management which has caught the imagination. We are stumbling backwards into the future, a typically British posture which allows one to look longingly towards a receding past whilst actually adapting to the future. Unheralded and unwittingly, our organisations are shaping a new society, because these new arrangements are not just the stuff of business: their logic, and eventually their appeal, will catch on everywhere, in all organisations.

Just think of it. Schools need not be the total institutions that they have always been. So much of what they do could be done else-where and by others. Computers in the home will be more effective than textbooks; work experience turns out to be an excellent way of learning social and technical skills (should we be surprised?); children learn best with adults and adults learn, too, when cast as coaches or teachers. The Open University, pioneered in Britain and now imitated across the world, is not only a distance-learning venture, it is an example of a contractual organisation (paying fees to writers, producers and tutors) with a professional core and federal structure. Fascinated by the University's technological in-novations, the world has not yet grasped the organisational inno-vations, but they provide the beginnings of a model for the other parts of education. If each school were the core of an educational network for all ages in its own community, there would be few lives in that community untouched, if only because more education would take place in the home.

And if schools, why not hospitals? To some extent, hospitals are already becoming the physical hub of a substantial network, with

211

many ancillary services contracted out; more equipment on loan to individuals but 'plugged in' to the hospital; more care and help offered by associated services – the Regional Health Authorities of Britain are really federal organisations, although they are, most of them, still managed as if they were Apollonian entities.

Or take fees, and their implications. More people paid on a fee basis means more people able to decide where and when to do their work. The 9-5 office routine, the daily commute and the home used as a hotel is not the lot of most people on a fee basis. Yes, they have to be part of a network, or of several networks. Many will do most of their work for only one or only a few large organisations. But they can connect with those networks or organisations by telephone and television, as well as by personal visits. More people will work *from* home if not *at* home, using their home as their base, rather as farmers and sales representatives have always done. This change in work patterns is not going to leave the home and its routines unaffected.

Professional organisations and fee-based earnings rely on qualifications and certificates to get started. It will be increasingly hard to get a job or a contract without some piece of paper to prove that you are competent. In the end, results may speak for themselves, but to start with the paper has to do part of the selling. A more Dionysian society heralds a Credential Society, suggesting the need for education throughout life, retraining and updating. Without qualifications and a professional network, the individual will be trapped in one of the new organisational villages, which, however well they are led and managed, will feel like prisons to some. Credentials, and a network, are the passports to leave as well as the permits to enter.

That is fine for those who can get credentials, but what happens to the rest in these professional, contractual organisations made for Athenians and Dionysians? The British census of population in 1981 revealed that the numbers of unskilled manual workers in manufacturing had fallen by 46.2 per cent, and semi-skilled by 22.6 per cent, while employers and managers had gone up by 18.6 per cent and own account workers by 16.0 per cent. The unskilled and the semi-skilled are not wanted, so what are they going to live on, or do? Is more unemployment an inevitable outcome of the more professional, contractual organisation?

And women? In the last twenty years the number of working

wives in jobs in Britain has grown faster than the numbers of men out of work. It is not that women are displacing men in their jobs, but that the new businesses and the new organisations want more part-time, short-term, semi-contractual workers, semi-skilled but reliable. Women fill the bill more easily than men, who still hanker for the permanent job with some sort of long-term career structure. The new structures and the new jobs may be insecure and many of them poorly paid, but they fit into the flexilives of many women, allowing them to be mothers and home-managers as well as workers. Among the semi-skilled the term 'house-husband' may become more common. Among the professionals, will women get their share of the jobs?

Perhaps enough has been said to demonstrate that the re-ordering of the gods and the redesign of our organisations is going to make a difference to the way most people live and to the way society functions. Because organisations provide the skeleton of society, any change in their ways affects all of us, whether we approve or lament. In this chapter, we look at the three major consequences for society:

● The decline of the employment society
● The new ownership
● The new paradigms

Each of them offers exciting opportunities, but they also give rise to

● The new questions

The questions may be old ones like, 'What do we live on?', or, 'How do we learn?', but they will require new answers in a re-organised society. If we don't try to answer them, we may be facing the way Rome faced at the start of her decline.

THE DECLINE OF ROME (AND BRITAIN?)

Gordon Rattray Taylor summarised the symptoms of Rome's decline.* His summary has disturbing echoes in several Western countries today:

* G. Rattray Taylor, *How to Avoid the Future*, New English Library, 1978.

1. *The break-up of small-scale farming, leading to urbanisation and the formation of a 'mass society', with massive immigration as a further factor causing cultural disintegration.*
2. *The break-up of the empire and the development of an adverse trade balance.*
3. *The issue of doles and benefits to the urban masses and their growing preoccupation with conflict and violence.*
4. *The passing of power to the prime functional group, the army (or, for us, the trade unions?), and their irresponsible use of this power.*
5. *The break-up of the aristocracy under middle-class expansion, followed by the destruction of the middle class in the interests of the lower classes.*
6. *A continuously escalating inflation, and even heavier taxation, to support the constant increase of army pay and social services.*
7. *The decline of public safety as armed bands, drawn from the middle classes as well as the masses, seek to make a living outside society.*
8. *In place of the lower classes, modelling themselves on higher ones, the process is revised and popular manners, dress, etc., are imitated.*
9. *The growth of superstition, belief in astrology and other occult systems, the turning towards prospects of bliss in another world.*
10. *The imposition of a wealth tax, followed by confiscation of property.*
11. *The steady mounting of external threats: food supplies becoming unreliable because of irrigation failures, soil erosion and the Third World's desire to keep its products for itself.*
12. *A reign of terror, in which spying, denunciation and torture are employed.*
13. *The decline of artistic and technical greatness.*
14. *Corruption and intrigue at unprecedented levels.*

There is still time to escape the full list.

The decline of the employment society

In 30 years' time, it may be as odd to talk of an employee as it already is to talk of servants. Yet only two generations ago, domestic service was one of the main categories of work. There was an 'upstairs' and a 'downstairs' in most middle-class homes. There are still cooks and gardeners, of course, but today we call them caterers and garden maintenance firms, because, if you think about it, the middle-class family has gone automated and contractual. The same work is done, but not by servants.

Already in the UK today, almost half of the 33 million adults of working age are *not* in full-time employment. No, they are not all unemployed, although too many are. Many are still in education, some are self-employed, more are part-time employed, and both of those categories are going up, while the rest are what the OECD quaintly but correctly call 'unpaid domestic workers'. Together, these categories add up to 16 million, or 47 per cent of the total. It will take another generation, perhaps, but the numbers of those prepared to call themselves 'employees', as opposed to 'independents', 'consultants', 'partners', 'associates', or 'members', will steadily diminish until they are in a definite minority. It may sound like playing with words, but new words are the heralds of change, they symbolise a significant change in the relationship of individual to organisation, and they sound some kind of death knell for the employment society as we knew it.

The employment society was a convenient idea – by guaranteeing a job to everyone who wanted one, society provided money, structure and identity to every household. Call it a form of social control if you want to, employment was certainly the thing that held society together and made it work. Social welfare could then be the insurance that Beveridge wanted it to be, a fall-back for the temporarily unfortunate. So pervasive has the idea of employment become that 'work' effectively means 'a job', and a person without employment passes into an empty space in society, without income, without status, without occupation – *sans* everything, as Shakespeare said of old age.

It is fashionable to blame unemployment on new technology, and there are those who hope that the lapse from full employment is only temporary, that the new technologies will grow new jobs and that we shall return ere long to the employment society in all its Apollonian splendour. The truth is probably more subtle and more complicated. Yes, indeed we are seeing, and will see more of, the phasing out of old ways and old industries, and the birth of new ones. This inevitably causes a lot of human displacement. But the new businesses and the new occupations require brains rather than brawn: fingers, not muscles. This is not just a difficult retraining problem, it actually signals the need for a different sort of organisation to cope with different requirements and different sorts of people. The days of the 'works' which dominated the town are gone for ever. To put it simplistically, the new technologies need Dionysians and Athenians, not Apollonians, as their main resource, and they, as we have seen, require a looser sort of organisation.

TOMORROW'S OFFICE TODAY?

LSI Logic, in Silicon Valley, under Wolf Corrigan provided The Economist* *with a vision of the workplace of the future. There is one huge room shared by administrative and management people. No private offices, but private meeting rooms. It is an almost paper-free office, people gleaning information from computer terminals or from neighbours. The place is eerily quiet, although there are over 400 employees, but each professional working there has over $100,000 of computing power to back him up. They estimate that, because of this equipment, each circuit designer at LSI Logic is producing four times as many designs, with greater reliability, than would have been possible only three years earlier.*

The results on employment? Wolf Corrigan saw two types of jobs disappearing – the little-skilled in manufacturing and servicing and the jobs of the middle manager. Any manager, he reckoned, had better be as technically skilled as his few subordinates if he wanted to keep on working.

THE NEW JOBS

In the 1970s, the United States created 19 million new jobs. 5 per cent were in manufacturing, 11 per cent in goods-producing industries and 12 per cent in the traditional service sector. 72 per cent were in the information sector (teachers, accountants, bankers, insurance brokers, lawyers, computer programmers and other people who process bits of information, or move them about).

* Reported in *The Economist,* 19 May, 1984.

The twenty-hour week is becoming more common as the propor-tion of part-time workers grows in all countries. Much of this new work goes to women, and much of it is in services where the work has often got sharp peaks which need extra staff at irregular intervals. Part-time work suits the services and it often suits women, who can combine it with household and child management. As a result, the proportion of women in work in OECD's biggest economies has risen from 50.5 per cent in 1975 to 55.9 per cent in 1982.

TRUNCATED CAREERS

To put it another way, the organisations of the new technologies will find it more economic to pay fees rather than wages to many of these new workers, whom they will require more intermittently and can manage by more remote control. The contractual fringe of the new organisations is likely to be large. Why employ someone all week when you only really need two days of their creative talent or their dexterity?

But some will still be employed, and in central and local govern-ment, in schools, hospitals and prisons, it is likely to be the majority. In others, it will only be the professional core. Employ-ment, however, is likely, even for those, to last for fewer years than it used to. A smaller, flatter organisation needs more people to leave it sooner, to provide promotion opportunities for those behind. The new organisations are likely to follow the armed services in stipulating varying lengths of service, from three to twenty years, to be reviewed at the discretion of the organisation, not the individual. Tenure, in universities, the professions and business, will increasingly have a terminal date put on it which will bring it closer to twenty-five years than the current forty-eight. Even for the professional core, in other words, employment will be only a phase of life, not much longer than the educational phase. Maybe the French are right in talking of the three ages of man – the age of learning, the age of working and the age of living. Maybe it will be as rare to hear someone in their sixties talk of their employ-ment days as it would be to hear them talk of their schooldays. Both would be phases of the past, a fount of memories, reminiscences and stories, but something left behind.

In practical terms, organisations will follow the universities in treating tenure for life as a rare and precious privilege. There will be more service contracts at all levels, more short-term appointments of a two- or three-year nature to a particular project or team (as already happens in research groups and in voluntary organisations). More appointments will be subject to review after five or seven years. Early retirement will become a norm, rather than an exception, for the expensive people – top management and specialists. It will be done in the interests of economy and efficiency and to prevent the organisation becoming an elderly ghetto or a gerontocracy, but the end result will be to limit employment to the middle years of life for most people.

THE 50,000-HOUR JOB?

It used to be that people worked for 47 hours a week (including overtime), for 47 weeks, for 47 years of their life. Multiplied out, that comes to just over 100,000 hours of employment in a lifetime.

Times are changing. The 35-hour week is common in many offices. What with public holidays, sick leave, absenteeism and paid leave, many people now have 10 weeks or more away from the organisation, leaving 42 weeks a year of work. A graduate may not start work until he or she is twenty-three or twenty-four and will often plan to leave before sixty, giving 35 years of active working life. That multiplies out to just over 50,000 hours in a lifetime.

We shall soon have halved the lifetime job. We shall have spent the gains of productivity on reducing employment, in hours and days and years.

The 50,000-hour job may not happen in the same way for all people. Some will take their hours in an intensive period of twenty years, working all the hours that they can find and then moving on, in mid-life, to other pursuits. Others will spread it thinly, working part-time for many years. Others will chunk it, interleaving periods in a job with periods in education, child-rearing or caring for their elders. Whatever form it comes in, a 50,000-hour employment life signals a lot of life beyond employment, a lot of time when every individual will define himself or herself in ways that have nothing to do with being employed in an organisation.

LIFE BEYOND EMPLOYMENT

What will they be doing? They will be unofficially employed, or, as they would put it, busy about other things. Work, with odd lags and sags, expands to fill the space available for it, and much of it will go to build up the unofficial or informal economy. People will use their new extra discretionary time either to make more money, in the black economy, or to save money, by doing for themselves what they used to pay others to do for them (the household economy), or to save other people money by doing things for them for free (the voluntary economy). It is all work, and some of it is paid for, but none of it is called employment. It is a world for small Zeus figures, for private Dionysians and illicit Athenians. There will also be those, sadly, who do nothing, who find it hard to live without the structure of employment, as well as its money, who need the traction of employment to pull them out of bed in the morning: Apollonians bereft of a temple. For those, the decline of the employment society is all bad news.

THE INFORMAL ECONOMIES

The Inland Revenue in Britain estimated that something like 7½ per cent of taxable income was undeclared and illegal. That would mean that the average household spent, between them, something approaching £1,000 p.a. in the black economy. Other estimates range from half of that to almost double. In Italy, some think it might be as high as 20 per cent of GNP, with many small businesses and self-employed people invisible to the state, while in the Eastern bloc countries it might even reach 30 per cent.

The perfectly legal household economy is hard to value. How does one cost the rearing of children, the growing of potatoes or the cleaning of houses? The best way to do it is to count the hours of labour instead. One such estimate* calculated the figure for the UK to be 51 per cent of all the hours worked, in the country.

Employment is going out of fashion because Apollonian organisations, like middle-class families after the Second World War, are

* R. Rose, *Getting By in Three Economies*, Centre for Study of Public Policy, 1983.

automating and contracting-out. As with the middle-class families, the work is still there to be done, along with some new and different work, but it will be done in new ways and in new kinds of organisations. It is a change of gods, triggered by structural changes in our economic life and by new technology, but far-reaching in the way it will affect the whole bone-structure of what used to be the industrial society. Whether we like it or not, more and more of us are going to have to follow Zeus and Dionysus for more and more of our lives. Apollo's temples, which have offered some sort of sanctuary for so many for so long, will not disappear – the new organisations have to be as tightly regulated as they are loosely structured – but they will be smaller and lower, with less room in them and more selection about both entry and exit. Even the people in these smaller temples may no longer think of themselves as employees, as we shall see.

The new ownership

Sheer size, and the complexity, inflexibility and accumulating slack which result from size, is a key factor in the flight from Apollo. But so is the reluctance to be owned by another, even if the pay is good. Marx was right – to be another's wage slave is wrong; it is alienating, ultimately humiliating and a denial of one's full freedom. No one wants to be a 'human resource' (the cold language of Apollonian organisations), no matter how well remunerated, if there is another choice. Marx was also right in seeing that, where capital and labour were in separate hands, there was inevitably conflict between the two, a conflict which in the end capital would always win, no matter how well protected labour was. In the end, capital expands by using as little labour as it can as productively as it may. That makes a lot of sense if you are the owner of the capital, or the agent of the owners; it makes much less sense if you are part of the 'as little labour as possible'.

The small businessman understands the problem in his gut. He knows that, if he wants to build up the business, at the outset he has to work all the hours he can for as little money as he can live on, to build up the assets, the goodwill and the turnover of the business. A good salary comes later. Even then, with a thriving business in hand, he knows that, if he wants to grow richer, he pays himself poorly but lets the business grow. He can make the trade-off because he is both capital and labour in one. The small farmer can make and understand a similar trade-off, because he too provides the capital and the labour himself. It is when they both get bigger and employ extra help that capital and labour become divorced, and, as in all divorces, arguments break out over the division of the property.

The employment organisations which grew up under industrial-isation magnified and formalised that divorce. The only way in which employees could benefit from a growth of capital was to ask for more wages. These were naturally resisted, because they de-tracted from the growth of capital, unless they could in some way be tied into even greater productivity. The adversary system of management and unions was born out of the divorce between capital and labour.

One interesting outcome of the gradual decline of employment and the rise of new forms of organisation may be a reconciliation of capital and labour. Dionysians do not like to be managed, or owned, by anyone. Not only, therefore, do they look for organ-isations of consent, in which they have a right of veto on any important decisions; they also look for organisations which in some way or other are 'theirs', not 'other people's'. Professionals work in partnerships, from choice, where capital increases belong to the partners. If formal partnerships are impossible, then universities, schools, hospitals, churches and voluntary bodies are at least non-profitmaking organisations, which means, in effect, that any surplus earned is put back into the organisation, to be spent, invested or given away with the consent of the members.

The Dionysian swell is likely, therefore, to result in more and more requests and demands by people in organisations for a share in the fruits of ownership as well as the fruits of labour. Even those remaining in the Apollonian centres of the new federal organ-isations will see themselves as professional staff, not as employees. At top management level, there are already share-option schemes in more and more businesses. Common in America, these schemes only became really tax-efficient after 1980 in Britain and are now growing rapidly. It is an obvious way in which to marry labour and capital, with the result that top managers do not, in those firms, usually think of themselves as employees but as co-owners, partners or as members of the corporation.

Why stop at top management? Why cannot everyone have a share of the spoils? The Industrial Participation Association in the UK estimated in 1983 that between 320 and 420 companies, employing 1.5 million people, had profit-sharing schemes of some sort. That is a start, but it is still less than 10 per cent of all those employed in industry or commerce. Furthermore, many of those schemes are discretionary – that is, a bonus is declared at the discretion of the board, making it look like benevolence, rather than one's rightful share in the capital. The pressures are bound to grow.

It is, after all, only ownership which really counts. That which you own you don't destroy or even kick. We don't break up the cookers, washing-machines and other household automata which have revolutionised our homes, because they are *ours*. People, on the other hand, have been known to kill the goose that lays the golden egg, if it is laying those eggs for others but not for them. We shall have to find more ways whereby those who work in organisations get direct financial benefit from the growth of capital. When that happens, technological change, which may cut labour but will increase the worth and value of the organisation, will be welcomed by people who are both sides of the coin at once, owners as well as workers.

SHARES IN THE STOCK

The new ownership will come in many forms. Most obviously, and perhaps most powerfully, it will come as a share in the stock of a business. Why could not a monthly paycheck be part salary and part stock? If this is, as yet, too fanciful, we shall certainly see more new businesses rewarding their founder-members with shares in their joint creation, a recognition that, whereas some will have contributed money, others will have provided expertise and specialist skills, or just sheer hard work. Companies going public for the first time will increasingly offer their shares at a discount to those who work for them; and when they shed bits of their business, the new trend of buy-outs provides a way for the workers to take on board the responsibility and the risk of owning a bit of their own business at a price that is low, to reflect the risk, but therefore within their reach.

CO-OPERATIVES

The extreme form of share ownership would be a full co-operative, where all the ownership is shared by the members of the co-operative. Because ownership is totally vested in the workers, these think of themselves as 'members', not as 'employees'. The marriage of capital and labour is complete. Ironically, however, since co-operatives started as a reaction against capitalism, they have always tended to reject the growth of their capital as a form of reward, calling profit 'surplus' and taking their rewards in the form of increased wages, dividends or bonuses. Partly, therefore, because of their ideological dislike of capital, many co-operatives have always been financially undernourished, without the resources to survive troughs and depressions, or the investment to take advantage of new markets or new technologies. By denying themselves the motives of their former users, the co-operatives are not only being irrational, they are being naive and self-defeating, given that they operate in capitalist market economies. It is not capital, after all, that has been at fault, but the way it was used by some at the expense of others. Happily, there are signs – in Italy and France, particularly – that the co-operative movement is coming to terms with reality.

ITALY CO-OPERATES

At last count,* there were almost 4,000 co-operatives in Italy, many of them in building construction, with lesser members in services and industrial production. It is said that only 5 per cent die each year, while as many as 25 per cent new ones are formed.

Financially fragile, they have improved their competitiveness by bonding together in consortia to compete for larger tenders and orders, which allows them to act big while staying small. They have also kept management to a minimum (co-operative law says there should be only one white-collar for every twelve blue-collars) and have used their federations to help raise money and to put pressure on the state and the banks to provide loans. The state, indeed, has been very supportive, passing laws in 1951, 1963 and 1978 to give specialist

---

* As reported by J. Thornley in *Workers' Co-operatives*, Heinemann, 1981.

status to co-operatives and to provide cheap capital. Idealism is strong among the co-operatives but today in Italy it is tempered by realism. As a result, co-operatives are now an important third sector in the economy.

TRUSTEESHIP

Thirdly, ownership can take a more constitutional form, with workers becoming the formal owners of the organisation, but with that ownership expressed collectively through a trust, which owns the company on behalf of the workers. Or, as in Britain's John Lewis Partnership, the workers can be the titular owners of the company but delegate their powers to an elected council. In these cases, capital seems to be not so much married to labour as put in trust for it, to be used on its behalf. It feels like ownership by remote control and less compelling to the individual than a direct share in the organisation's assets.

THE SCOTT BADER COMMONWEALTH

Ernest Bader was a dynamic Swiss businessman of strong Christian convictions, who went to Britain, settled there, and built up a thriving business. In the 1950s, he started to hand over the business to his workers, although he remained chairman. The shares of the business (The Scott Bader Company Limited) are now wholly owned by the Scott Bader Commonwealth, a trust, on behalf of the employees. His hope was that by this means capital and labour could be re-united, giving more meaning to work, more responsibility for their destiny to the workers, and removing any sense of exploitation by the owners. An array of democratic mechanisms was set up at the same time to allow the workers, now also members of the Commonwealth, to express their views in the management of the company, including four directorships on the company board.

Does it work? 'To a degree,' would perhaps be the best answer. No one at Scott Bader feels owned by anyone else, but they do not feel that they own the place, either. Ownership vested in the Commonwealth and not in individual shares has somehow been put into quarantine – it won't contaminate, but you can't get at it.

REPRESENTATION

Fourthly, ownership can be expressed by representation. Where it is impossible, as in the state corporations or state services, to have a share in the capital, or where it is difficult, and perhaps meaningless because miniscule, as in very large business operations, at least ways can and should be found of giving the employee some say in the way the capital is used. Representative democracy, as the way to enfranchising the worker, has been favoured by managements, by governments and by the European Commission. Some would do it with worker directors, some by works councils or by more bottom-line participation in the day-to-day decisions of management. It is, perhaps, the only way for employees to exert some control over their own destinies and to share in the future of their organisation if capital is inviolate. The trouble is that no one seems to want it very much (see below), perhaps because they realise that it is a mere shadow of the real thing.

WORKERS AND DEMOCRACY

A survey* of British workers' attitudes to more representation and say in their companies produced the following results:

Only 4 per cent of employees specify 'campaigning to get employees on the board of directors' as a priority for trade unions.

Only 10 per cent of employees mention 'workers having seats on the board of directors' as one of the four things they would most like to achieve.

Only 17 per cent mention 'getting employees a bigger say in running the organisation they work for' as being an important objective for trade unions.

Only 8 per cent think it important for workers to have a bigger say in management decision about finance and investment.

* Reported by Opinion Research and Communication in 'Worker Aspirations and Revised EEC Proposals on Worker Involvement', 1983.

Only 20 per cent think it important for workers to have a bigger say in the day-to-day running of the company they work for.

Only 3 per cent think it important for union officials to have seats on the board of directors.

In the large corporations of state and private enterprise, in local government and the state services, the employee culture will remain ingrained. There seems no real possibility in these organisations for capital to be married to labour. We may, however, expect the feelings of professionalism to be increasingly expressed in a right to be consulted, not through representative democracy, but directly. These places will have to lean over backwards to become organisations of consent, precisely *because* they cannot turn their workers into owners. Representation, however, is not the easiest or best way to do it, while direct democracy requires small units – where everyone can, if need be, be fitted into one room or one shed – federally linked. If Dionysians cannot be partners, they at least want the right to shout, 'No', and to shout it themselves.

A share in the ownership of the organisation will always remain the best way to keep one's freedom in that organisation. Dionysians and Athenians will, we may be sure, be looking for more ownership to replace their dependence on the Apollonian structure. If they cannot get ownership, then the right to be consulted, personally, will become more pressing; in other words, organisations will have to get smaller until the individual, not his or her representative, can be heard at the top.

The new paradigms

'Paradigm' is a word made fashionable by T. S. Kuhn, writing about the way science advances. A paradigm is essentially a set of assumptions; change the set and you change the view. A whole new way of looking at things can release new insights and new energies. When Copernicus suggested that, instead of the sun encircling the earth, it was the earth and other planets going round the sun, he did not actually change anything except the way we saw things, but he did set science on a new course.

Similarly, new sets of assumptions about people, work and organisations are going to put society on a new course. It may be a chicken-and-egg process – difficult to say which at any time is cause and which effect – because organisations are so entwined in daily life and daily values; but it is less important to be able to say what started it than to be clear what 'it' is that has changed.

THE FEMININE STRAIN

The changing role and status of women is a good example of the chicken-and-egg syndrome. It is not the Apollonian crisis that has caused the women's liberation movement, nor the other way round. but the move towards more task and person cultures that has definitely made it easier for women to become properly involved in organisations, at the top and in the middle, as well as at the bottom; whilst the pressure in society at large for women to have the same career and work opportunities as men has allowed a more feminine strain to infiltrate organisations. It is appropriately symbolic that Athena is a goddess, while Dionysus was the favoured god of those who might be called the liberated women of ancient times.

The feminine strain shows itself not just in the physical presence of more women but in a heightened awareness of creativity, sensitivity, personal relationships and feelings, personal worth and individual differences. Men care about these things too, of course, some of them more than some women, but a predominantly male culture will keep such things under cover and control and will promote toughness, discipline and impersonality. The feminine strain is more noticeable in the Athenian and Dionysian cultures, the male characteristics in Zeus and Apollo.

The more Athenian or Dionysian the organisation, therefore, the greater the feminine strain and the easier it is for women to have a proper influence. Advertising agencies, market research firms. television production teams, schools, hospitals and law courts are all arenas where women are increasingly prominent, even if they had to fight hard at first to overcome the male control of some Dionysian strongholds, as in the law courts or the hospitals. Apollonian and Zeus organisations, however, remain predominantly male in sex and attitude, as the composition of the boards of most European industrial companies will remind us – hardly a female name on any of them. The decline of Apollo has to be, therefore, an opportunity for women.

So, as we have seen, is the growth of the contractual organisation. No doubt much of the work is semi-skilled, irregular in hours and poorly paid, but the evidence is that, though it could be better, it is better than nothing and better, for many women, than full-time employment, which leaves no time for anything else. The employment of women has actually increased in all European countries while the unemployment of men has been accelerating.

The results are often exciting, often confusing. Work roles in households get reversed, blended or confused. Women may find it easier to take on new work roles but still difficult to unload the caring and home-making roles, partly because men may not want them, partly because women may want to hang on to them. Men, it seems, like hoovering, washing-up and cooking (the proactive tasks) but are less keen on dusting and child care. How does a woman decide when to leave career for motherhood, even if only temporarily? Should men also be expected to give up their careers for a period of child-rearing? Do husbands accompany their wives to their official functions when the male officials have their wives by their side, or is a woman's work something she does on her own, often under her maiden name? Does the language of 'and partner' rather than 'and wife', which more and more official invitations now use, tell us something about the emergence of the feminine strain, or only confirm the fragility of marriage? These are some new questions for a society which is having to work with a new paradigm of women. That paradigm does not treat women as men, which is merely to perpetuate the old paradigm but relax the entry restrictions giving permission to women to act like men; the new paradigm treats women as different but as good as men, with their own talents, gifts and particular needs. It is an exciting paradigm, offering chances to both men and women to develop more aspects of themselves, to explore new roles and to take on new relationships. It offers an escape from stereotyping, from forced dependency of female on male, and the possibility of more partnerships of equals – proper Dionysian pairings. It is happening, in part, because the changing cultures of our organisations allow it to happen. In Japan's Apollonian world, women are still seen as the home and family managers for their men.

CONFUSING PARADIGMS

*I work from home and at home. My wife helps with my correspond-
ence, does the typing, answers the telephone, manages my diary –
much as a secretary would, in fact, and she is paid accordingly.*

*She used to answer the phone by giving her name, thereby identi-
fying herself as one of the family. This seemed to embarrass and
confuse many callers, who still think of work being done in office or
factory or shop and see home as a private sanctuary – 'Oh, I am sorry
to bother you,' they would say, 'I could ring some other time.'*

*She then took to answering the phone, during normal office hours,
as 'Charles Handy's secretary'. This worked beautifully for all those
calling from an office, often secretaries themselves, but it caused
anger among some women friends who phoned in. 'How demean-
ing,' they said, 'how could you put yourself down like that? Why
don't you use your own name? You are a person, aren't you, not a
piece of property?'*

*You really need to know whether it's an Apollonian or a Dionysian
calling before you answer the telephone!*

THE CREDENTIAL SOCIETY

It will be a more flexible world. People will move jobs more often
because jobs will be shorter. They may work, part-time or self-
employed, for two or more organisations at once. Many will turn
their hobby or their profession into a tiny business on the side,
others will be forced into self-employment as the positive alternative to unemployment. Offices will be the focal points of networks,
with many people telecommunicating (by telephone or computer)
much of the time, travelling in to meetings when need be. The
offices and shops will increasingly be on the fringe of cities rather
than in the middle, in order to enlarge their catchment areas (see
below), whilst more homes will turn the garage or the back room
into a study or a workshop. Time, for most people, will be more
discretionary, up to them how to use it; although many people will
probably choose to use it to do more work to make more money,
some will delve deeper into self-sufficiency or community work. It
will be a more flexilife world, with fewer people able to define
themselves, Apollonian-style, as an ICI man or a Shell woman.

ISOCHRONES

Draw a line on a road map to mark how far you could travel, by car, rail or bus, from your home in an hour. You have now drawn an isochrone, which is like a contour on a map, except that it joins points that are the same distance away in time, *not the same height.*

If you live on the edge of a city, your isochrones will be very jagged, taking you perhaps 12 miles into the centre of the city in one direction or 60 miles in another. Add in aeroplanes and it gets even more jagged.

Motorways and ring roads make a lot of distance to isochrones. The big ring road around London will eventually pull London's centre of gravity outwards when people realise that the isochrones for an office on the ring road are much bigger than for one in the centre of the city, giving it a much bigger catchment area.

Empty commuter trains, perhaps?

Flexilife sounds fun, and it can be. People will end up with portfolios of work rather than one occupation which saw them through life. Instead of having to get money, status and fulfilment out of one job, they can be shared out a bit over different parts of work and life, with money coming from one activity, perhaps, but status from something that provides little financial reward. It will be a more Dionysian world.

It will also be a more insecure world. Dionysians get security from their professionalism. A doctor is, as long as he stays within the law, always a doctor. She, or he, might not be a good doctor, but even bad doctors can still practise. Self-employed people, be they artists or artisans, have no long-term contracts to keep them alive. Instead, they rely on their skill and expertise, for saleable skill is the ultimate security of a flexilife existence. But, to be saleable, a skill needs to be certificated, at least in the early years of practice. In time, the work done is its own diploma, but no one is going to ask you to do the first lot of work without some assurance that you can do it. A name on a business card with 'plumber' or 'publicity' underneath it is no guarantee in itself that the bearer can either plumb or publicise. Credentials, in other words, will be an essential but, alas, not sufficient starting point.

Credentials may guarantee you the chance of work and money in a Dionysian society, but if work, or at any rate paid work, is no

longer the whole of life for all of life, if there are going to be big
chunks of time, during or after one's working life, which are for
other things, then credentials alone will not define you or your
success. They will, however, free you to be more than your official
work, more than your credentials.

Replacing the employment society by the credential society may
therefore allow society to develop many more models and definitions of success, the good life and fulfilment. A full-employment
society divided life into the job – and leisure. Success was conventionally defined as success in the job, although many always knew,
and others often found, that it was things outside the job which
mattered most: the family, the garden, sport or the community. The
employment society is by its nature materialist and careerist,
because those are its motivating weapons. If no one needed money
or career advancement, Apollonian structures would lose their
grip. A more Dionysian society will have plenty of materialists, no
doubt, and we should be grateful for that, for we need their wealth-
creating drive, but there must also be other models to choose from.
Quality in life is not totally dependent on quantity, and some will
use their new freedom and their new discretionary time to develop
new interests, to travel more, or to lead a simpler life, to invest in
their families, put a toe into local politics, get involved in voluntary
work, or just to read more, watch more television, or talk with
friends. Success will have, I hope, many faces, of which the careerist
professional will be only one.

For some, this freeing-up of pathways will be confusing. Choice is
often more worrying than no choice. The point of life will be less
obvious if money is no longer the main criterion. How will we judge
people? How will we judge ourselves? How will we know whether
our prospective son- or daughter-in-law has good prospects when
'prospects' can be so widely defined? The new paradigm offers a
cafeteria of possibilities for life; it is an opportunity to choose one's
own set of credentials and a life-style to fit. It will lead to an
interesting and varied society, but also one that will be confusing to
many, particularly to those who are not naturally Dionysian, or who
do not find credentials easy to come by and have valued the routine
and the security of employment. Sadly, the professionalisation of
the Apollonian cultures that remain will mean that those who are
least able to cope with life beyond employment will be among the
first to be pushed into it. The credential society will not be every-

one's dream and might well be the basis for a new class divide – those with credentials and those without.

The new questions

The exciting possibilities of new patterns of organisations, jobs and life should not blind us to the problems, and in particular to the three key questions.

- What are we going to live on?
- How are we going to educate ourselves?
- How do we protect ourselves?

These are the enabling questions of the new scenario. If we don't get them right, we shall divide society into those who can work, have jobs and make money, and those who cannot. It will be a society of escalating envy and resentment, in which those who make money will resent paying high taxes to keep alive those who don't or can't work, whilst these in turn will resent their dependency and envy the privileges and the life-style of those in jobs.

Money and education are the pathways to freedom. Without them, a person is trapped, physically and psychologically. It is no use advising people to 'get on their bikes' and look for work, as one employment minister did in Britain, if they don't have bikes, let alone cars, in the first place (and at that date less than 10 per cent of Britain's unemployed did own a bike); if they can't sell their houses or find another one on over-subscribed housing lists; or if they don't have the skills required in the new jobs. Money and education are the most sensible investments any society can make in its citizens, particularly the less fortunate ones, but they have to be seen as an investment, not a grudging handout. If the investment is not made, we might well be heading for a Gor-Saga society. It is an investment, however, which we cannot wait for society as a whole to make up its mind about; organisations will themselves need to take a lead if they want to end up in a world worth living in.

THE GOR-SAGA SOCIETY

In her novel, Gor-Saga,* *Maureen Duffy describes, as a backcloth to*

* Methuen. 1981.

the plot, a world in which the meritocracy, in their professional jobs, has taken over. Control of the technology gives to the officials of organisations control of information and the power to run people's lives and even, maybe, to create life of the sort they want.

Excluded from this society are the 'nons', those without proper jobs, who live in encampments on the edges of cities, or deep in the country. Violence is rife and even voluntary agencies have to become armed guerillas in order to be effective. The cities have become ghettoes for the rich and for the tourist, and passes are needed for the best of the suburbs.

There are trains and buses and television and all the paraphernalia of life, but it is proper life only for the credentialled few and a jungle existence for the many, a world in which 'word processor' has become a polite word for a machine-minder and 'pensioner' means anyone, of any age, who can not provide for themselves.

WHAT ARE WE GOING TO LIVE ON?

Put rather starkly, if we are working half the hours we used to and if we can look forward to twice as many years after employment, we ought to be putting aside, as a nation or as individuals, four times as much money for our retirement. Nothing like that is happening, although it could be argued that, in Britain at least, people have been over-investing in their pensions for years, because it was so tax-effective, and have therefore been unwittingly preparing for the kind of future which is in store.

That would be true if everyone had been doing it, and if pensions were universally seen as an individual's accumulating capital rather than his right to a wage or salary after he has left employment. As it is, early leavers or frequent movers lose most of the organisation's contributions and fund the fuller pensions of those who stay. Organisations, and their pension funds, will need to recognise the realities of modern organisational life, of truncated careers and flexilives, if they want to make it easier for people to move out, to sub-contract or to work part-time.

Dionysians have individual pension plans and so-called 'portable pensions' will surely become more common as Dionysians become more fashionable in and around organisations. But portable and personal pension schemes are inevitably more expensive; or, putting it the other way round, they produce lower pensions, because they cannot take so much actuarial account of all those early leavers and frequent movers. In the new scenario, therefore, we will, most of us, be poorer than we would have been, unless we do something.

The 'something' has to start with increased contributions, by organisation and individual, but these will not be forthcoming unless and until people really understand that careers will be shorter and life after employment longer. It is critical to their own futures that managers and employees understand how organisations are changing. To make last-minute provision, as happens today when top executives retire early, will be ruinously expensive when it happens on a larger scale. To make no last-minute provision, on the other hand, can be to condemn a loyal colleague to poverty, for it is unrealistic to expect the state to find the funds to make up the difference. Brave talk of reducing the official retirement age always peters out when the cost is calculated. In the end, a large part of an individual's later-life money has to come from mid-life savings.

Savings, or deferred pay if you like to see it that way, will never, however, be enough for most. Many will want, and need, to top it up with some marginal work, often at low or marginal prices. Fortunately, the more Dionysian nature of work will make this possible for anyone with a saleable skill or talent and the energy and zeal to sell it. People will be pushed towards part-time self-employment because they are still young enough to work and to want the rewards. For some, however, it will not be making money but saving money which will be important – doing things for themselves, instead of paying out money to others to do them. Self-sufficiency is a form of domestic import substitution, just as effective as increasing exports. But self-sufficiency is only another form of self-employment, except that it is done for oneself, not for others.

The central message is clear. Necessity is going to make Dionysians of us all, later if not sooner. Individuals had better adjust to this – and organisations would be sensible to help them in that adjustment, particularly by making better financial provision for their life beyond employment – because no state is going to be able to afford to do it adequately.

The state, however, could usefully start to regard unemployment benefit, supplementary benefit and pensions as basic incomes, and not as alternatives to income. Then, any earnings over and above these basics would not be penalised so heavily. Current rules make entrepreneurship a crime for anyone out of work, when it ought to be the best possible medicine for them and for society. We need, in fact, to rethink our whole approach to welfare now that full-time jobs are the prerequisite of only half the adult working population. We could make a start by banning the word 'unemployment' and talking of 'temporarily self-employed', like actors or writers; of people who need to supplement their income but are still in the working population; of Dionysians, not failed Apollonians.

HOW ARE WE GOING TO EDUCATE OURSELVES?

Money, however, as so often, is only part of the problem, even if it is the part that hurts, the presenting problem. If a Dionysian life is going, at some stage or other, to be forced on all of us, we shall have to learn new skills, new habits and new attitudes.

Schools have long been Apollonian organisations, educating people for Apollonian lives in formal organisations. As we have seen, there are signs that schools, like other organisations, will change into something more like networks, with more Athenian and Dionysian characteristics, but the change won't be in time to affect or interest any of those likely to read this book. For them, the institutions of education will have to be the work organisation, with help whenever possible from the further and higher education system.

The first requirement, after all, of a Dionysian life is a saleable skill or talent. Examination results, a career of ever more important management jobs, a record of international or industrial experience, are of little use unless they can be turned into a product that someone wants. In self-employment, unlike employment, it is not the individual that people are interested in, but the product he or she is offering. Professionals, therefore, have it easy, because their qualification is in effect a license to sell their skill. Professionals can be Dionysians outside or inside the organisation, and it is easier for them to move away and practise on their own account than it is for someone whose main job has been to co-ordinate and manage. What does a manager do without people to manage?

THE DE-SKILLED EXECUTIVE

The account executive was depressed. He had just been made re-
dundant from his advertising firm, at the age of forty-eight. He was
anxious for another job, but at his age there were few openings in the
advertising world.

'What are you good at?' I asked.
'Running an account group in an advertising agency,' he replied.
'Well, that won't get you very far.'
'I know, but that's all I'm any good at.'

I suggested that he ask twenty friends or associates over the next
two weeks to tell him one thing he was good at. Two weeks later, he
came back with a list of twenty talents. He was excited but puzzled.
'Not one of them mentioned running an account group!'

Working on, and developing, his unsuspected talents opened up
new avenues and new kinds of work. Organisations can keep bits of
you hidden from yourself.

More people need more opportunities to discover talents and
abilities which they can turn into products and useful work. 'Continuing education' needs to become more of a reality and not just a
way of learning a new hobby or improving one's holidays with
rather better languages and a knowledge of history. Pre-retirement
education should be about the development of skills and the
capacity for self-employment, rather than lectures about keeping fit
and maintaining the home.

In time, maybe, governments will pick up the idea of educational
credits for people in mid-life, to be cashed in at the institution of
one's choice at a time of one's choice. In time, more schools will
make their skills available to all in the community and not just to the
kids. In time, it will become easier and more respectable for people
over forty to take part-time degrees and time off work to study.
Organisations, however, would be wise not to wait for governments
but to make it their responsibility to see that individuals equip
themselves for life beyond employment whilst they are still in
employment. It is, after all, as important to equip someone to earn
money as it is to give them money – and it might be cheaper.

Asking organisations to equip someone to be independent
sounds like asking them to plot their own downfall. But good
Dionysian organisations know that their strength lies in their best

individuals, despite the risk that those individuals are always the ones who would find it easiest to leave. Keeping people dependent has never worked, in families or organisations. Organisations need therefore to think of themselves as schools, although schools of a very different sort, places where individuals can acquire, develop and practise skills which will be useful all their lives; and they need to encourage individuals to acquire relevant qualifications which will be their passport to self-employment at some stage. They need, in other words, to encourage people to acquire the means to freedom, even if they sometimes set themselves free before the organisation would have wanted it. Better that than a group of dependants growing older and more scared of the world outside.

HOW WILL WE PROJECT OURSELVES?

Money and education are the pathways to self-employment, but it remains an insecure and ill-protected way of life for most. They may have a skill, a willingness to work, aptitude and talent, but selling themselves is another matter. The self-employed home-worker has traditionally been the most exploited of all workers and there is little sign that this has improved much, although the technology has changed from the loom to the computer terminal.

The traditional professions have their associations, supposed to maintain standards as well as to seek for fair rewards. Some self-employed have agents, who sell and negotiate on behalf of their artists or their actors or their writers. Some form co-operatives, to share facilities or to promote their wares. Others join networks, loose associations, which print lots of names, convene conferences, publish newsletters and generally provide a way of keeping in touch.

We shall need to see more of each. In a sense, the guilds need to be re-created, both to set standards and to look after the interests of their members, because those potential members will be up against strong forces. Their markets will, in many cases, be organisations, not individuals, and organisations can deal roughly with people smaller than themselves, paying them late, bargaining down the rate of pay, keeping contracts short, insisting on unreasonable delivery arrangements. Not all organisations will act responsibly.

The role of the unions is critical in all of this. The unions emerged as the protector of the employee. Will they continue to interpret this as meaning the protection of the individual *only* as employee, or will they broaden their scope to include the individual in any relationship with the organisation? It is in their own interest to broaden their mandate, for the decline of employment will otherwise inevitably mean the decline of unions as their membership continues to soak away. Employment *à la carte* is the message of the future. If the unions stick to only one dish, they will effectively signal their own demise.

CHANGE OR DECAY?

Many organisations do not change; they only fade away, and others grow up to take their place. Unable to contemplate a future different from all that they have been used to, they continue to beaver away at what they know best how to do, working harder and more efficiently on a diminishing task. Education, for instance, is the growth sector of every society, yet in Britain schools are contracting or closing and the educational profession is in recession and retreat; meanwhile, computer manufacturers, book publishers, video film makers, language schools and, above all, the Manpower Services Commission of the Department of Employment, are booming away. Education, yes, but not in schools, it seems. Indeed, as educational networks become more common and more available, we may see the school-leaving age reduced, leaving individuals, perhaps financed by vouchers, to choose their own sources of learning, while schools contract even more.

Unions may be turning their backs on the future, but they are only copying firms who are reluctant to change their patterns of employment, their promises of careers for all, or their assumptions that the place can only function if everyone is at work all the time.

Unusually, however, and fortunately, their destiny is in their own hands. Organisations may usually wither and decay instead of changing, but it does not have to be that way. This book is written in the hope that if more managers understand what is happening and what possibilities are open to them, then more will experiment with the future, instead of ignoring it. Change, after all, in the Anglo-Saxon tradition, does not come about as a result of edicts from the centre but because of new case-law, which after a time becomes established practice, incorporated in the law of the land. It is more experiments we need, to change organisational fashion, even if some, as is their wont, do not come off. Without them, our society may well decay as its organisations wither.

INDEX